The Shadow of a Year

History of Ireland and
the Irish Diaspora

SERIES EDITORS

James S. Donnelly, Jr.
Thomas Archdeacon

The Shadow of a Year

The 1641 Rebellion
in Irish History and Memory

John Gibney

The University of Wisconsin Press

Publication of this volume has been made possible, in part,
through support from the **Anonymous Fund**
of the College of Letters and Science
at the University of Wisconsin–Madison.

The University of Wisconsin Press
1930 Monroe Street, 3rd Floor
Madison, Wisconsin 53711-2059
uwpress.wisc.edu

3 Henrietta Street
London WC2E 8LU, England
eurospanbookstore.com

Printed in the United States of America

Library of Congress Cataloging-in-Publication Data
Gibney, John, 1976–
The shadow of a year: the 1641 rebellion in Irish history and memory / John Gibney.
p.   cm. — (History of Ireland and the Irish diaspora)
Includes bibliographical references and index.
ISBN 978-0-299-28954-6 (pbk.: alk. paper)
ISBN 978-0-299-28953-9 (e-book)
1. Ireland—History—Rebellion of 1641—Historiography.
2. Ireland—Historiography.   I. Title.
II. Series: History of Ireland and the Irish diaspora.
DA943.G42   2013
941.506—dc23
2012010169

I admired the histories of the late Professor J. C. Beckett, especially the clarity of his writing, and when we met and I told him so, he was glad. As he thanked me, he remarked, "Of course, they're prejudiced," with a very sly twinkle. What this has always seemed to me to imply is that there is no such thing as a "true" history. Each is a version of what has taken place, and everybody who writes is coming from somewhere.

John McGahern

Contents

Illustrations

Acknowledgments

Most of the research and and much of the writing of this book took place under the auspices of a Government of Ireland fellowship held at the Moore Institute, National University of Ireland, Galway. Earlier versions of parts of the text have been published as "'Facts Newly *Stated*': John Curry, the 1641 Rebellion, and Catholic Revisionism in Eighteenth-Century Ireland, 1747–80," *Éire-Ireland: An Interdisciplinary Journal of Irish Studies* 44, no. 3–4 (Fall/Winter 2009): 248–77; "Walter Love's 'Bloody Massacre': An Unfinished Study in Irish Cultural History, 1641–1963," *Proceedings of the Royal Irish Academy* 110C (2010): 217–37; and "Protestant Interests? The 1641 Rebellion and State Formation in Early Modern Ireland," *Historical Research* 84 (Feb. 2011): 67–86. I would like to thank, respectively, the Irish American Cultural Institute, the Royal Irish Academy, and the Institute of Historical Research for permission to reproduce this material. I would also like to thank the Board of the British Library, the Board of the National Library of Ireland, the Board of Trinity College Dublin, Dublin City Archives, and the Honourable Society of King's Inns for permission to quote from unpublished material in their possession.

On a personal level, a number of people made my life much easier in the course of working on this book, most especially Nicholas Canny, Carmel Connolly, Emily Cullen, Eamon Darcy, Kevin Forkan, Ted McCormick, Edward Madigan, Christopher Maginn, Brian Ó Conchubair, Grace O'Keefe, Kate O'Malley, Orla Power, and Jim Smyth, who all provided encouragement and support of one kind or another. Karl Bottigheimer generously responded to my query about the late Walter Love. Aidan Clarke, Christopher Fox, and Hiram Morgan provided me with unpublished material. I naturally wish to thank the staffs of the various libraries that I used in the course of my research, but I should single out Aedin Clements (Notre Dame), Kieran Hoare (National University of Ireland, Galway), and Gerry Kavanagh (National Library of

Ireland) for going above and beyond the call of duty. Elizabethanne Boran, Eamon Darcy, Kevin Forkan, Brian Hanley, Jason McHugh, James McConnel, Robin Usher, and Kevin Whelan provided me with all kinds of arcane references and sources. Brendan Kane furnished me with a copy of a useful book and Jane Ohlmeyer kindly submitted to an interview. Tommy Graham extended invitations to discuss the topic before audiences in Letterkenny, Derry, the National Library of Ireland, and the Electric Picnic in Stradbally; Micheal Ó Siochrú invited me to speak to another audience at Trinity College Dublin. Guy Beiner commented on the introduction, and Aidan Clarke provided me with a forensic commentary on an earlier version of the manuscript, thereby improving it immeasurably. James S. Donnelly nudged it toward the finishing line with exemplary patience. Eileen O'Neill prepared the index. Breandán Mac Suibhne deserves some credit for the title whether he likes it or not. I can only apologize to any colleagues or friends whose assistance I have forgotten. Finally, I owe profound debts to my family and, last but never least, to Liza Costello.

The Shadow of a Year

Introduction

On 22 October 2010, in the Long Room of Trinity College Dublin, Mary McAleese and Ian Paisley launched an exhibition about the Irish rebellion of 1641. On the face of it, they were an unlikely duo. Prior to her election as president of the Republic of Ireland, McAleese (a Belfast Catholic whose family home had been burnt out by loyalists in the 1970s) was perceived by some to represent particularly conservative forms of Irish Catholicism and nationalism—a "tribal time bomb," as one commentator had put it.[1] As for Paisley, despite his transition to a seemingly mellow old age, he remained the epitome of an unyielding Protestant loyalism, whose career as both demagogue and Democratic Unionist leader was synonymous with the "Troubles" and had indeed been an integral part of them. Hence the existence of what might be, to a casual observer, an incongruous double act: between them, McAleese and Paisley represented the opposing political and religious traditions on the island of Ireland, from which the principal actors in the conflict in Northern Ireland had sprung over the previous five decades.

But this was the entire point of their presence, and on this occasion both were in a gracious mood. The conflict that erupted in Northern Ireland had been the latest manifestation of an enduring historical dichotomy between Catholic and Protestant on the island of Ireland. The seemingly atavistic nature of this conflict arose in part from the fact that it had never been adequately resolved and had continued to fester after being largely corralled into the six counties of Northern Ireland following the British partition of 1920. But the ultimate origin of such sectarianism is to be found long before the twentieth century. From the latter half of the sixteenth century onwards, Ireland was reconquered by English governments based in Dublin. In the aftermath large tracts of the country, especially in the northern province of Ulster, were colonized in

the early decades of the seventeenth century by tens of thousands of British
settlers, the majority of whom were Protestants of one kind or another. The
exhibition being launched by McAleese and Paisley concerned the single most
significant event of this period: the rebellion of 1641, in which Irish Catholics rose
up against the British Protestant colonists who were seen to have supplanted
them. They were assumed to have done so with appalling brutality, and so the
insurrection of 1641 has traditionally been viewed as the first explicitly sectarian
conflict in Irish history. It has been remembered as the first of many such
conflicts, but the launch of this exhibition in Trinity was more concerned with
how it had been *misremembered*. According to McAleese, when it came to the
events of 1641, "facts and truth have been casualties along the way and the
distillation of skewed perceptions over generations have contributed to a situation where both sides"—Catholic and Protestant—"were confounding mysteries
to one another." The significance of overcoming such misunderstanding was
spelled out by Paisley, who claimed that "to learn this story, I believe, is to
know who we are, why we have had to witness our own trouble, and why we
live in a divided island."[2] Within such statements was a recognition that the
events of 1641 had left a stark and enduring legacy.

McAleese and Paisley spoke on the 369th anniversary of the outbreak of the
rebellion—or of the rising, depending on one's perspective.[3] Regardless of what
one called it, the event that marked its outbreak was relatively straightforward.
On 22 October 1641 Sir Phelim O'Neill, MP for Dungannon (among other
titles), called at Charlemont fort in Armagh under the pretext of dining with its
governor, Toby, Lord Caulfield. O'Neill seems to have depended on their
presumably cordial relations to gain entry, and having done so, his followers
produced weapons and proceeded to take over the fort. Similar events happened
across Armagh and Tyrone during the next two days. That this was part of a
larger scheme for a rebellion also became evident on 22 October, when, far
from the epicenter of the uprising in Ulster, the government in Dublin learned
of a plan to capture Dublin Castle and appropriate its arsenal. Having been
warned, officials ordered the imprisonment of all those who were accused or
suspected of involvement in the conspiracy. But that did nothing to impede the
widespread revolt that soon followed.

The immediate context of the insurrection was the political crisis across the
three Stuart kingdoms engendered by Charles I's attempt to impose episcopacy
on Presbyterian Scotland, an effort that had prompted the Scots to revolt in
1637. Charles was unable to defeat the Scots and sought to strengthen his forces
by raising an army in his Irish kingdom. But before this force could be brought
to bear on the Scots, they invaded northern England, occupying it as far south

as Newcastle and declaring that they would withdraw only under terms ratified by the English parliament. This, along with the fact that Charles now needed English forces to deal with the Scots, forced the calling of the "Long Parliament" in November 1640. The original purpose of the Irish army was now redundant, but given that a large, overwhelming Catholic force had been raised to impose the king's will on the Scots, concerns began to emerge that it might be used to impose his will on the English instead. This fear was accentuated by sectarian factors: a Catholic army was anathema to Protestant England, and especially to an English parliament that seemed militantly Protestant in its disposition. To some elements of elite Catholic opinion in Ireland, this new reality was disconcerting on two fronts.

There were many types of Catholic in early Stuart Ireland. One category was that of the "Old English"—the term given to those descendants of the original Anglo-Norman colonists who, while remaining loyal to the crown, had also retained their loyalty to the Church of Rome. As Catholics, they were dissident by definition, and throughout the reign of Charles I they had sought to square this circle, seeking some toleration of their religion and secure ownership of their lands in return for their loyalty to the crown. The fact that neither objective had been achieved by 1641 had left a lingering uncertainty that was now being compounded by anti-Catholic rumblings sounding across the Irish Sea, from both the English parliament and the Scots. While the Old English certainly considered using force to secure their position in the early summer of 1641 (after all, the Scots had successfully done something similar), by the end of the year their inclination to do so had faded. Indeed, the crisis across the three kingdoms was abating. After successful negotiations with the Scots there were suggestions from within the English parliament that it could now be dissolved. The fact that it would not be dissolved for almost twenty years largely arose from the fact that an insurrection erupted in Ireland.

The most significant and numerous segment of the Catholic population in Ireland were the native Irish themselves. They had been peripheral to many of these events, but their religious adherence meant that they could not be wholly disinterested bystanders. They too had shared the fears of the Old English about the possible intentions of the English parliament, but thanks to their recent historical experience, the grievances of the Irish over the uncertain ownership of their lands were rendered even more acute than those of their coreligionists. The massive plantation of Ulster in the early decades of the seventeenth century had largely been conducted at their expense, as many of them had been dispossessed of their lands and stripped of their status. Compounding these festering realities was the fact that the Irish played virtually no part in any of the negotiations that had been conducted throughout the crisis. They were excluded, and to paraphrase Michael Perceval-Maxwell, they had become alienated and isolated. Taking their cue from the Scots, they thus had recourse to arms.

The original purpose of the conspiracy headed by O'Neill seemed straightforward enough. The Catholic gentry of Ulster sought a position of security and strength from which to negotiate with Charles I on the issues of concern to them: security of land and religion. Indeed, at no point did O'Neill and his fellow conspirators disavow their loyalty to the crown: quite the opposite. They claimed to have acted as loyal subjects in defense of their rights. Some of them, such as O'Neill, would later seek to bolster their legitimacy and garner support by claiming to have a commission from Charles I to do so. But the fact that this could later be used as propaganda against them arose from the unintended consequences of his actions.

The limited capture of key positions in Ulster for specific purposes gave way to a popular rebellion directed at the English Protestant colonists who had settled there under the plantation of Ulster. As the rebellion fanned out from its core in Armagh and the authority of the government collapsed, much of what happened in the weeks that followed amply illustrated that many of the Catholic Irish insurgents intended to exact a heavy price from those settlers, whom they explicitly targeted for attack.[4] Some of these attacks stemmed from little more than banditry and robbery; some arose from socioeconomic grievances. But alongside short-term considerations were deeper resentments. A visceral anti-Englishness became evident as settlers were attacked in ways that seemed to foreshadow both their eradication and that of the culture they had brought with them to Ireland. Naked sectarianism was evident as the symbols of Protestantism (such as bibles) also came under attack. Taken as a whole, the winter of 1641–42 saw almost ritualized attempts to wipe out the physical, cultural, and religious presence of the Protestant colonists in Ireland.

It is this aspect of the rebellion that had traditionally garnered the greatest attention. And it rests on a significant core of truth. Protestants were very deliberately killed in attacks. There were also instances where prisoners were deliberately slaughtered en masse. Others were killed indirectly: the stripping of prisoners in the depths of winter often became a death sentence in itself. The torture of captives, the drowning of Protestants in Belturbet and Portadown, mass killings in Sligo and Shrule, the desecration of recently killed corpses in Kilkenny: there is no mistaking the fact that such things happened. Nor can there be any avoidance of the fact that Protestant forces were capable of equally brutal killings during both the initial insurrection and the war that followed. But it was the murder of innocent Protestants that became the iconic motif of 1641, one that would resonate through centuries of British and Irish history. As an anonymous English pamphleteer remarked in an anti-Catholic diatribe in

1680, "We may call Popery a bloody religion, if at least we may afford the name of religion to a thing made up of idolatry, usurpation, and cruelty."[5] And, he continued, for particularly heinous examples of such cruelty,

> we need not look any further back than the present age: in the rebellion of Ireland wherein there were more than three hundred thousand innocent Protestants destroyed, and this in a base treacherous manner, without any provocation[;] no age, sex, or quality being privileged from massacres and lingering deaths, by being robbed, stripped naked, and so exposed to perish by cold and famine, or else suddenly hanged, their throats cut, drowned in rivers, bogs, and ditches, or else murdered with exquisite torture: wives ravished before their husbands faces, children forced to hang up their own parents, others compelled against their consciences to own the Romish superstitions and swear thereunto in hopes to save their lives, and presently murthered, as if they designed to destroy souls as well as bodies: and such beastly cruelties acted as the most barbarous heathens would blush to practise. All which being acted within these 40 years, I hope is not yet, nor ever will be forgot.[6]

This author got his wish: over two centuries later, in 1909, Frederick MacNiece, a Church of Ireland minister in County Antrim (and the father of the poet Louis), bemoaned the fact that it had not been forgotten, as he hoped "to God we had the wisdom not only to remember but to forget. Surely there is no true wisdom in recalling year after year the story of wrongs inflicted upon Protestants in 1641."[7]

The fact that MacNiece felt compelled to point this out illustrates the enduring power of the recollection. According to another Ulsterman, the historian A. T. Q. Stewart, "The 1641 rebellion is perhaps the most important episode in the history of Ulster since the plantation, yet it is one of the least discussed. Like an unseen planet whose presence is revealed only by its influence on other celestial bodies, the rebellion betrays its significance in later events: the more one explores Ulster history, the more one becomes aware of its occult force. Sooner or later in each successive crisis, the cry is raised of '1641 come again.'"[8] Stewart was an historian of unionist sympathies, and he may have written from experience: his assessment of 1641 came after the bloodiest period of the "Troubles" in the 1970s. But if anything, it is an understatement: the symbolic import of 1641 made it one of the most important events in the history of modern Ireland, let alone Ulster, and much of that importance arose from the manner in which it was perceived by subsequent generations. In the 1960s an American historian of Ireland, Walter D. Love, correctly observed that the significance of 1641 in the centuries after the event rested on perception rather than reality, for just as "Protestants wrote histories that were alive with Catholic rebellions and massacres" and "justified the penal laws as necessary protection against an unforgivably and ineradically rebellious people," so Catholics "wrote histories to protest against the penal laws; they laboured to show that the rebellions and massacres were really provoked by Protestants and that most past troubles were caused either by the Protestants themselves or by the unfortunate division of the country, by law, into two hostile bodies."[9]

The significance of such sectarian arguments was straightforward enough. From the 1640s onward, a Protestant paradigm of the *rebellion* as an attempt at wholesale sectarian massacre had been constructed and, indeed, had received official sanction via the official commemoration of the rebellion by the Church of Ireland on 23 October each year (one that lingered until at least the end of the eighteenth century).[10] In this reading of 1641 the grievances of Irish Catholics, prompted as they were by the experience of dispossession and plantation, were disregarded, and the rebellion and its perceived brutalities were attributed to their innate bigotry and brutality. This interpretation was used as a pretext for both the Cromwellian reconquest of 1649–53 and the subsequent confiscations of the 1650s. It was also deployed to justify both the substantive maintenance of these confiscations after the restoration of the monarchy in 1660 and the "penal laws" of a later era. To uphold this "Protestant" version of 1641 was to justify the continued dispossession and disenfranchisement of Irish Catholics on the grounds of justice and prudence.

But there was also a Catholic interpretation of 1641 that depicted it as a *rising*, an event with a far greater legitimacy than any mere "rebellion." In this reading, Protestant allegations of Catholic atrocities were downplayed or dismissed; indeed, some Catholic polemists went so far as to argue that the maintenance of this Protestant version of 1641 was merely a cynical justification for relegating Irish Catholics to the status of a dispossessed and oppressed underclass. But should the Protestant interpretation of the rebellion be successfully challenged, then a key historical justification for the existence of a sectarian state in eighteenth-century Ireland could be undermined. This was the context, for example, in which the eighteenth-century Catholic physician and activist John Curry articulated a Catholic perspective on the rebellion in his own writings on Irish history. To dismiss the allegations of a massacre of Protestants was to provide a further weapon in the ongoing debate over the readmission of Irish Catholics to political and social rights—the so-called "Catholic question."[11] Such disputations would recur against the backdrop of later events: the 1798 rebellion, the struggle for Catholic Emancipation in the 1820s, and the campaigns for Home Rule in the second half of the nineteenth century, to name but three. And as Walter Love put it in the early 1960s, "the two traditions went right on, and they have continued, bombast and all, into the present day."[12]

What actually happened in 1641? Attempts to answer that question have, over the centuries, tended to generate more heat than light. But the rebellion left to posterity an unprecedented and almost unique body of evidence: a massive quantity of contemporary testimonies collected from survivors of the rebellion in the 1640s and 1650s. These "depositions" have been in the possession of Trinity College Dublin since 1741 and are arguably the most controversial collection of documents in Irish history, for they have usually been assumed to prove that the rebellion was indeed a sectarian war against Protestant settlers. Some of the depositions do indeed contain lurid reports of atrocities visited on Protestant settlers by Catholics, both real and rumored; the tiny proportion of the depositions that had made their way into the public domain over the centuries played a role in sectarian arguments by seeming to illustrate this perspective. Very few people had ever tried to systematically examine the entire collection of depositions, largely because the originals are notoriously difficult to decipher and to make sense of. But by 22 October 2010 this obstacle appeared to have been finally overcome, as the depositions were made fully accessible online. Between 2007 and 2010 Trinity College had spearheaded a hugely expensive and massively ambitious project to transcribe, digitize, and publish all of the depositions. Mary McAleese and Ian Paisley were in Trinity not just to launch an exhibition; they were also there to officially launch the website on which the testimonies were now available for public perusal. The symbolism of their presence was related to this stunning novelty above all else, and both seemed well aware of it as they implored the audience to learn from the riches of the website. For McAleese testimonies such as these "should inspire us to keep on working to ensure an end forever to such suffering." Paisley seemed to echo this sentiment. "Let us introduce these parts of our history in the right way to our children."[13] It is worth pausing to consider what these "parts of our history" actually consisted of.

The 1641 depositions are bound into thirty-one volumes, arranged by county and containing approximately 8,000 testimonies taken from Protestant survivors of the rebellion (and some Catholics), along with certain associated documents.[14] They were presented to Trinity College on the centenary of the rebellion, in 1741, by John Stearne, the bishop of Clogher. He had bought them between 1702 and 1708 from the widow of John Madden, a collector who had obtained them at some point from Matthew Barry, the clerk of the Irish privy council. Precisely when they had been arranged by county is uncertain, but it clearly proved confusing to posterity. In order to make sense of the depositions, they have to be unscrambled, and this means that their origins have to be explained.

The manner in which the depositions are arranged is misleadingly neat: it hides at least five major categories of documents, along with a scattering of other testimonies. The first set of documents consists of the original depositions, taken by a commission of Anglican clergymen appointed on 23 December 1641 and headed by Henry Jones (dean of Kilmore and future stalwart of the Protestant interest). The original motives for collecting them were to obtain a record of the material losses of Protestant settlers in order to provide for their relief and to gather information on the rebels, but within a matter of weeks the commissioners' remit was expanded to inquire into murders. These accounts were copied in 1645–46 by Thomas Waring, the clerk of the commission, who may have feared that the originals were to be destroyed at the behest of the Confederate Catholics and who later conveyed these copies to England; the ones that survive make up the second set of documents. The third consists of depositions taken in Munster between March 1642 and July 1643 by a second commission headed by Philip Bisse, the archdeacon of Cloyne, which were intended to augment the original set, none of which had come from Munster. The fourth set of documents consists of various testimonies taken by officials throughout the 1640s, while the final category consists of the examinations taken between 1652 and 1654 by seventy commissioners appointed to gather evidence of atrocities and murders committed since the rebellion in order to prosecute the perpetrators. The depositions were used at later junctures when the issue of Catholic guilt for crimes allegedly committed in 1641 could have a bearing on events—for example, during the Cromwellian settlement of the 1650s and in the attempts to revise the settlement after the restoration of the monarchy in 1660.

Bound together as they are, the depositions make up an uneven but extraordinary collection, seemingly without parallel in early modern Europe. The way in which they are arranged may be confusing, and the spelling, format, and handwriting within them might be erratic and inconsistent throughout, but within this jumble is a huge amount of information on colonial life in Ulster, the course of the rebellion, and most obviously the allegations of crimes and atrocities committed during it. Admittedly, the depositions are "just one side of a story of murder, [of] atrocity, and the fact that we've got [only] one side of it is highly problematic."[15] This is a valid qualification, but it does not undermine their potential value: the depositions offer a window into the experience of Protestants during the rebellion, not to mention the lives they had led before it.

Yet the reality is that the manner in which the depositions have been used and abused over the centuries places a much greater emphasis on death than on life. There is no doubt that some of the depositions contain accounts of killings, and numerous descriptions of such actions are indeed horrific. While some of these testimonies were exaggerated, others were not. But most of the depositions made no mention of killings of any kind. Of those that did so, some were eyewitness accounts, whereas others reported hearsay and rumor. The confusing and haphazard manner in which the depositions were collated meant that such distinctions could be lost on those few scholars who actually looked at them. The English cleric Ferdinando Warner, for example, examined at least some of the depositions in the eighteenth century but then dismissed them all as worthless on grounds that suggest a certain degree of confusion; it seems that he simply did not understand what he was looking at and instead based his assessment of 1641 on documents that were far less problematic. This was plainly inadequate, but Warner deserves some credit for one simple reason: he actually looked at the originals. And very few people had ever done so.

The bloodcurdling descriptions of Catholic atrocities that copperfastened the image of 1641 as a sectarian bloodbath came from the tiny proportion of the depositions that had actually been published.[16] Prior to the publication of Mary Hickson's extensive anthology of the depositions in 1884, perhaps no more than two hundred of the original testimonies could be considered as being in the public domain in any sense whatsoever. These had originally been published in the 1640s in works by Henry Jones and Sir John Temple. Thomas Waring, who had copied the originals, apparently planned to publish more of them but never did, so those writers who followed in the footsteps of Jones and Temple did so quite literally. Attempts either to prove or disprove the perennial allegation that in 1641 there had been an effort to exterminate Protestants were generally based on depositions that had conveniently been published in the seventeenth century, and for very specific purposes. But this was wholly inadequate, for it was generally assumed that the handful of depositions that had been published were representative of the whole, when in reality they were anything but. The vast majority of the depositions were generally ignored. So the evidence with which one might have proved or disproved the allegations of a massacre was actually there; the problem was that virtually nobody bothered to look at it. In this regard the debate over the precise nature of the 1641 rebellion that took place over the centuries was essentially an unreal one. But it was no less vigorous for that.

At some point in the early 1960s the American historian Walter Love read *The Leopard*, Giuseppe Tomasi di Lampedusa's epic novel of the Italian *risorgimento*. In it was a passage he decided to record: "Nowhere has truth so short a life as in Sicily; a fact has scarcely happened five minutes before its genuine kernel has vanished, been camouflaged, embellished, disfigured, annihilated by imagination and self interest; shame, fear, generosity, malice, opportunism, charity, all the passions, good as well as evil, fling themselves on the fact and tear it to pieces; very soon it has vanished altogether."[17] The problem that this passage implied was bound to engage the interest of an historian: the necessity to look for the reality of an event behind the layers of distortion that could become attached to it over time. Broadly speaking, this was a task in which Irish historians took a particular interest during the latter decades of the twentieth century. But while this passage from *The Leopard* could have struck a responsive chord with any number of Irish historians, the scholar who took note of it was an outsider whose career was shaped in a very different milieu, and it seemed to speak to his particular interests.

Walter Love grew up in a Mormon family in Salt Lake City, Utah, and was a graduate of both the University of Chicago and the University of California, Berkeley; he held successive posts at Emory University in Atlanta and the University of Bridgeport in Connecticut before he was killed in a car accident in 1966.[18] Prior to his premature death he had been working on a project that in hindsight seemed far ahead of its time, at least in Irish terms: a study of the manner in which 1641 had been represented, debated, and argued about in print from its outbreak until the end of the nineteenth century.[19] While his book remained unfinished, Love's notes and research materials were bequeathed to Karl Bottigheimer, an American historian of early modern Ireland whom he had originally met in Dublin, and who deposited them in the library of Trinity College Dublin in the 1970s.

Love's papers consist of a bewildering jumble of material: notes, files, drafts, jottings, and assorted papers both in longhand and typescript; some correspondence; and in a piquant testament to his industry, hundreds of call slips from the National Library of Ireland. Collectively, these provide a road map into the intricacies of the contested historiography of the insurrection of 1641, the problems that writing a book of this kind might present, and the material with which one might attempt to write it.[20] Love's surviving papers demonstrate that he was working on what would have been, first and foremost, a study of historical *writing*. His academic background lent itself to this, and the broad contours of his career suggest that a recurrent interest in the writing of history brought him to Irish history, and thence to the contested memory of 1641.[21]

It is difficult to be entirely sure of the title of his unfinished book, but the surviving fragments of the text are filed under a phrase that recurred again and again in both his papers and published work: the "Bloody Massacre."[22] The book was to have a tripartite structure, opening in the eighteenth century in order to illustrate the "two sets (opposing and contradictory) of feelings" about the events of 1641.[23] The subsequent section would move back to the seventeenth century to illustrate "what happened to create this story."[24] Love conceived of the rhetorical trick of writing this segment from his own "personal experience," and thought to end it by using the depositions to reveal how the massacres were exaggerated as they made their way into print. This would lead to a third section dealing with the nineteenth century and with what he viewed as "the next obvious problem": why the advent of "scientific" history in the nineteenth century did not lead to a resolution.[25] The absence of such a resolution "projects part four, which I may or may not do, the problem of what actually happened."[26] Yet this was not Love's priority. The crucial question he sought to answer was "how did the original story get formed, assuming it is false and can be destroyed. Or perhaps it is true; then too, one might ask how it got formed in such a way that such violent exception can be taken to it and seem plausible for good historians to write it."[27]

Walter D. Love was a very good historian. His tragic death robbed his peers of what would surely have been a groundbreaking study (an echo of which is to be found in this current, and surely inferior, book). But the project to which Walter Love had dedicated himself was not the kind of project that Irish historians were likely to have undertaken in the 1960s. Instead, he was working on precisely the kind of intensely subjective historical writing that many of his Irish contemporaries would almost certainly have dismissed. The emergence of professional academic history in twentieth-century Ireland is usually ascribed to the various initiatives of J. C. Beckett of Queen's University, Belfast, Robert Dudley Edwards of University College Dublin, and T. W. Moody of Trinity College from the 1930s onward, often in a rather eulogistic and uncritical manner.[28] Their endeavors were driven by an acute awareness that the writing of Irish history had usually been shaped by the competing religious and political affiliations of those who had written it. Strictly speaking, there was nothing specifically Irish in this, other than its distinctly Irish manifestations: the existence of both nationalist and unionist versions of Irish history, often corresponding to older confessional (both Catholic and Protestant) narratives of the Irish past. But despite an awareness of this latent subjectivity on the part of these "new historians," and their resultant ambition to correct this problem, there seemed little inclination to probe the reasons why such polemical histories had come into being in the first place, and why they might continue to exist. Even as late as the 1970s Moody himself simply took their existence for granted and argued that the so-called "myths" of Irish history needed to be critically interrogated in the light of empirical reality as revealed by historians.[29] It is hard to argue against that proposition. Yet at the same time it is a crude assumption, for it took little cognizance of the role that such "myths" had actually played in Irish history, or of the processes by which they were recalled, reshaped, and reinvented down through the centuries.

1641 was remembered. Of that there could be no doubt. In William Carleton's story "Larry McFarland's Wake" (1812), the eponymous Larry drowns in a bog hole while drunk. His dissolute life is inevitably followed by an impressive wake, and amid much singing, boozing, and smoking, visitors paying their respects "might see a knot of ould men sitting together, talking over old times—ghost stories, fairy tales, or the great rebellion of 41."[30] Similar murmurs were picked up in April 1836 in County Londonderry, when collectors for the unpublished memoirs compiled by the Ordnance Survey of Ireland noted that "there are many traditions relating to the troubles of 1641."[31]

The precise manner in which 1641 was remembered at this oral, subaltern level is largely obscure, for reasons explained below. The version of 1641 being remembered might also be difficult to discern; Carleton—himself a native of Tyrone—remained noncommittal. But hints of its essential significance can be detected. In his preface to the collection to which the tale of the unfortunate Larry McFarland belonged, Carleton helpfully observed that "the English reader, perhaps, may be skeptical as to the deep hatred which prevails among Roman Catholics in the north of Ireland against those who differ from them in party and religious principles; but when he reflects that they were driven before the face of the Scotch invader, and divested by the Settlement of Ulster of their pleasant vales, forced to quench the fires on their fathers' hearths, and retire to the mountain ranges of Tyrone, Donegal, and Derry, perhaps he will grant, after all, that the feeling is natural to a race treated as they have been."[32] The 1641 rebellion was one of the episodes that lurked behind such sentiments, for as we shall see, it provided much of the pretext for the continued dispossession of the Roman Catholics of whom Carleton spoke. In a similar vein the French traveler Gustave de Beaumont, writing in the 1830s, observed that "it is impossible to travel in Ireland without meeting a ruin which was the witness of some sanguinary struggle; it is scarce possible to stir a step without treading on land which, by the fortune of civil war, has not passed through the hands of three or four sets of possessors, the last of which, remaining master, represents that cause that triumphed. The vanquished may be seen beside the conquerors still full of the recollections of more prosperous times. . . . The wounds made by the wars of religion are those which are still the deepest and most grievous in Ireland."[33]

Again, the shadow of 1641 lurked behind such observations, with their recognition of the power of religion. As the exemplar of sectarian war in Ireland, 1641 had been a cornerstone of Ireland's sectarian history from the seventeenth century onward. But it was remembered in differing ways by those who would concern themselves with such sectarianism and its implications. The question of how the Irish past was remembered cannot be divorced from the question of who was remembering it. And this forces consideration of the vexing issue of "collective," "historical," or "social" memory.[34]

The most obvious problem to overcome while trying to make sense of such awkward concepts is perhaps the most enduring: the inevitable tension between the individual and the collective. Is "collective memory" a contradiction in terms? Rather than proceed from a potentially tricky assumption, it might be more useful to examine how the individuals who make up both communities and cultures—Catholic and Protestant—remember the past in overlapping and convergent ways. Graham Dawson usefully defined cultural memory as "the representation by a social group of processes, events, or experiences that have taken place or are believed to have taken place in its past; that articulates its sense of a lived connection between past and present, and the meanings it makes of that connection."[35] Remembrance certainly acquires meaning, but remembrance is not the same as remembering: a particular version of an event can be reconstructed by individuals and communities whose lived experience lies a long way away from that event. The version that is summoned into existence might diverge wildly from the reality of what actually happened. There is never simply an unbroken line of transmission across the centuries; instead, there is a process of regeneration that is shaped by the conditions of the historical moment in which it takes place.[36] This observation brings us back to Moody's dichotomy between history (reality) and myth. But it also implies that between the reality and the "myth" is a process that transforms one into the other. Equally, the distinction between history and myth is not the only dichotomy of this kind. The notion that "history" and "memory" are antithetical by nature is nothing new, but the fluidity between the two is worth considering. This inquiry can bring us to a distinction between "social memory" and "historical reconstruction"; the latter can reveal things that play no part in the former, though in certain circumstances such reconstruction can also play a part in shaping "social" memory into a different pattern.[37] But we need to be clear about what "memory" in this context actually means. If it simply refers to a pattern of remembrance, it does not automatically mean that this pattern reflects the reality of what is being remembered. "Memory" can also denote a particular representation of the past—of what was *believed* to have happened. Or as Moody put it, a "myth." While it was one thing to attempt to destroy myths, a far more challenging task would be to examine them, understand them, and explain them. The empirical basis of the so-called "new history" in Ireland was quite capable of attempting to dispel myths, but its methodological basis was arguably incapable of explaining them.[38] Hence the significance of any attempt by a historian to grapple with these so-called myths, which was precisely what Walter Love was trying to do by writing about the historiography of 1641.

Let us assume that "history" and "memory" are indeed antithetical, and that the same can be true of "history" and "myth." But, crucially, one can be transformed into the other. Traditions of remembrance might fade over time, but they could still survive, to be reinvigorated at certain junctures. The fluid and organic nature of these transmitted traditions could be married to the ostensible precision of the written word in what one scholar defined as a "cognitive reappropriation of the past."[39] Written history could become a tool to reinvigorate myths as much as to refute them. And what this book is largely concerned with is that written history.

My original ambition was to emulate the work of Guy Beiner by analyzing the folk history and social memory of the 1798 rebellion.[40] But the rich collections of the National Folklore Collection (NFC), used by Beiner to great effect, lacks a comparable body of material for the 1641 rebellion. It simply does not register— a stark reality that I was extremely surprised to encounter. Nor does the NFC's schools collection cover the six counties of Northern Ireland, so the gap in the folkloric record is all the more pronounced. The oral tradition remains largely obscure, which is most unfortunate, though I have endeavored to incorporate such fragments as I could find. Thus the focus of my book is on the printed word, with the contested historiography of 1641 at its heart. This choice was dictated by the sources that were available, and my focus on certain historians is driven by the fact that only a handful of scholars even attempted to get beyond traditional sectarian assumptions about the nature of 1641. It is this handful who set the terms of the debate, such as it was.

One might legitimately observe that this study is more concerned with what was written than with what was read. The reason for this tilt is the simple fact that, as Toby Barnard observed, "past readers seldom tell us in any helpful way how they responded to their books."[41] Not every reader is as helpful as the un- known individual who, on reading an eighteenth-century edition of a history of Ireland, underlined the passage that described 1641 as "this last bloody rebellion, wherein the inhabitants of almost all the Pale, although all of them of English descent, have conspired with the native Irish for to shake off the government of the crown of England and utterly to extinguish the reformed religion, with all the professors thereof, and quite to root them out of Ireland."[42] This passage obviously resonated with this reader, who noted at the bottom of the page that these events were "like the year 1798." He or she had drawn a continuity between these two upheavals. But their precise meaning for that reader remains lost to historians. And even this tantalizing fragment is the exception rather then the rule. We simply do not—cannot—know with any certainty how, or by whom, ideas about the past were received. One can attempt to plug this gap. For example, analyzing the contents of a library (as Barnard himself has done) can offer a hint as to the preoccupations and interests of its owner.[43] But this approach must be tempered by Anthony Burgess's dictum that owning a book is the perfect substitute for not reading it. After all, the most notorious account of the 1641 rebellion was Sir John Temple's *The Irish Rebellion*, originally published in 1646. But in the latter half of the seventeenth century it was borrowed from the library of Trinity College Dublin only four times in twenty years.[44] Thus, when it comes to making assumptions about the manner in which texts were read (if they actually were), one must proceed with caution. To analyze the reception of texts, and of the ideas that they contained, is to step into a field fraught with difficulty. Book reviews, for example, provide some useful hints about how books were received. But while I have made some use of them, reviews can furnish only a narrow and unrepresentative set of responses to a text. The little that can be captured is a fraction of what might ideally be corralled. I have endeavored to indicate points at which the works I discuss met an audience, but as the reception of ideas remains difficult to assess, my focus is on the manner in which they were articulated and propounded in print. Hence the purpose of this discussion is to put forth a series of suggestions about how historical writing, and writing about history in its broadest sense, can be integrated into or influence broader patterns of remembrance. Readers can hopefully draw their own conclusions.

After this excursus let us return to 1641. How was the insurrection remembered and represented, and to what ends? For it was obvious that inaccurate and misleading depictions of it became crucial ideological touchstones. The existence of a "collective identity based on myths, and more particularly myths of origins," is merely one strand of memory, and the shift to a written record—1641 was rapidly and extensively entrenched within print culture—could allow for the formalization of such remembrance.[45] But 1641 was remembered insofar as it was relevant to those who did so. As 1641 passed into history, it was reconstructed and reincorporated into distinct interpretations of Irish history that drew much of their rationale from the perceived continuity of the past with the present. I borrow from Pierre Nora in viewing 1641 as a *lieu de mémoire*, a "place" or "site" of memory, to be invested with meaning as the present dictated.[46]

This perspective is valid for many dates that have been recalled throughout Irish history: the afterlives of the Gunpowder Plot, the Siege of Derry, the 1798 Rebellion, the Easter Rising, and the Irish Civil War all come to mind, and all have been subjected to scholarly scrutiny.[47] I have attempted to add 1641 to this list, for its importance arises from its afterlife as much as from its constitutive events. There was nothing unusual about the past being interpreted at the behest of the present. In nineteenth-century Germany, for example, competing Protestant and Catholic narratives of the German experience of the Thirty Years' War (1618–48) retained deeply loaded meanings, especially since Protestant narratives of the war came to be defined in nationalistic terms as "a struggle for German freedom."[48] The parallel with Ireland is obvious, and not just in terms of the period under scrutiny: differing versions of 1641 bolstered differing versions of Irish history, and by extension, differing visions of the Irish present. Protestant writers, for example, often linked 1641 with the Cromwellian settlement, for one had justified the other and continued to sanction its maintenance. Conversely, their Catholic counterparts sought to undercut or sever this connection by trying to disprove or downplay such atrocities as had taken place, or even by denying their very existence.[49] Between these two poles there lay considerable ground for debate; what was being said was perhaps of greater importance than who was saying it. It is impossible to dispute the fact that a rebellion or a rising broke out in Ulster on 23 October 1641. What always have been disputed are its nature and purpose. The rising became part of political and sectarian discourse in Ireland, both explicitly and implicitly, whether consciously or unconsciously. It was remembered: that is not in dispute either.[50] This book is concerned with the manner of such remembrance in order to test Walter Love's observation that one "might find out a lot about three centuries of conflict in that broken world of Irish life by studying the historiography of the massacre."[51]

The approach that I have chosen is designed to reflect the dialectic of much of that historiography, and in many ways follows in the unfinished footsteps of Walter Love, whose conception of the subject has helped to shape my own. In particular, I have benefited from his extensive identification of sources, though I have sought to expand the range of the material that might be used to make sense of the subject. Chapter 1 examines the construction and perpetuation of the "Protestant" version of 1641 as sectarian massacre, from the 1640s to the middle of the nineteenth century. Chapter 2 examines the construction of a Catholic counterargument over the same period of time. These debates over the true nature of 1641 did not progress or develop in meaningful ways prior to the latter decades of the nineteenth century, so chapter 3 examines the attempts to replace these contested images of the rebellion with a definitive and scholarly account in the second half of the nineteenth century; also explored are the failure of these efforts and the eventual manner in which they became the subject of reflection and serious inquiry. While each chapter can stand alone, none is hermetically sealed from the others: all three make up a connected whole.

And there are caveats to be entered, for there is much more to be said on this subject. Quite apart from my concentration on the written word, one might reasonably question my emphasis on extremes, given that the dominant trend in Irish historiography over the past thirty years has been to probe the ambiguous complexities of reality rather than to dwell on the simplicities of perception and prejudice. But this book is ultimately about such simplicities, hence the deployment of such catchall terms as "Catholic" and "Protestant." It is designed to set out the broad contours of an argument and is intended to open up its topic rather than to draw a line beneath it. For the sake of producing a manageable book I have been obliged to be selective, and the material used here has been restricted to the English language; sources in French, Irish, Latin, and Spanish will almost certainly provide other scholars with opportunities to contribute to the study of the contested remembrance of 1641.[52] The sources that I have used are like icebergs, revealing only fractions of the mentalities that lie beneath them. The manner in which the beliefs that fostered such mindsets were actually disseminated is not my primary concern here; I focus tightly on what those beliefs and interpretations were in the first instance. The sheer scale of the subject means that this book is perhaps more of an essay than a piece of exhaustive research, but this caveat does little to alter the essential objective: to look at how, where, and when 1641 was remembered and, of course, *why*.

I

"The Sad Story of Our Miseries"

Protestant Interpretations
of the Rebellion, c. 1641–c. 1840

John Gamble was a doctor and a native of Strabane who had been educated in
Edinburgh and served in the British army; he later settled in London and then,
in the early decades of the nineteenth century, made a number of trips home.
He wrote down his impressions of these trips and in doing so left a fleeting
record of a visit made in 1812 to an inn near Dungiven run by a Presbyterian
who had sworn to have but one drink a day, and that in the morning. Gamble
was thereby deprived of a prospective drinking companion after dinner, so
instead, to occupy his time, he picked up a book that another lodger had left
down:

> It was Sir William Temple's account of the rebellion of 1641. I carried it to
> my room. Sir William was a great statesman, a polished gentleman, and
> elegant scholar. Such is the character historians give him. We must not
> judge an author by his book, else I should pronounce him very undeserving
> of the praise so lavishly bestowed on him. Of all the accounts of the above
> unhappy period, his is the most partial, the most exaggerated, and the
> most absurd. On reflection, he was himself highly dissatisfied with the
> performance and would not suffer it to pass through a second edition. But
> the mischief was already done.[1]

Gamble made one mistake: he attributed this book to the diplomat and writer
Sir William Temple and in doing so questioned his illustrious reputation. But it

was not the work of Sir William Temple; rather, it had been written by his father, and Gamble was right not to understate its influence. Sir John Temple's *The Irish Rebellion* (1646) was probably the most famous—or infamous—depiction of the events of 1641, a work that could still, in 1887, be sarcastically described as "an almost infallible witness against Catholicism."[2] Its notoriety over the centuries rested on its status as a canonical "Protestant" account of 1641. Temple's work, based as it was on the more lurid of the testimonies taken from Protestant survivors of the rebellion, painted 1641 as little more than a vicious sectarian massacre. It also provided an interpretation of its origins that depicted it as both unjustified and unexpected, a judgment that further damned those who had taken part in it. But irrespective of the debates that later sprang up about its events, there was no question but that the outbreak of a rebellion in Ireland on 23 October 1641 was largely unexpected. So too were its legacies.

Representing a Rebellion: Henry Jones, Sir John Temple, and the Construction of a Protestant Paradigm

Sir John Temple himself had been the master of the rolls in the Dublin administration in the early 1640s, and on 2 September 1641 he told one correspondent that "this kingdom gives nothing worth your knowledge."[3] But within weeks of the outbreak of rebellion in the following October, the government of which Temple was a part was receiving reports that the insurgents were massacring Protestants or, in a judgment that foreshadowed a standard theme of much subsequent propaganda, that they fully intended to. According to the lord justices, John Borlase and William Parsons—the officials then in charge of the government in Dublin—by 5 November 1641 it was obvious that "the rebels have with great multitudes proceeded in their outrages even to great cruelty against the English and Protestants in all places they came."[4] Amid the devastation "they give out publicly that their purpose is totally to extirpate the English and Protestants."[5] Borlase and Parsons warned:

> If supplies of men, money, and arms come not speedily forth [out] of England hither, it cannot be avoided but the kingdom must be lost, and all the English and Protestants here destroyed. . . . And certainly this kingdom and the lives of us all here, and all the Protestants in the kingdom, were never in so great danger to be lost as at this instant, no age having produced in this kingdom an example of so much mischief done in so short a time as now we find acted here in less than a fortnight's space, by killing and destroying so many English and Protestants in several parts, by robbing

and spoiling of them and many thousands more of his Majesty's good subjects, by seizing so many castles, houses, and places of strength in several parts of the kingdom, by threatening the English to depart or otherwise they will destroy them utterly, and all their wickedness acted against the English and Protestants with so much inhumanity and cruelty as cannot be imagined from Christians even towards infidels.[6]

It is worth bearing in mind, given the manner in which later polemicists tried to dismiss the allegations of Protestants by casting doubt on the testimonies of survivors, that such allegations predated the collection of those testimonies. The rebellion was also blamed on "the incitement of Jesuits, priests, and friars."[7] If details were required, in November the lords justices claimed that in Ulster the rebels had taken Protestant men, stripped them, blinded them, and cut off their hands, "that they might endure the greater torment during the few hours left of their life, wherein is observable the most inveterate and virulent hatred they bear to the English nation."[8] By mid-December they were depicting the actions of the insurgents in terms such as these: "Nor is their malice towards the English expressed only so but further, even to the beasts of their fields and improvements of their lands, for they destroy all cattle of English breed and declare openly that their reason is because they are English, so great is their hatred not only to the persons of the English but also to every species of that nation, and they destroy all improvements made by the English and lay waste their habitations."[9] It was inevitable that reports of this nature were directed toward London, as English assistance would be required to suppress the rebellion. It seemed reasonable to expect such assistance to be forthcoming: even aside from a sense of Protestant solidarity, fears were rife that the atrocities (and intended atrocities) being reported would soon be transposed to England once the Irish turned their attention across the Irish Sea.

The rebellion came to play a crucial role in political discourse in England throughout the civil wars of the 1640s. The first printed accounts of atrocities committed against Protestants in Ireland appeared within a week of the rebellion breaking out (again, prior to the collection of the depositions), and between November 1641 and June 1642 the Irish rebellion accounted for a great deal of printed "news" in England (in April 1642 alone 37 percent of the London bookseller George Thomason's book purchases referred to Irish affairs, though this figure rapidly declined thereafter).[10] Indeed, the rebellion came to play a major role in ensuring that there was an English civil war in the first place, and the inflammatory role that Ireland played within the wider British crisis was continually stoked by print. The outbreak of the Irish rebellion had already prompted widespread fears in Wales and southeast England that Irish rebels would soon arrive in Britain. Rumors of their impending arrival were bolstered by the tales carried to Britain by Protestant refugees from Ireland, and "given that the plantation in Ulster had been a fairly recent project, a good number of the refugees must have been originally born in England or Wales and were consequently returning to their place of birth for relief" (a fact that may have strengthened their veracity).[11] A testimony from Ireland gives an indication of what such accounts may have related. In February 1642, during the siege of a castle in Clare, one of the defenders recorded that "the enemy would daily in our sight [draw] forth their skeins and swords, flourishing them, swearing many dangerous oaths that ere long they would drag us forth and hack us to pieces, terming us Puritan rogues and all the base names that might be invented, vowing that shortly Sir Phelim O'Neill and at least 40,000 soldiers would come into Thomond and not leave a Protestant living."[12]

The original rebellion spearheaded by Phelim O'Neill was wholly un-expected, but what seemed to be the sudden, brutal, and indiscriminate murder of innocent Protestants soon acquired a totemic status. While atrocities against Protestants did indeed take place (and were most frequently associated with the Ulster counties of Armagh, Fermanagh, Monaghan, and Tyrone[13]), rumors and expectations magnified these events into horribly lurid instances of Catholic savagery. Protestants were depicted as having been murdered without mercy, often by gleeful rebels who were only too happy to dispatch them. And the ends they met were apparently dreadful. Protestant men, women, and children were apparently roasted alive, drowned, eviscerated, hanged, stabbed, and tortured—often inventively, at great length, and in huge numbers. These depictions were perpetuated within the explosion of printed material that accompanied the outbreak of the civil wars, as the perception that the Irish rebellion was charac-terized by horrendous cruelty rapidly became entrenched.[14]

The initial printed reports of a massacre were seemingly derived from accounts presented to the English House of Commons in the first week of November 1641: "God in his mercy look upon us in these great straits and extremities, and deliver us out of the hands of these viperous and bloodthirsty people, who [are] satisfied with nothing but blood."[15] Many of the same types of atrocity were reiterated in these publications: the drowning of prisoners, brutal killings of children, the disemboweling of pregnant women. Such depictions drew on long-established tropes of Catholic atrocities stretching back to the Reformation: events such as the Marian persecutions in England, the Saint Bartholomew's Day massacre in France, and the excesses of the Spanish in both the Americas and the Netherlands made up a pantheon of Catholic brutality into which 1641 could easily be integrated.[16] Accounts that dwelled on the deliberate sectarianism of the Irish corresponded to, and became part of, a

Protestant tradition of martyrology exemplified in England by Foxe's *Acts and Monuments*.[17] Admittedly, such lurid versions of events often dealt with the expectation of a massacre rather than its occurrence, as intention was conflated with reality.[18] But statements of intent could be plausible: one tract confidently asserted that "the plot it was this, that in one day the castle of Dublin and all the king's forts in Ireland should have been taken, and all the Protestants' throats cut throughout all that kingdom."[19] This was not the invention of an English pamphleteer: it was a neat summary of the information provided to the authorities in Dublin by the informer Owen Connolly on the eve of the rebellion.[20] In other words, allegations about what the rebels in Ireland were doing (or intended to do) were coming from seemingly authoritative sources in Ireland. Even aside from their supposed intentions, there was no shortage of works that claimed to illustrate what the rebels had actually done.

A sample gives a flavor of how 1641 was presented to contemporaries. On 20 December 1641, in Bantry, Co. Cork, one John "Davenant" [*sic*], a pilchard fisherman, was attacked by some of the Irish. His children and his wife were roasted on a spit before him (his wife was also "abused") before his tongue was cut out and his legs and genitals were cut off, and finally these "unparalleled blood suckers" roasted him alive.[21] A similar account from Kinsale related the ordeal of John "Dabnet" (presumably the same person) and in doing so expanded on the story: the children had been forced to roast each other on spits, Dabnet's tongue had been cut out when he refused to abjure his religion, and his wife had been drowned in a well.[22] Other reports from Munster, as presented to the English parliament, told of further tortures inflicted upon Protestants: the rebels blinded and castrated Protestant men. Children were boiled alive, pregnant women were disemboweled immediately after giving birth, and then their babies were killed. Hundreds of Protestants were drowned after having been thrown from bridges, and rape became widespread.[23] A letter, apparently written by the Earl of Cork and printed in London, repeated assertions that rebels had tortured and executed English prisoners near Barrymore and then massacred the Protestant inhabitants indiscriminately; pregnant women were supposedly disemboweled here too.[24]

Such allegations were not restricted to Munster. In 1642 a markedly religious tract placed great emphasis on the intentions of the rebels, who "resolved upon a general massacre of all the Protestants throughout divers counties in the country."[25] It told of the murder of the Dublin merchant Sir Arthur Champion in Fermanagh, and of the alleged massacre of three hundred English Protestants in Fermanagh on the same day: "Some they would not give leave to say their prayers before there end, others had their noses and ears cut off, being cruelly tortured before they dispatched them; some women had their hands

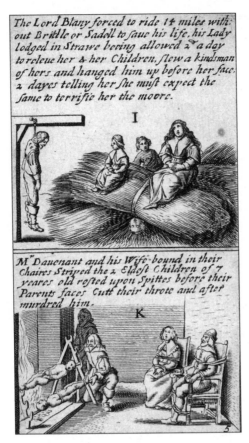

The Lord Blany forced to ride 14 miles without Brittle or Sadell to saue his life, his Lady lodged in Strawe beeing allowed 2 a day to releue her & her Children, slew a kindsman of hers and hanged him up before her face 2 dayes telling her she must expect the same to terrifie her the moore.

I

M Dauenant and his Wife bound in their Chaires Striped the 2 Eldest Children of 7 yeares old rosted upon Spittes before their Parents faces Cutt their throte and after murdred him.

K

Proof from James Cranford, *The Teares of Ireland*, London, 1642. The lower panel depicts the torture of "Mr Davenant" and his family. (courtesy of the National Library of Ireland)

and arms cut off, yea jointed alive to make them confess where their money was"—a telling suggestion that at least some of the rebels were motivated by more earthly concerns. In an aside hinting that the rebellion was directed at colonial authority as much as at Protestants per se, the same author noted that "above all others (ministers excepted) they were most fierce against the king's officers."[26] Yet glimmers of hope could be recorded too: while a refugee convoy was stripped outside Belturbet, in an early instance of what became a recurring theme, God's favor toward Protestants in Ireland was revealed in the deliverance accorded to many of them (including the Puritan minister Faithful Teate), and the author of a tract that described this event went on to beseech the English parliament for assistance.[27] But not all reports were as optimistic as this one; another pamphleteer told how 1,500 Protestant refugees from Belturbet were stripped of their clothes and continually attacked by the Irish. Children were flung into a river near Cavan town with pitchforks, while the rest were driven into the river to drown; those who could swim were clubbed to death at the water's edge.[28] At Kilworth in Cork a "gentlewoman" was hanged on a gate and disemboweled. Her servants and children were also killed, and more Protestants were disemboweled. Women were raped, while others were tortured with hot irons and whipped to death. Small children were impaled on hooks through their throats. Pregnant women were yet again disemboweled, and the fetuses trampled on. A minister was flayed to make a drum "that the heretics may hear the sound of it."[29] In Kilkenny another minister was beaten to death as his pregnant wife was raped and disemboweled by the rebels.[30] In the towns of Armagh and Loughgall both English and Scots were murdered, and the insurgents raped women and dashed the heads of children on stones before impaling them on pikes, "and so running with them from place to place, saying that those were the pigs of the English sows."[31]

The rebels had "shed abundance of English blood and have vowed to destroy all the Protestants now living in Ireland."[32] The pope had ordered Catholics to massacre "heretics," and Catholics were instructed to "study your brains daily to invent instruments of tortures."[33] Indeed, "the rebels' tyranny is so great that they put both man, woman, and child (that are Protestants) to the sword, not sparing either age, degree, sex, or their reputation."[34] In the immediate aftermath of the rebellion the image that was being presented to English audiences was that of a wholesale and horrific attempt at sectarian genocide in Ireland.

It should be made clear that the atrocity stories recounted above were not statements of fact; they were propaganda and were used as such. But they undoubtedly had an impact. In London, for instance, some of the tracts mentioned above were read and believed with mounting horror by the Puritan artisan Nehemiah Wallington.[35] Many of the same types of atrocity were reiterated in contemporary pamphlet literature, including the drowning of prisoners, brutal killings of children, and the disemboweling of pregnant women. While British settlers in Ireland had indeed come under brutal attack, accounts of what they had endured were often exaggerated in the telling. In many pamphlet accounts the various strands of the rebellion—the capture of Dublin Castle and the attacks on settlers—were often collapsed into a single narrative. The massacres were depicted as indiscriminately sectarian. The inherent barbarity of the Irish was another theme. Many of their alleged victims were children. Sexual violence became another recurring allegation, even though it was not necessarily reflected in the depositions collected later (modesty may have ensured that such attacks were not always recorded). But the reports of pregnant women being disemboweled and of men being castrated had a stark symbolic meaning: this was a root-and-branch assault on the colonists. Its cruelty was aimed at their extermination.[36] As the rebellion gave way to the wars of the 1640s, such accounts of the rebellion continued to play a role within the conflicts raging throughout the Stuart kingdoms. But even aside from this kind of propaganda, the views of many Protestants who had actually lived through the upheavals of 1641–42 were to be found in another corpus of material from which polemicists would later draw.

On 16 March 1642 Henry Jones, the dean of Kilmore, who headed the commission that collected the original depositions, presented a selection of extracts from them to the English parliament that was subsequently published as *A Remonstrance of Divers Remarkeable Passages Concerning the Church and Kingdom of Ireland* (1642). This was, first and foremost, an attempt to solicit assistance for Irish Protestant refugees from the English parliament.[37] It was also an exercise in simplification: the *Remonstrance* sought to emphasize the blamelessness of Ireland's Protestants for the fate that had befallen them.

It was probably inevitable that sooner or later the specific events of 1641 would come to be located within a wider sectarian discourse. By the early 1640s it had become a standard assumption for Protestants in both Britain and Ireland to view themselves as combatants in an international struggle against popery, both in the islands in which they dwelled and in the broader arenas of Europe and the Atlantic world.[38] In the case of Ireland, with its traditional links to Catholic Europe and its location within the emergent British empire, this Catholic threat seemed disturbingly close to home, and Jones rapidly contextualized the Irish rebellion within this framework. The vast bulk of the *Remonstrance* consisted of extracts from depositions recorded by Jones and his colleagues. Within these testimonies, taken down in the chaotic aftermath of the rebellion, rumor and hearsay were reproduced alongside eyewitness accounts, a practice that served to magnify their cumulative effect. The litany of horrors that these documents purported to reveal consisted essentially of appendices to an account of the rebellion that prefaced them and was derived from them. According to Jones and his colleagues, "There hath been beyond all parallel of former ages a most bloody and antichristian combination and plot hatched by well-nigh the whole Romish sect, by way of combination from parts foreign with those at home, against this our church and state, thereby intending the utter extirpation of the reformed religion and the professors of it."[39]

The rebels had apparently expected assistance from France and Spain, the two great Catholic powers of Europe. They had also received the blessing of the pope for their enterprise, which was to be linked to uprisings in both England and Scotland. The Irish rebellion in this reading had been planned for a long time, perhaps decades; Jones also supplied the Committee on Irish Affairs

Title page of [Henry Jones], *A Remonstrance of Divers Remarkeable Passages Concerning the Church and Kingdom Of Ireland*, London, 1642. (courtesy of the National Library of Ireland)

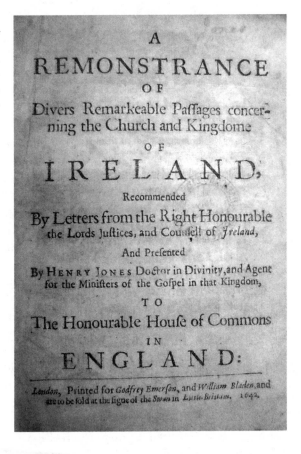

A
REMONSTRANCE
OF
Divers Remarkeable Paſſages concerning the Church and Kingdome
OF
IRELAND,
Recommended
By Letters from the Right Honourable the Lords Juſtices, and Couſell of *Ireland*,
And Preſented
By HENRY JONES Doctor in Divinity, and Agent for the Miniſters of the Goſpel in that Kingdom,
TO
The Honourable Houſe of Commons
IN
ENGLAND:
London, Printed for *Godfrey Emerſon*, and *William Bladen*, and are to be ſold at the ſigne of the *Swan* in *Little-Britain*, 1642.

appointed by the English parliament with a prophecy found in Newry predicting a massacre of Protestants in Ireland.[40]

His broad interpretation proved potent. It was malleable enough to misrepresent events to suit its purpose. For example, the Confederate Catholics were depicted here as a dastardly Catholic coalition who fully intended to facilitate the "wicked and devilish design" of "a general extirpation, even down to the last and least drop of English blood."[41] But it had been this assumption of universal Catholic guilt and, more concretely, the militant response of the government to the outbreak of the rebellion, that had compelled the Old English to throw in their lot with the insurgents in the first place: the creation of the Confederate Association was the result. As for what the rebellion had consisted of, "What pen can set forth, what tongue express, whose eye can read, ear hear, or heart, without melting, consider the cruelties, more than barbarous, daily exercised upon us by those inhuman, blood-sucking tigers!"[42] This view of the rebellion as sectarian genocide would be stoutly restated by the first truly canonical account of 1641, and the one that later caught John Gamble's eye: Sir John Temple's *The Irish Rebellion*.

Temple was one of a number of senior officials in the Dublin administration who had been imprisoned in 1643 in what was effectively a royalist coup (he was rightly suspected of having parliamentarian sympathies); and soon after this, he began to work on his history of the rebellion. It was first published in London in 1646 by Samuel Gellibrand, a London bookseller specializing in theological works who was presumably the father of the Edward Gellibrand who published one of two editions of Temple's book to appear in London in 1679, at the height of the Popish Plot. There seems to have been another edition printed during the 1670s, though Temple himself denied consenting to this one (despite numerous requests to do so).[43] Indeed, during the Popish Plot Roger Lestrange, the English licenser of the press, claimed that he had been told some years previously not to license any works on Irish history without the approval of the then viceroy, James Butler, Duke of Ormond, and other senior figures— a stricture that would naturally have applied to Temple.[44] The subject matter was too inflammatory.

Despite this official view, the value of Temple's work as a sourcebook, packed with lurid testimony, gave it an influence wholly disproportionate to its actual publication history. Its subject matter gave it a particular relevance that ensured its republication at certain junctures. For example, the first Dublin editions were printed by the Dublin Presbyterian Patrick Campbell (described scabrously by one contemporary as having a "natural aversion to honesty"[45]) on either side of the Jacobite rebellion of 1715. The 1713 Dublin reprint came in an edition that also contained William King's *State of the Protestants* (perhaps an inevitable combination, given contemporary fears about the intentions of the Jacobites).[46] In 1716 Campbell augmented this version still further by including Sir Henry Tichborne's account of the siege of Drogheda in 1641—an omnibus warning against the perils of popery in general and the Stuarts in particular.[47]

Probably the best-known edition of Temple's work was published in 1724 by the prominent Dublin printer Aaron Rhames. He may have done so very deliberately. A note on the flyleaf of a copy in Marsh's Library states: "Mr. [Aaron] Rhames reprinted this book, being very scarce, the D[uke] of [Liria], when in Ireland anno 1723 having bought up all the copies he could find of it in order to destroy the memory of so black a period. And some of the Irish Roman Catholics have had the confidence since to deny even the truth of the fact and treat it as a Protestant fable."[48] The Duke of Liria was James Stuart Fitzjames, second Duke of Berwick; he was the grandson of James II, whose mother was Patrick Sarsfield's widow. The intervention of this most prominent of Jacobites

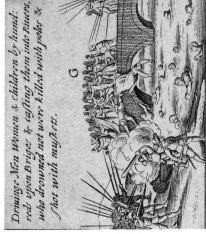

Proof from James Cranford, *The Teares of Ireland*, London, 1642. (courtesy of the National Library of Ireland)

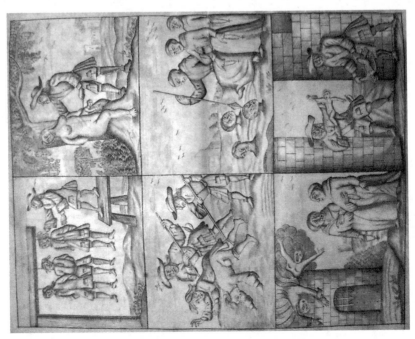

THE

Irish Rebellion:

OR, AN

HISTORY

Of the Beginnings and first Progress of the

General Rebellion,

Raised within the

Kingdom of IRELAND,

UPON

The Three and Twentieth Day of *October*, 1641.

Together with the

Barbarous Cruelties and Bloody Massacres

which ensued thereupon.

Publish'd in the Year 1646, by Sir JOHN TEMPLE, Kt. Master of the Rolls, and one of His Majesty's most Honourable Privy-Council within the Kingdom of IRELAND.

THE SIXTH EDITION,

Reprinted from the best *London*-Edition, 1679. wherein several entire Sentences, omitted in all the *Irish*-Editions, are truly inserted; many other Omissions, Errors and Mistakes carefully supplied, corrected, and amended. To which is also prefix'd, The late Act of Parliament, made the Fourteenth and Fifteenth Years of King CHARLES II. for Keeping and Celebrating the Twenty Third of *October*, as an Anniversary Thanksgiving in this Kingdom.

To which is added,

Sir *HENRY TICHBORNE's* HISTORY of the Siege of DROGHEDA, in the Year 1641.

As also, The whole Tryal of CONNOR Lord MACGUIRE, with the printed Copies of the Indictment, and all the Evidences against him, Together with the *Pope's* Bull to the Confederate Catholicks in *Ireland.*

DUBLIN:

Printed by and for AARON RHAMES, and are to be sold by the Booksellers, MDCCXXIV.

Frontispiece and title page of John Temple, *The Irish Rebellion*, Dublin, 1724 ed. (courtesy of the National Library of Ireland) would surely have had a sinister implication in any struggle for the memory of 1641. The title page of the 1724 Dublin edition claimed it to be the sixth edition, reprinted "from the best *London*-edition, 1679," allegedly with sentences that had been omitted from the Irish editions being reinserted and with numerous mistakes corrected. This version also included Tichborne's account of the siege of Drogheda, along with an account of the trial of Conor, Lord Maguire (presumably to bolster Temple's enduring sectarian message). But what made Rhames's edition distinctive was that it included a sequence of six etchings that made up a rare (and influential) pictorial representation of 1641: three Protestants being hanged; a Protestant woman stripped naked and tied to a tree with her small child while a rebel advanced on her with a knife; Protestants being driven into a river with pikes, with more Protestants being finished off in the river by a trio of sinister Jesuits (two of whom seemed to go on to burn the inhabitants of a castle alive); and finally, two rebels preparing to smash the skulls of two small children off a wall. Later visual depictions seemed to take their cue from these images, which were themselves inspired by the stock atrocities that were seen to have defined 1641.

Yet Temple's *Irish Rebellion* rarely receives adequate attention from scholars.[49] This may arise from the fact that, as its title suggests, it was a fairly straightforward work requiring little further explanation. *The Irish Rebellion* was a deeply polemical text and was recognized as such virtually ever since its first publication, but its purpose gave it its significance and was set out in the preface—to reveal to readers "the sad story of our miseries."[50] Temple placed great emphasis on both the veracity and the variety of the evidence he presented and readily cast himself in the role of "public informer,"[51] one whose clear objective was "that there may remain for the benefit of this present age, as well as of posterity, some certain records and monuments of the first beginnings and fatal progress of this rebellion, together with the horrid cruelties most unmercifully exercised by the Irish rebels upon the British and Protestants within this kingdom of Ireland."[52] To prove this point, Temple, with the assistance of unknown collaborators (one of whom was probably Henry Jones) obtained access to, used, and published some of the depositions that purported to describe those "horrid cruelties" (though they amounted to little more than a bare, if lurid, handful).[53] But herein lies the basis of his book's enduring notoriety: by quoting from and printing a fraction of the depositions, Temple provided the "circumstantial detail and explanatory framework"[54] that would dovetail neatly with the purposes of later Protestant polemicists who took an interest in 1641.

Temple was no advocate of conciliation toward the Catholic Irish. Rather, he proposed "a wall of separation betwixt the English and the Irish" as a preventive measure to ensure that future generations of Protestants might be saved from any future rebellion.[55] His own definition of his purpose was revealing—"to provide some general account of the losses suffered by the British."[56] And this naturally begged a question: What was the extent of those losses?

In March 1643 the lord justices Borlase and Parsons claimed that 154,000 Protestants had been killed since 23 October 1641. They took this figure from the unsubstantiated assertion of Robert Maxwell, an Armagh clergyman of Scottish extraction. They then deployed it to block conciliatory overtures to the Confederates by providing an English audience with a stark reminder of the scale of what Irish Catholics had supposedly done.[57] Determining the death toll would prove to be an enduring preoccupation, and the means used to do this down through the centuries ranged from assiduous calculation to arbitrary guesswork. Contemporary pamphlets provided estimates ranging from 10,000 to 1,000,000 (though the latter figure may have been a printer's error), but the numbers usually hovered in the region of 100,000 to 300,000.[58] Temple himself opted for the latter figure, claiming that between 23 October 1641 and 15 September 1643 (the date of the first cessation of hostilities with the Confederates), "above 300,000 British and Protestants [were] cruelly murdered in cold blood, destroyed some other way, or expelled out of their habitations, according to the strictest conjecture and computation of those who seemed best to understand the numbers of *English* planted in *Ireland*, besides those few who perished in the heat of [the] fight during the war."[59]

His estimate was thereby qualified. Temple did not know the precise numbers involved; instead, he seems to have relied on the rough calculations of a person, or persons, with some knowledge of the plantations in Ulster. But his estimate was also ambiguous. Precisely how many were murdered or destroyed, and how many were simply expelled? Temple deployed a rhetorical sleight of hand that would naturally appeal to those programmed to expect the worst, and which was combined with a far more specific objective—his explicit intention to authoritatively describe "the cruelties exercised by the Irish."[60] His claim that many of the deponents had died soon after presenting their testimony seemed to intensify their veracity; the depositions stood as their valediction. Indeed, there were reasons to be adamant on this point. Any doctoring of the record would inevitably have implications for the future, as the Irish would seek to "palliate their rebellion . . . under the name of a holy and just war."[61] He explicitly rejected any basis for Catholic grievances, such as those contained in the remonstrance presented by the Confederate Catholics to royalist negotiators at Trim in 1643. This had placed the blame for the outbreak of the rebellion firmly on the Dublin administration of which Temple had been a member: it was probably unsurprising that he dismissed it.[62] Instead, he went so far as to claim that it had been intended to garner sympathy for the rebels and assistance for the rebellion from "foreign states abroad as well as discontented powers at home."[63]

It is debatable whether Temple set an agenda for future Protestant analyses of Ireland and the Irish or whether he was simply reiterating a point of view that was already established. To explain the hostility of the Irish toward the English, Temple dwelled on religion and ethnicity, both of which he now inextricably linked.[64] He adopted a claim (originally made by Giraldus Cambrensis in the Middle Ages) that the suffering of the Irish was a punishment for their sin; and in such a reading the English became the instruments of God's wrath, having been punished for their own sins by the rebellion but having been given a chance to redeem themselves by their survival.[65] The savage and barbarous nature of the Irish, and their unremitting hostility to the English, was a running theme in his narrative as it approached its terminal date of 1641 (he implicitly conceded that the loathing was mutual).[66] He also painted a picture of forty years of relative peace and harmony prior to the outbreak of the rebellion (albeit one underpinned by the assumed existence of a hidden and deep-rooted Catholic conspiracy); his picture on the one hand eroded any basis for claiming that the rebellion had its origins in anything other than the savagery of the Irish and, on the other, served as a counterpoint to the brutality he related.

Temple almost certainly composed *The Irish Rebellion* to bolster the case for a prospective reconquest of Ireland under the auspices of the English parliament, the better to block the possibility of an alliance between Charles I and the Confederate Catholics; 1641 was very much part of contemporary politics in both islands.[67] Structurally, his book was an unwieldy and disjointed text, but as with Jones's work, its ideological and physical core consisted of the section in which Temple outlined the plot and narrated "some of the most notorious cruelties and barbarous murders committed by the Irish rebels, attested upon oath, as they appear in several examinations annexed in the margin."[68] Alongside these depositions, Temple's *Rebellion* was liberally studded with various other kinds of documentary evidence.[69] As we shall see, by the end of the 1640s the interpretation of the rebellion articulated and encapsulated by Jones and Temple had influenced both the English parliament's eventual reintervention in Irish affairs and the fact that many of Ireland's Protestants would align themselves with it. This "Protestant" interpretation of 1641 continued to play a role in Britain and Ireland throughout the remainder of the decade, especially when the English parliament finally turned its attention back to Ireland in 1649.

Ascendancy and Commemoration: Securing a Protestant State, 1649–1745

The Cromwellian reconquest of Ireland that began in August 1649 is usually discussed in terms of outcomes rather than objectives. To be precise, it is usually defined by the New Model Army's sanguinary assaults on Drogheda and Wexford, events correctly perceived as without precedent among the many brutalities of the civil wars across the Stuart kingdoms. Oliver Cromwell was by no means the most anti-Catholic of English Puritans, and while the atrocities at Drogheda and Wexford can be attributed to a combination of ruthlessness, the desire to make examples, and—certainly at Wexford—an unforeseen loss of control over his troops, Cromwell seems to have been disturbed by what he had witnessed. His oft-quoted justification for the slaughter at Drogheda has the uneasy tone of a *post-facto* rationalization—that the massacre was "a righteous judgement of God upon these barbarous wretches who have imbrued their hands in so much innocent blood" (presumably that of the Protestant victims of 1641).[70]

As we will see, many writers drew a line of continuity between the rebellion of 1641 and the Cromwellian invasion of 1649. One of the more florid examples of this practice came from the pen of Thomas Carlyle in 1846, in the relevant section of his edition of Cromwell's *Letters and Speeches*, where he declared that "Ireland, ever since the Irish rebellion broke out and changed itself into an Irish massacre, in the end of 1641, has been a scene of distracted controversies, plunderings, excommunications, treacheries, conflagrations, of universal misery and blood and bluster, such as the world before or since has never seen. The history of it does not form itself into a picture, but remains only as a huge blot, an indiscriminate blackness, which the human memory cannot willingly charge itself with!"[71]

He continued in this vein for a while longer. The passage can be read as a fevered attempt at evoking chaos. Yet it can also be seen as an example of a particular rhetorical trope that often appeared in certain English writings about Ireland, namely, the depiction of Ireland in irrational terms as a country—and by extension a people—impervious to the reasoned judgments of modernity, and instead motivated by the most atavistic and irrational of impulses. Carlyle's rhetoric also obscures the more hardheaded reasons for the parliamentarian invasion of Ireland in 1649. A key motivation had been the strategic necessity to defeat the royalist forces there, especially after the 1649 treaty between the viceroy James Butler, Earl of Ormond, and the Confederate Catholics that seemed once again to presage an alliance between them. Cromwell had argued that "they will in a very short time be able to land forces in England and put us to trouble here," and declared, "I had rather be overrun with a Cavalierish interest than a Scotch interest; I had rather be overrun with a Scotch interest than an Irish interest; and I think of all this [the Irish interest] is most danger- ous . . . for all the world knows their barbarism."[72]

The perception of 1641 as sectarian massacre was part of this outlook and had provided an additional pretext for the invasion. Much of the atrocity propaganda generated by the rebellion had, after all, been printed in England for an English audience. (Though while these tracts seemed to shape English perceptions of the rebellion, they did not guarantee unanimity about its origins and nature.)[73] The belief that the rebellion had seen a widespread massacre of Protestants proved crucial in consolidating English domestic support for the reconquest of Ireland.[74] Perhaps in an effort to bolster continuing support for the war in Ireland, another tract published in London in 1650 (by "special authority") asserted that the Irish rebellion had merely been one part of a long- standing Catholic plot to wipe out Protestants across the three kingdoms; the Catholic clergy had supposedly instigated it, and the Spanish were alleged to have attempted to land weapons in Ireland for the rebels.[75] This tract was the work of Thomas Waring, the clerk of the commission that had collected the depositions, and the official who had secretly transferred them to England in October 1646. The exhaustive account of Irish cruelty that this work contained was explicitly culled from the depositions, and while the perpetrators were deemed to be "merely a kind of *reptilia*, things creeping on their bellies,"[76] they had still been capable of "tortures and murders such as (I am confident) cannot be paralleled by story in any former age or country."[77]

If Cromwell assimilated the version of the rebellion espoused by such polemicists, he was hardly alone among Englishmen. His own opinion of 1641 was evident in his response to the declaration of the Irish Catholic bishops assembled at Clonmacnoise in December 1649, where they agreed that the New Model Army was bent on exterminating Catholicism in the three kingdoms by exterminating the Catholics who professed it.[78] Cromwell's ferocious reply ("for the undeceiving of deluded and seduced people") damned the Catholic clergy as agents of Antichrist and justified his conduct of the war, not least because the massacres of 1641 had yet to be avenged.[79] But Cromwell the man was not the Cromwellian regime; he was in Ireland for only nine months, and the "Cromwellian" reconquest was carried out by the New Model Army and its Irish Protestant adherents. During the 1640s many Irish Protestants had thrown in their lot with parliament, seeing it as the best guarantor of their interests; Henry Jones and the Munster grandee Roger Boyle, Lord Broghill, are perhaps the most obvious examples. If, as Toby Barnard has argued, the period between 1641 and 1660 was decisive in ensuring the transition of the settler communities from viewing themselves in ethnic terms as an English interest to viewing themselves in religious terms as a Protestant interest, then the sense of danger provided by the sectarian conflicts of the 1640s, and especially the initial rebellion, was the catalyst that both created the change and cemented it.[80]

The 1649 invasion and the settlement that followed the successful prosecution of the war in Ireland were shaped by a number of intertwining factors, at least some of which rested on the sizeable rock of the original rebellion. The impulses that 1641 had fostered did not lose their potency. Indeed in the 1650s, in the absence of any ongoing Catholic rebellion in Ireland, depictions of Catholic atrocities abroad were brought to bear on Ireland instead. It was reported in 1655 that some of the persecutions of Protestants in Piedmont at the hands of Catholic forces—events that were usually perceived as having been particularly savage—had been carried out by Irish regiments in the French service.[81] In Dublin, reports of such atrocities were "less strange to us when we heard that the insatiable Irish had a hand in that blood. If our transplantation [does] not go on, they may chance to give us the dregs of that cup to drink."[82] Measures to forestall such an unwelcome prospect were unlikely to meet with opposition from Irish Protestants. The ideological basis of the Cromwellian settlement lay in the visceral antipopery and insecurity generated by the recollection of 1641. This was reflected in the legislation that was to give effect to the settlement.

Its key planks had been authorized by the Rump Parliament even before the war in Ireland had been concluded. The formal title of the "Act of general pardon and oblivion" of February 1652 spoke for itself, but among a number of named crimes that were not to be pardoned under its aegis (such as treason and sexual and religious offenses), the law very specifically excluded "any person or persons who have had any hand in the plotting, contriving, or designing [of] the rebellion of Ireland, or in aiding, assisting, and abetting the same."[83] Within this there were, admittedly, exemptions for those who had submitted and remained loyal to parliament, or for those who had (or would have) their estates confiscated and sold. But given that these measures were essentially a belated response to the original rebellion, or at least claimed to be so, the prospect of according lenient treatment to those involved in it proved contentious (though the bitter legacy of 1641 had not stopped the Cromwellians from recruiting Irish Catholics as required).[84] In May 1652 a report was presented to parliament about a meeting of the Cromwellian army in Ireland at which the various treaties made with Irish forces across the country had been discussed. Given that the "blood-guiltiness" of the Irish was taken for granted, such agreements prompted unease and were a key topic of the discussion related to "our dealing with those

who yet continue in rebellion."[85] It was at this point that the seemingly ubiquitous Henry Jones, who apparently possessed the original depositions and was
now scoutmaster general of the parliamentarian army, produced an account of
some of them:

> And so deeply were all affected with the barbarous wickedness of the actors
> in these cruel murders and massacres (being so publicly in most places
> committed) that we are much afraid our behaviour towards this people
> may never sufficiently avenge the same; and fearing lest others, who are at
> a greater distance, might be moved to the lenity we have found no small
> temptation in ourselves, and we not knowing but that the parliament
> might shortly be in pursuance of a speedy settlement of this nation, and
> thereby some tender concessions might be concluded through your being
> unacquainted with these abominations, we have caused this enclosed
> abstract to be transcribed and made fit for your view.[86]

As published, this account was no more than a skeletal outline of allegations of
atrocities culled from various depositions and stripped of any context; there
was an obvious comparison to be made with Jones's earlier *Remonstrance*.[87] In
August 1652 he was ordered to inquire once again into the "murders, massacres,
and robberies which have been committed upon the English and Protestants in
Ireland," especially in Leinster and Munster.[88] This was the prelude to the
establishment of the High Courts of Justice that would prosecute those impli-
cated in the rebellion. Phelim O'Neill himself was convicted and executed in
Dublin in March 1653. But the assumption about the nature of the rebellion that
underpinned Jones's commission also influenced the legislation that facilitated
the settlement of the 1650s.

The "Act for the Settling of Ireland" of August 1652 was explicitly formulated
in the successful aftermath of the war. It stated that while "it is not the intention
of the parliament to extirpate that whole nation," a number of categories of
rebels were to be completely exempted from pardon. These included all those
who had been in arms or had assisted the rebellion before 10 November 1642
(the date of the first sitting of the Confederate General Assembly); all Catholic
clerics, who once again were collectively assumed to have encouraged and
abetted the "murders or massacres, robberies or violences committed against
the Protestants and English"; a wide spectrum of named Irish and Old English
figures; anyone who had not been employed as a soldier under English control
after 1 October 1641; anyone who had attacked or killed any forces under
English control; and finally, anyone in arms who did not submit to parliament
within twenty-eight days. In a manner that foreshadowed the 1665 Act of
Explanation, others outside these categories were to have their estates confiscated

and were to be recompensed with either one-third of their former land or other land elsewhere. It was, however, left to the discretion of the civil and military authorities to apply these strictures to anybody who did not fall into the stipulated categories. A submission would guarantee pardon, but the caveat relating to the confiscation of land would still be applicable. A variant of this requirement also applied to those Catholics who had not adhered to the Commonwealth (presumably meaning the English parliament) consistently between October 1641 and March 1650; they were automatically to lose one-third of their land and would be reassigned the equivalent of their remaining lands elsewhere at official discretion. Any loopholes relating to inheritance that might have interfered with these stipulations were automatically closed off.[89]

This was the Cromwellian settlement on paper. It was predicated on the Protestant interpretation of 1641 formulated over the previous eleven years; and having influenced the Cromwellian reconquest, that interpretation now helped to shape the principles behind the postwar settlement. The actual implementation of the settlement, however, proved untidy and contentious. The various claims of those Protestants entitled to benefit from it would not be resolved before 1660, and the allocation of lands arising from it was contested for much of the remainder of the century. But thanks to the principles that underpinned the settlement, these were disputes that Irish Catholics would not be a part of. The Cromwellian land settlement effectively survived the Restoration; the forcible transfer in the 1650s of perhaps half of the available land in Ireland from a Catholic elite to a Protestant elite was adjusted rather than reversed.

One of the crucial components of the restoration of the monarchy in May 1660—possibly the only ideological component—was the requirement that all laws passed by successive "usurping" governments after 1649 be considered null and void. In Ireland the implication of this provision was the reversal of the Cromwellian settlement. Consequently, those Protestants who had benefited from it vehemently opposed the prospect. Having correctly discerned that the monarchy would be restored sooner or later, they had mobilized rapidly to defend their interests long before the return of Charles II was finalized.[90] Indeed, in the immediate aftermath of the Restoration reports had reached Dublin that dispossessed landowners were exploiting the uncertainty of events by seeking to reclaim their estates by force.[91] The implications were obvious.

The fragmented members of the Protestant interest in Ireland were briefly united by the recognition of a common danger. They successfully lobbied the returning Charles II to permit a general pardon to those Irish Protestants who had been Protestants on 23 October 1641 and, more ambiguously, to those Catholics who had maintained their "good affection."[92] This commitment, contained in the Declaration of Breda that heralded the restoration of the monarchy, also deferred any modification of the settlement to an Irish parliament that would meet at some point in the future, for, in Aidan Clarke's words, "it was essential that the land settlement should survive, in short, not merely because individuals had profited, but because it was the basis of a reconfiguration of power which excluded Catholic competition in a new colonial Ireland. The condition of Protestant survival was that the community should be made invulnerable to the forces that had almost destroyed it in the 1640s."[93] Just as this arrangement could be justified by recourse to Protestant security, its maintenance could be exploited by recourse to Protestant fears. Unsurprisingly, the maintenance of a particular view of 1641 became integral to ensuring that this new dispensation survived; and in doing so, its ideological function was secured.[94] In the negotiations between Catholic spokesmen and the crown after the Restoration, the loyalty of Irish Catholics had been emphasized, and the injustice of any blanket denunciation of Catholics was highlighted.[95] Pleas such as these were, however, disregarded with a simple reply: "it is no new experiment in Ireland to dispose of lands forfeited by rebellion"[96]

The crucial point was this: the recollection of a particular version of 1641 played a role not only in shaping the emerging identities of Irish Protestants but also in helping to fashion the state in which they dwelled. There was a degree of ideological continuity between the 1662 Act of Settlement (and its successor, the 1665 Act of Explanation) passed in the Irish parliament of 1661–66 that effectively upheld the Cromwellian settlement, and the act of 1652 that had actually created it. The act of 1662 proceeded from the assumption that the "unnatural insurrection" of 1641 was "a formed and almost national rebellion of the Irish papists . . . to the destruction of the English and Protestants inhabiting in Ireland . . . , forasmuch as the rapines, depredations, and massacres committed by the said Irish and popish rebels and enemies are not only well known to this present parliament, but are notorious to the whole world."[97] It should be said that the divisive nature of the land settlement itself was recognized by some Protestant commentators in the 1660s and 1670s (including, perhaps ironically, Sir John Temple's son[98]), but tentative efforts by Catholic lobbyists to force a review of it in the early 1670s proved unsuccessful. As one assessment of the settlement concluded, "If two acts of parliament passed with so great deliberation, so universal a consent, and executed with so good success be not a good title, nothing in the world can be. If this foundation be shaken, no other can be laid."[99]

But there was an ironic consequence. The maintenance of the dispossession of a sizable chunk of Catholic Ireland, on the grounds that they had rebelled in 1641, continued to fuel Protestant fears that they remained in the shadow of a potential repeat of the rebellion. Facts on the ground exacerbated their concerns. In the 1650s Sir William Petty had organized the "Down survey," the massive and pioneering land survey that had facilitated the Cromwellian confiscations, and in or around 1672 he composed *The Political Anatomy of Ireland*, in which he placed great emphasis on the significance of the 1640s; the decade lay at the heart of his analysis of a postwar society.[100] He also attempted to quantify the obvious reality that Protestants in Ireland were vastly outnumbered by Catholics. Petty estimated that the Irish population consisted of 200,000 English, 100,000 Scots (deemed Presbyterian), and 800,000 Irish (deemed Catholic).[101] The Irish in his view were inevitably linked to a foreign power in the form of the Catholic church, and the land settlement remained the key source of division on the island.[102] There was a conclusion to be drawn from this analysis: if the Irish did indeed have legitimate grievances, then it followed that their discontent with the new colonial order did not arise from any inherent degeneracy. But any solace that this may have provided was tempered by a deep and lingering discontent among the Irish over their losses in the 1650s.[103] For as long as Irish Catholics had reasons to feel aggrieved at their lot, there was always the possibility that they might attempt to reverse it with another rebellion.

Other Irish Protestants could (and would) attempt to counter this prospect by deploying a more traditional analysis. In 1676 Henry Jones, whose long career culminated in his appointment as bishop of Meath, preached a sermon at Christ Church in Dublin. It was a reminder to Protestants of the danger they still faced, for "Ireland . . . *is above all other nations in Europe influenced by the power of Rome* . . . ; *Of this we have had memorials of former ages, some of them fresh and bleeding.*"[104] More explicitly, Jones queried, "Can the *bloody butcheries of poor Protestants by the cruel* Irish *in* Ireland be in this forgotten, when about *one hundred thousand* perished *anno* 1641? Yet to that impudence is that now risen, as to disavow any such rebellion of the *Irish, or such their murders of the innocent Protestants in* Ireland; *but daring to aver on the contrary that they themselves were the sufferers, and that by the* English *and Protestants.*"[105] Four years after Jones's sermon, the Popish Plot saw the publication in London of another substantial account of 1641—Edmund Borlase's *History of the Execrable Irish Rebellion*.[106] The author was the son of Sir John Borlase, one of the lord justices in Ireland at the time of the rebellion. His father's contemporary Jones provided a glowing preface to the book, possibly because, as part of his extensive documentary appendices, Borlase had recycled Jones's 1652 *Abstract*.[107] The utility of such a work in the midst of this crisis was obvious: in 1679 the book was recommended from the pulpit of Saint Patrick's Cathedral in Dublin in front of a presumably uncomfortable Ormond during the annual commemorative sermon on 23 October.[108] But despite its presumed topicality, the book was poorly received and unsuccessful (though it would receive a new lease of life as a sourcebook in the eighteenth century).[109] Timing might have rendered such a new account redundant; in 1679 Temple's iconic work had been republished twice in London, and perhaps more pertinently, the Protestant interpretation of the rebellion was by now legally enshrined within the structure of the de facto Irish Protestant state. The 1641 rebellion may indeed have served as a foundation myth of sorts. But by being embedded in the legislation that underpinned the Restoration settlement, 1641 was also one of the foundations for what had been built, and for what later seemed to come under threat during the reign of a new king.

The Catholic revival that took place in Ireland after the accession of King James II in 1685 was naturally of great interest to Irish Protestants, as its logical purpose was to supplant them on the grounds that they themselves had supplanted Irish Catholics. The mere accession of a Catholic king was sufficient to fuel the fears of Protestants across the Stuart kingdoms, but Irish Protestants proved particularly concerned. Two decades after Petty's demographic assessments, they were still vastly outnumbered by Catholics, and James's reign seemed to give them other reasons to be fearful. Under the auspices of James's viceroy, the Old English Richard Talbot, Earl of Tyrconnell, there was a policy of official discrimination against Protestants on the grounds of Catholic redress, which dovetailed with (and arguably encouraged) widespread and increasing popular sectarianism directed against Protestants.[110] Even prior to the outbreak of the war, Tyrconnell, according to one Protestant grandee, had said that he "would let loose the rabble Irish upon the English and lay the kingdom in ashes."[111] Alongside concerns about the intentions of the Catholic elite were more popular fears exemplified by incidents such as that of the "Comber letter"—a report found in December 1688 in the County Down village of the same name, in which it was reported that "all our Irishmen . . . are sworn to fall on [and] to kill and murder man, wife, and child."[112] The ethnic distinction bespoke the religious one. The plight of Irish Protestants and the outbreak of war after 1689 generated a great deal of printed propaganda, much of which was intended to solicit English and Dutch assistance. There is an obvious parallel with the explosion of printed material that had been harnessed to a similar purpose in the 1640s, as it was increasingly clear that the plight of a later generation of Protestants in Ireland was being interpreted in terms redolent of an imminent repeat of 1641.[113] The assault on Protestants by Tyrconnell and his forces "so nearly resemble their beginnings in their last so horrid rebellion in Forty One."[114]

The obvious conclusion to be drawn was articulated in a sermon preached before Irish Protestant refugees in London on 23 October 1690—the anniversary of the rebellion—which ominously stated that Protestants in Ireland would have to remain vigilant, for by their actions the Catholic Irish had proven themselves to be irredeemable.[115] From a Protestant perspective parallels with 1641 were by no means far-fetched. According to Archbishop William King of Derry, writing after the war in his capacity as a staunch defender of the Protestant interest: "If they hated us so much in 1641 that without provocation, and whilst in possession of their estates, they rose as one man and attempted to destroy us; if they were so set on it that they ventured to do it without arms, discipline, or authority on their side, and where the hazard was so great that it was ten to one if they succeeded; what could we expect they would do now, when provoked to the height by the loss of their estates, when armed, disciplined, and entrusted with the places of strength, power and profit in the kingdom?"[116]

And just as a settlement of Ireland followed the crisis of the 1640s and 1650s, so another followed the Williamite victory of 1691. The perennial fears of Irish Protestants in the 1690s were compounded by their unease at the perceived lenity of the Treaty of Limerick that had ended the war; William and his commanders did not automatically share the anti-Catholicism of their Irish Protestant allies. As a result, the relatively generous terms of the treaty were gradually rolled back from the 1690s onward by a succession of legislative measures intended to safeguard the Protestant interest in Ireland: the "popery" or "penal" laws. Given the nature of the settlement of the 1660s, it is worth reflecting on the purpose of the more piecemeal "settlement" of the 1690s, especially the penal legislation that ultimately flowed from the Williamite victory and that gave formal and unprecedented expression to the new balance of power in Ireland.[117] Even in the 1640s the perceived events of 1641 had prompted occasional calls for anti-Catholic measures that resembled the eventual penal laws;[118] for Irish Protestants such occurrences illustrated exactly why they needed to remain vigilant with regard to their Catholic enemies. As one commentator in 1695 argued, "Considering the principles of Irish papists, together with their inhuman butcherly actions in 41 and the blood and treasure that both then, and now again have, and is like yet further to be spent and spilt in its fuller reducement . . . , for these and the like reasons it seems not only reasonable but even just and equitable to endeavour as much in us lies, by all reasonable and prudent ways, the prevention of the like evils for the future."[119] The piecemeal formulation of the penal laws was a piecemeal solution to the dilemma that Irish Protestants had faced in the decades after 1641. They were a logical continuation rather than a new departure, and were underpinned by the same inchoate impetus—the fear of a Catholic enemy.

Circumstances continued to justify such drastic measures. As William King plaintively asked in 1719, "How will the Protestants secure themselves or England secure Ireland when all the commonality are papists?"[120] Admittedly, by the time that he wrote, circumstances may have changed, as the Jacobite rebellion of 1715 had not fulfilled its feared potential in Ireland, and thus the Jacobite threat could be seen to have receded. But equally, the potential danger posed by Catholics was not confined to the ambitions of the Stuart Pretender. In 1717 the Irish House of Commons sought to highlight the "fatal consequences" that would ensue should the outlawries prompted by the events of 1641 and 1688 be reversed. The effectiveness of such attainders "was so well understood that no outlawry of any person guilty of the rebellion of 1641 was reversed until the time of the government of the late Earl of Tyrconnell, about the year 1687, when the design to extirpate the British and Protestant interests and to establish popery as the national religion was openly and avowedly declared." (A royal assurance not to tamper with these outlawries was finally forthcoming in 1728.)[121] Within this parliamentary action of 1717 lay an interpretation of recent history that wholly disregarded the chronological markers so beloved of later historians. It ultimately rested on the danger exemplified by 1641, a danger that was to be borne constantly in mind lest the settlement stemming from it be disregarded at the expense of those Protestants who had benefited from it.

In the years following the restoration of the monarchy in 1660 there had been a variety of sporadic and uncoordinated attempts to exclude Catholics from power and influence in Ireland. But after 1691 the same impulses found fuller and, in theory, more complete and comprehensive expression: the penal laws collectively reflected a desire to contain what was seen to be a genuine threat. For as the preacher of a sermon in Dublin on 23 October 1735 said to his congregation, "I do not pretend to say anything concerning the laws which are in force against popery but this; that they are only to be justified on the grounds of civil self-defence."[122] The model for the threat that they were intended to forestall, at its most basic level, arose from the subject that justified the sermon: the perception that 1641 had been nothing more than an attempt to exterminate Protestants. And each year the Protestants of Ireland were to be presented with a reminder of this.

In 1642 the Irish administration ordered that the outbreak of the rebellion in the previous year was to be commemorated "until by authority of parliament it shall be made a law to be delivered over to posterity."[123] It was not until 1662 that an Irish parliament managed to do this. The same assembly that passed the Act of Settlement formalized a Protestant interpretation of the rebellion by passing into law, apparently at the behest of Roger Boyle, now Earl of Orrery, and other militant Protestant spokesmen, an act to commemorate its outbreak.

The act stipulated that each year on 23 October (the anniversary of the rebellion) a sermon was to be preached in all Anglican churches giving thanks for the deliverance of Protestant Ireland from what was seen to be the imminent destruction it had faced in 1641. No work was to be done on that day, and attendance at the sermons was mandatory; reminders were to be issued to the congregations on the preceding Sunday. If no sermon was prepared, the text of the act itself, and the interpretation of the rebellion that it contained, was to be read out in its stead. The fact that such a "conspiracy so generally inhumane, barbarous, and cruel" had been permitted to proceed was deemed to be a judgment of God on Protestants, while its discovery and the assistance in suppressing it that eventually came from England provided a glimmer of redemption and thus the necessity for thanksgiving.[124] The Church of Ireland built on this law by incorporating into its liturgy distinct new forms of prayer to commemorate the rebellion; these appeared in the Irish edition of the Book of Common Prayer in 1666 and would remain in it until 1859.[125]

The degree of ideological cohesion that such official commemoration gave to the fractious Protestant interest should not be underestimated. But from an early stage the divisive nature of such an essentially sectarian commemoration was also obvious, and it would be challenged.[126] The provocative potential of celebrating an event that provided a justification for wholesale dispossession was noted by figures such as Ormond, who as viceroy (1662–69, 1677–84) exercised an unofficial veto over the publication of the anniversary sermons and other works (such as Temple's) that dealt with the rebellion.[127] But the remembrance and commemoration of 1641 was not purely dependent on sermons or the written word. It should be seen as part of a broader pattern of Protestant commemoration that had developed in British political culture from the later sixteenth century. Events that were seen as especially significant to British Protestants—the defeat of the Spanish Armada, the discovery of the Gunpowder Plot, the execution of Charles I, and the restoration of his son (all of which were also observed in Ireland, just as sermons commemorating 1641 were occasionally preached in England[128])—had come to be celebrated and remembered in an official and very public fashion.[129] The anniversary of 1641 was distinctly Irish, but the rhetoric and events that accompanied it shared many characteristics with the anniversaries that had been deemed worthy of notice across the Irish Sea. What these celebrations entailed in Ireland seems to have been quite straightforward. On 24 October 1775 the *Freeman's Journal* noted that "yesterday, being the anniversary of the Irish rebellion in 1641, was observed in this city with the usual commemorations of that event."[130] Besides being the occasion for sermons, 23 October was also marked by public ceremonials. According to one official observer, on the anniversary in 1733 the peers assembled at the new Parliament House on College Green, prayed, adjourned, and made their way to Dublin Castle, after which "His Grace the Lord

Lieutenant went to Christchurch in state . . . [and] at dinner proclaimed his majesties [sic] style."[131] It seems safe to say that the peers were not the only ones to celebrate. Beyond such elite ceremonials—which could be extended to army officers and members of the gentry—the anniversary featured equally traditional accompaniments: the ringing of bells, gun salutes, bonfires, parades, public illuminations, and "other demonstrations of public joy,"[132] all helped along by large-scale public drinking, with the alcohol often provided by the authorities or aristocratic patrons. Commemoration of 23 October might not possess the mass appeal of the anniversaries of William of Orange's birthday (4 November) or the Battle of the Boyne (1/12 July), but it could still attract crowds.[133] Such public rituals had a part to play in perpetuating awareness of the event in question, and by implication the version of 1641 that was being highlighted. Those who turned up to celebrate were likely to be conscious of the pretext on which they did so; and given that Catholics sometimes attempted to attack or disrupt such celebrations, the meaning of 23 October was presumably not lost on them either.

At the core of such commemoration was the anniversary sermon itself.[134] Though these were rarely printed prior to 1690, the events of James's reign dispelled any lingering official doubts about the wisdom of either publishing them or of patronizing the anniversary. Toby Barnard's study of the sermons illustrates how the subject of 1641 became a springboard for broader discourses on a wide range of issues that contemporary listeners might wish to consider. The same could be said of the ritualistic public celebrations of 1641, which could become focal points for articulating attitudes and beliefs that might be quite removed from the subject at hand.[135] But the justification for remembrance and commemoration, of whatever kind, was the outbreak of the original rebellion. The issues that this presented served as a common thread that ran through sermons preached on a bewildering range of topics. A perennial theme was naturally the danger of popery and the necessity for Protestant deliverance. For instance, in 1716 the popish threat was still perceived to be afoot in the form of Jacobitism (though the Hanoverian succession could be depicted as another divine mercy); one preacher expressed a firm belief in the relevance of 1641 as a warning to his parishioners.[136]

The utility of the messages contained in the sermons varied over time and space and were dictated by the inclinations of the clerics who composed them. Their delivery from the pulpit ensured that the messages would reach a wide audience, including both those who heard them and those who may have disseminated what they heard in church to widening social circles outside it. Admittedly, given the vast corpus of these sermons, one cannot automatically ascribe unanimity to either their broad meanings or their immediate purposes. But the sermons rested on assumptions about the atrocious nature of both the rebellion and Catholicism. In 1735 one cleric felt compelled to tell his flock that "the circumstances of that great event are so well known that I shall not trouble you with a repetition of them."[137] In this instance, those assumptions were presumably unchanged.

It is difficult to determine the full nature and extent of popular responses to this public recollection of 1641, which had effectively been abandoned in Dublin by the 1790s.[138] Arguably, this state of affairs in the capital city suggests that the iconic power of 1641 may have been fading against the backdrop of fundamental shifts in Irish society in the late eighteenth century. Equally, the changed situation might also reflect the fact that the Protestant establishment was detaching itself from overtly sectarian commemorations in the early years of the nineteenth century.[139] The continuance of the prayers commemorating the rebellion in the Book of Common Prayer until 1859 may well have been an oversight; it was abolished by the statute that officially abolished the English state commemorations that had prompted the celebration of 23 October in the first place. But given that the commemorations that marked the anniversary of 1641 drew on a British model, it is worth considering just how 1641 was perceived and recalled in the neighboring island.

1641 in British Protestant Discourse

In 1705 no less a figure than Daniel Defoe penned a manifesto on behalf of Dissenters that justified "exclusive laws" as a necessary defense against Irish Catholics.[140] After all, he noted, "how was thy massacre in Forty-one a flaming beacon to illuminate the world and tell *England* what was coming upon her! Giving her timely notice to take care of herself and leading the way to her safety with the blood of 200,000 innocent betrayed Protestants."[141] Such rhetorical flourishes were nothing new; the events of 1641 had been firmly ensconced in British political discourse since the 1640s. Indeed, one of the most inflated attempts at estimating the death toll from the rebellion had come from the pen of as notable an author as John Milton in 1649. Milton wrote *Eikonoklastes* as a *post facto* justification for the execution of Charles I; in it he sought to indict Charles as the "prime author" of the rebellion and ensuing massacre. This tack naturally begged the question of scale, so Milton took the original estimate by the lord justices of 154,000 dead "in the province of Ulster only" and ventured that the addition of this figure to those for the other three provinces "makes up the total sum of that slaughter in all likelihood four times as great."[142]

The repetition of a litany of Irish atrocities in Britain was slightly different from its Irish counterpart, for it lacked the immediate relevance that it was presumed to possess in Ireland. Instead, 1641 became part of the pantheon of foreign popery that provided the critical impetus for anti-Catholicism in eighteenth-century England and, by extension, for the development of a distinctive British Protestant identity.[143] The continuing vitality of English antipopery was driven by the lurking persistence of the French threat; and 1641 was usually retained within the British Protestant calendar. But in English terms the recollection of 1641 had an element of abstraction to it by virtue of distance, even if the original rebellion had been intertwined with crucial events in English history. There was a notable divergence in attitudes, for example, between those Anglican bishops actually born in Ireland and the English-born bishops, generally Whigs, who were parachuted into Irish sees in the reign of George I to dilute a Tory majority among the Irish bishoprics. Irish-born bishops were usually satisfied that the Catholic threat had been nullified and were more concerned with that posed by Dissenters. English-born ecclesiastics, on the other hand, viewed Catholics as the greater danger and occasionally invoked 1641 as they did so.[144] But these differing opinions did not make the polemical potential of 1641 redundant.

The specter of a massacre of Protestants in Ireland had been dangled in front of the English parliament when elements of the nascent Whig opposition unscrupulously promoted the allegations of dubious Irish informers during the Exclusion Crisis of 1679–81.[145] The template for the nature of this specter was obvious. In 1682 the published diary of the parliamentarian lawyer and politician Bulstrode Whitelock dismissed the validity of the standard *post facto* justifications for the rebellion (fears of dispossession and discrimination): "Upon these pretences and manifest untruths they ground their taking up of arms."[146] Whitelock provided a sample of the consequences in his account of the storming of Drogheda:

> The rebels storming the town were repulsed, they in other places executed horrid tortures upon the *English*, they murthered the Lord *Caulfield* basely, hanged one *Blaney*, tortured a woman to force her to hear mass, drowned many hundreds, men, women, and innocent children, in the rivers, some they sent to sea in a rotten vessel without any sails or rudder, to be cast away, and great numbers of the *English*, after they had done all drudgeries for the rebels in hopes of mercy, had all their throats cut by them; and with some of them the execrable villains and monsters would make themselves pastime and sport before their death, trying who could hack deepest into the *English-mens* flesh; and so with the highest torture and cruelty mangled them to death.[147]

Similar, if more heartrending, details of Irish cruelty were provided by other English writers: "Innocence could not protect the sucking babes (for they said, *nits would make lice*), and more than twenty times, when the poor babes, to see the mother hanged, have cried out *Mammy, Mammy*, they have stuck it through the belly and, upon a halberd's point, reached it up to kiss its dying mother, laughing to see how with his expiring breath it would kiss the dead mother as she hung, *crying* till it died at her lips, *Mammy, Mammy*."[148] Such accounts were consistent with a scattered, fragmentary, but nonetheless coherent canon of atrocity literature.

A truly iconic British account of 1641 came with the eventual publication of the Earl of Clarendon's posthumous *History of the Rebellion and Civil Wars in England* (1702–4).[149] Henry Hyde, Earl of Clarendon, had been a leading English royalist both during and after the Restoration. In this version of the 1640s (portions of which had already been plagiarized by Edmund Borlase), the author's primary interest in Irish affairs was related to the impact of the rebellion on England, where it had "made a wonderful impression on the minds of men and proved of infinite disadvantage to the king's affairs."[150] As for the rebellion itself as portrayed by Clarendon, "a general insurrection of the Irish spread itself over the whole country in such an inhuman and barbarous manner that there were forty or fifty thousand of the English Protestants murdered before they suspected themselves to be in any danger."[151] While he did not elaborate on the details, his estimated death toll soon achieved canonical status, for the proximity of 1641 to British events sustained its resonance in British politics. In 1704, for example, it was deemed necessary to furiously refute the suggestion, made in a controversial edition of the memoirs of the parliamentarian and Non-conformist minister Richard Baxter, that King Charles I himself had sanctioned the massacre of Protestants in 1641.[152] In 1680 Edmund Borlase had tried to include material that supposedly proved the same allegation in a projected second edition of his history; he seems to have intended to reinsert material cut by Roger Lestrange, who, as licenser of the press, requested certain alterations "to clear the king of the outrages in Ireland."[153] The material in question related to the alleged commission from Charles I to the Irish rebels in 1641, further allegations about the cruelty of the Irish prior to the rebellion, and charges that Charles had been willing to "aid himself out of Ireland against the parliament."[154] These additions, had they been made, would surely have heightened the relevance of Borlase's work to an English audience during the Exclusion Crisis by conjuring up fears of the Catholic Irish and of the Stuarts' supposed affinity with them. By 1721 an edition of his history was being advertised in London that apparently contained the material that had been excised.[155]

Here was the recent past being harnessed to contemporary disputes. In the case of Charles I and his alleged guilt for the events of 1641, the older dispute was being bandied around by Whigs and Tories who seemed to perceive their predecessors at work in the 1640s. This perception was certainly true of Ormond's biographer Thomas Carte, who entered this dispute at exhaustive length to attempt to exonerate Charles I and, by implication, the exiled Stuart dynasty itself.[156] The recollection of 1641 was also stoked by the continuing vitality of Jacobitism. In 1714 "the papists in Ireland" supposedly grew insolent and were prepared to revolt; this alarm in turn gave rise to "the inexpressible terror of the *Protestants*, who are in daily fears of a MASSACRE"—fears grounded on "lamentable experience."[157] But none of these various polemicists departed from the essential premise that in 1641 there had been a "bloody rebellion and massacre" in Ireland resulting in "the murder of so many hundred thousand Protestants."[158] The political utility of this premise was evident in other instances. Jonathan Swift, for example, invoked the specter of 1641 on a number of occasions, and unlike an author such as Whitelock, he blamed the English parliament for provoking the rebellion. But he did not dissent from the assumption of its atrocious nature, though he bemoaned the manner in which the loyal Old English were so often conflated with the Catholic Irish who were deemed to have perpetrated the massacres. Writing from Ireland for an English audience, and holding the firm conviction that the circumstances that led to the civil wars had not been fully consigned to the past, Swift used 1641 as a tool with which to attack Whigs in general and Presbyterians in particular.[159]

The 1641 rebellion played a role not only in purely political discourse; it was also useful in arguments of a more philosophical nature. Among the more contentious accounts of the rebellion to emerge in the eighteenth century was that of David Hume in his *History of Great Britain* (1754–62).[160] Hume's work attracted notice largely owing to his stature, but the controversy surrounding his account also arose from the less edifying reality that he simply regurgitated the versions of 1641 previously placed in the public domain by Temple and Whitelock, on both of whom he relied extensively.

Hume's version, like many others, contextualized the outbreak of the rebellion against the backdrop of a crisis across the three kingdoms. He argued, as had Temple, that peace and prosperity had been the norm under the plantations: "The inveterate quarrels between the nations seemed, in a great measure, to be obliterated; and though the landed property forfeited by rebellion had been conferred on the new planters, a more than equal return had been made by their instructing the natives in tillage, building, manufactures, and all the civilised arts of life."[161] The implication was that gratitude should have been forthcoming. As for the religious fault lines introduced by the plantations, British Protestants were inclined toward Puritanism because they had "before their eyes all the horrors of popery."[162] Hume perceptively noted that by alienating themselves from the monarchy, the colonists had forfeited the protection of the only power that could preserve them from the Irish. Deeply hostile to the Irish on racial grounds, Hume was well aware that the revolt took advantage of the weakened position of the crown, and that the Catholic Irish feared repression at the hands of parliament. But he used remarkable rhetoric in his description of the rebellion itself, during which, he declared, "death was the lightest punishment inflicted by those enraged rebels: all the tortures which wanton cruelty could devise, all the lingering pains of body, the anguish of mind, the agonies of despair, could not satiate revenges excited without injury, and cruelty derived from no cause."[163] Though he professed to avoid mentioning the worst details out of decency, Hume cited the rebels' brutality toward women and children and the horror of Protestant prisoners at being forced to murder their relatives before being dispatched themselves. Perhaps unsurprisingly, he dwelled on the sectarianism of such acts and claimed that the "bigoted assassins" had assured their victims that, as heretics, they would have to endure much worse in the afterlife; these Protestant victims, he concluded, had been slaughtered in the course of "an event memorable in the annals of human kind and worthy to be held in perpetual detestation and abhorrence."[164] Hume's purpose was to elevate the virtue of reason by highlighting the extreme pitfalls into which religion could lead the unwary and the overzealous. The same strategy was used by his contemporary Voltaire, who, despite being surprisingly scrupulous in his historical writings (if somewhat unsympathetic to the Irish), wholeheartedly believed in the reality of the massacres and was unwilling to brook arguments to the contrary; he leant instead, as many had done before him, toward an interpretation of 1641 that placed it on a par with the Saint Bartholomew's Day massacre in his native France.[165]

Regardless of the more subtle purposes to which such accounts were put, they continued to perpetuate a visceral perception of the rebellion as sectarian genocide. Such an interpretation of 1641 could also be found in Catharine Macaulay's later *History of England* (1763–83).[166] This too seemed to suggest that there was a rationale for the rebellion, given that so much land had been "fraudulently and forcibly obtained from the inhabitants," albeit "in that barbarous country."[167] Macaulay added a new twist to the old assumption that Ireland prior to 1641 was a peaceable and prosperous land of plenty; in her work it was also one in which the inhabitants were the beneficiaries of English liberties.[168] But this was a misleading picture, for when the rebellion broke out, it was made infinitely worse, according to Macaulay, by "the wanton exercise of more execrable cruelty than had ever yet occurred to the warm and fertile imagination of Eastern barbarians."[169] Macaulay's text also leant heavily on the works of Temple, Borlase, and Clarendon (among others); it was quite literally underpinned by a sequence of footnotes in which a particularly lurid and ferocious account of the rebellion was set forth, alongside lengthy rebuttals of all attempts to mollify the assumption of Catholic guilt.[170] In this sense it differed little from Hume. And this alignment presents a paradox, for both Hume and Macaulay were perceived to have written their histories from opposing ends of the British ideological spectrum. At the most generalized level Hume was assumed to have provided a Tory version of British history; Macaulay was understood to have furnished a Whig riposte. Politics notwithstanding, both could be seen as representatives of a progressive, quasi-liberal tradition. Yet both provided their readers with fundamentally identical versions of the Irish rebellion of 1641 as genocidal sadism prompted by little more than hatred based on superstition. The rebellion retained its abstract power as an exemplar of barbarism in a manner far removed from its resonance in Ireland.

This is not to say, however, that it could not possess a visceral connotation in England. Alongside such elaborate works, in which a particular version of 1641 was assimilated into master narratives of English and Stuart history, more immediate exigencies prompted simpler accounts redolent of the propaganda of the seventeenth century. At a moment of crisis such as the Jacobite rebellion of 1745, the specter of Catholicism could be conjured up by tracts that simply reprinted terse and brutal extracts from depositions that had long been in the public domain.[171] The tensions that arose in England in 1780 against the backdrop of the imperial crisis and the Catholic Relief Act of 1778 (which ultimately led to the anti-Catholic Gordon Riots of June 1780) could be met with the explicit republication of anti-Catholic tracts from 1680.[172] Or equally, the story could simply be told anew. The notably militant Protestant Association of Newcastle, which in 1780 organized a petition to the English parliament signed by 7,661 people demanding the repeal of the relief act, was led by James Murray, the proprietor of an anti-Catholic monthly called *The Protestant Packet; or, British Monitor*.[173] In December 1780, over three issues, it published a familiar version of the story of 1641 for a new readership.[174] "There are many Protestants," its readers were told, "who have heard of the *massacre in Ireland* in general and are yet unacquainted with the springs of that fatal catastrophe and the manner of execution." This periodical drew the lesson: "As the intelligent reader will see a strong likeness betwixt the fate of affairs in *Ireland* before that bloody rebellion and many things in the present circumstances of *Britain*, he cannot but conclude, at least, that Protestants should be on their guard against dangers to which they *are* or *may* be exposed."[175]

After all, "*popery is always the same*."[176] Once again, Ireland was described as a land of peace prior to 1641, but in keeping with the contemporary tenor of the piece, *The Protestant Packet* alleged that the insurrection was facilitated by the indulgence of the government toward Catholics, who had acted all along at the instigation of their clerics and with the connivance of Charles I, "plotting the utter ruin and overthrow of *Protestants* and their religion—the total extirpation of the English laws, customs, and people from Ireland!"[177] This account explicitly linked the plot back to the papacy, and, having conjured the specter of 1641, *The Protestant Packet* asked the Protestant reader whose zeal against popery might prove wanting "whether he does not see a near relation betwixt the affairs of *Ireland* before the rebellion and what has been going on in *Britain* for some years past?"[178] As the Jacobites were supposedly still intent on the destruction of Protestantism, the utility of an appeal to history was manifest. The Irish rebellion was once again cast as a purely religious war, and the nature of its events were usefully lumped together under such headings as "drowning," "burning," "suffocation," "burying alive," "ripping," and "hanging."[179] Finally, as for the number of Protestant victims involved, Temple's suggestion of "not less than 300,000" was again uncritically adopted.[180] Little had changed.

1641, 1798, and the Crisis of Irish Protestantism in the Early Nineteenth Century

In March 1793, in the course of a debate in the Irish House of Lords on the Catholic relief bill of that year, the bishop of Cashel, Charles Agar, saw fit to remind his fellow peers about the dangers of popery. He did so by reading them a long and lurid extract about 1641 from David Hume ("an author generally supposed not favourable to popery").[181] "And now, my lords," cried Agar, "I call upon you to know whether this will not vindicate our ancestors and shew that they were through hard necessity compelled to defend themselves by laws against Roman Catholics, and not through wanton choice or persecuting bigotry."[182]

There was nothing unusual in disinterring an account of 1641 in the service of Protestant ascendancy. What was unusual was that Agar chose David Hume to provide one. This illustrates the circular dissemination of the received Protestant version of the rebellion; by the 1790s a British rather than an Irish account of 1641 could be seen as eminently serviceable and useful by a scion of the Irish ascendancy. But Hume's version had drawn heavily on the canonical account provided by Sir John Temple, and given the influence achieved by Temple, it is worth glancing backward in time to look at how *The Irish Rebellion* made its presence felt toward the end of the eighteenth century.

Temple's work had reappeared in London in 1746 in an edition printed for James Brindley (self-styled "bookseller to His Royal Highness the Prince of

Wales"), James Hodges, and Mary Cooper. Alongside major alterations to the format and typesetting, this collaborative edition changed what had previously been a fulsome subtitle to a more succinct "history of the attempts of the *Irish* papists to extirpate the Protestants in the kingdom of *Ireland*." It should not be forgotten that this was being published in the aftermath of the '45; the Jacobites unwittingly put Temple in demand (which might explain the collaborative publication), and his work was "now reprinted for the perusal of all Protestants as the most effectual *warning*-piece to keep them upon their guard against the encroachments of popery" (though a second London edition in the same year, published again by Cooper, dispensed with this latter suggestion).

The Irish Rebellion reappeared in Ireland in 1766, but in Cork rather than Dublin. What was described on the frontispiece as "the seventh edition" was published by subscription from the hands of the prominent Cork publishers George and Phineas Bagnell; the heightened agrarian and sectarian tensions that wracked south Munster in the early 1760s seem to have prompted a renewed demand for it (at least among the "middle ranks" of the Protestant community).[183] The activities of agrarian movements such as the Whiteboys (and later, the Defenders) could be interpreted in purely sectarian terms, as their intimidating and often violent attempts to force the redress of various grievances relating to enclosures and the payment of tithes were often directed at an overwhelmingly Protestant landed class, not to mention the Church of Ireland. It was inevitable that these activities could be seen as a possible prelude to an impending Catholic rebellion or massacre, to be aided by a French or Spanish invasion. They could also be described in terms—for example, with regard to the stripping of Protestants in the depths of winter—that unmistakably echoed accounts of 1641 such as Temple's.[184] A continuity between past and present was easily constructed. Indeed, the Bagnell edition seems to have been published in the second half of 1766—*after* the series of hangings of suspected Whiteboys, most notably the priest Nicholas Sheehy, that had taken place in March and May of that year: "If this chronology is correct, then one can suggest that Temple's *Rebellion* gave retrospective legitimacy to the actions of the Tipperary gentry in this momentous year."[185] But the final, and in some ways most significant, edition of *The Irish Rebellion* to be printed in either Britain or Ireland appeared in London almost half a century later and was also to be harnessed to the exigencies of the day. The London edition of 1812 published by Robert Wilks transformed a seventeenth-century text whose form had largely remained static into the recognizable style and format of the early nineteenth century. But the change in style did not imply any change in substance; quite the opposite. The 1812 edition reproduced the text of the 1746 frontispiece, the better to keep Protestants "upon their guard against the encroachments of popery." It also had a brand new preface, dated 29 September 1812 and written by the Whig lawyer Francis Masares.

Masares's preface was a direct response to ongoing demands in Britain and Ireland for Catholic emancipation—the greatest symbol of the formal readmission of Catholics to the British polity and consequently the greatest symbol of how the Protestant ethos of that polity was being eroded. Masares perceived the prospect of emancipation as a danger "to the safety of the present happy constitution," as settled and confirmed in 1688–89.[186] Why? Because of "the continued and incurable spirit of hostility" manifested by Catholics toward "the government of England when administered by Protestant sovereigns."[187] Consequently, warnings from history were required to alert the public to the danger in their midst. Masares provided the usual tableau of Catholic atrocities, from the reign of Elizabeth I to the Gunpowder Plot and finally 1641. With respect to the last, he supported and repeated Temple's suggestion that Ireland had been civilized by colonization and had existed in a blissful idyll prior to the outbreak of the rebellion, which was instigated by "the wicked suggestions of their priests as to enter[ing] into a general massacre," with even women and children to be wiped out, "and this abominable resolution they did, in a great degree, execute on the appointed day and for many weeks and even months afterwards."[188] Masares blamed the alleged massacre on Catholic acceptance of the pope's spiritual authority, which, he noted, was not being repudiated by contemporary proponents of emancipation. The logic of this observation was simple. Catholics remained under the thrall of their priests, just as they had been in 1641, and the consequences could yet prove as terrible as before.

Masares seemed ignorant of the Irish publishing history of Temple's work. He assumed that the 1746 edition (which he was republishing and acknowledged as a response to the '45) was only the second. He helpfully added another account of 1641, but asserted that Temple "is generally allowed to be so faithful and exact as not to need such confirmation."[189] Irrespective of this assurance, the 1812 edition contained extracts from another work about another event— namely, passages from Sir Richard Musgrave's massive account of the more recent rebellion of the United Irishmen in 1798. Specifically, the extracts consisted of passages relating to the activities of the Defenders in County Armagh (especially the atrocious mutilation of the Barkely family of Forkhill in 1791), the undoubtedly sectarian massacre of Protestants at Scullabogue in County Wexford in June 1798, and various documents and testimonies relating to the 1641 rebellion in Wexford, concluding with a bloodthirsty and uncompromising confession of faith supposedly found in the possession of a priest in Gorey and allegedly composed after 1641, an event to which the confession alluded approvingly.[190]

One can understand the appeal of such purely sectarian interpretations. For example, it is extremely difficult to argue that the burning to death of 113 Protestant (and 11 Catholic) prisoners in a barn at Scullabogue on 5 June 1798 was devoid of any sectarian motivation.[191] And there is little doubt that in Forkhill on the night of 28 January 1791 a party of men violently assaulted Alexander Barkely, a Protestant weaver and schoolmaster. They cut out both his tongue and that of his brother-in-law before slicing off three fingers of Barkely's right hand. They inflicted almost the same mutilations on his wife, a foretaste, so the attackers said, "of what he and those like him should suffer."[192] The key phrase is "those like him." It would appear that Barkely, having previously clashed with members of the local Defenders, fully intended to testify against a number of men at the impending Armagh assizes—hence the symbolism of cutting out his tongue. In this light "those like him" would seem to refer to prospective informers.[193] But for Protestant contemporaries, in Forkhill and further afield, the phrase carried a purely sectarian resonance: "those like him" meant Protestants. This interpretation of this uniquely brutal attack resonated for generations, indeed centuries.[194] And it corresponded to a particular template. The succession of Catholic atrocities compiled by Masares, of which the attack on the Barkelys was one, "clearly prove that the sentiments of the great body of the common people of Ireland, who profess the Roman-Catholick religion, and of the Romish priests by whom they are implicitly directed, continue still as hostile to their Protestant fellow-subjects (whom they call *hereticks*) as they were at the time of the said detestable massacre in the year 1641."[195] Consequently, Catholic emancipation should not be granted without the abjuration of papal authority. Yet this conclusion was almost an afterthought. Its relevance to a crucial contemporary issue was one thing. The symbolic import of yoking the events of 1641 and 1798 together into a single sectarian paradigm was another matter entirely. Masares, however, was not the first to attempt to advance such an argument; this had been the very reason why Sir Richard Musgrave had written his *Memoirs of the Different Rebellions in Ireland* (1801) in the first place.[196]

Born into an upwardly mobile Protestant gentry family in County Waterford, Musgrave eventually acquired quite a reputation for extremism. According to his fellow MP Jonah Barrington, "except on the abstract topics of politics, religion, martial law, his wife, the pope, the Pretender, the Jesuits, Napper Tandy, and the whipping-post," Musgrave "was generally in his senses."[197] He had embarked on a political career that consisted of sitting as MP for Lismore in Waterford, and little else. But his ideological trajectory was of far greater import. Musgrave came from a region that had witnessed considerable agrarian unrest in the 1760s and 1770s, and later, as high sheriff of Waterford in 1786–87, he had proven ruthless in prosecuting those accused of Rightboy activity (even flogging one unfortunate prisoner personally). Musgrave was one of many Protestant MPs who balked at "the prospect of admitting Catholics to the political process."[198] In the 1790s he wrote a number of tracts attacking the French Revolution, which he vehemently opposed. These had the significant consequence of bringing Musgrave into the orbit of an increasingly militant English loyalism, and toward the end of the decade occurred the event—the 1798 rebellion—that ensured his true significance to posterity, not as a participant but as its erstwhile chronicler. It would be more accurate, however, to say that it was Musgrave's *interpretation* of 1798 that guaranteed his fame. In his ultra-Protestant reading of 1798 the secular republican ideals of the United Irishmen did not count for anything. Neither did the ferocious government repression that had preceded their rebellion. For Musgrave there was one overarching explanation for the sanguinary excesses of 1798 and one alone: popery.

In the years prior to the rebellion he bluntly interpreted agrarian unrest in Waterford as the prelude to both a French invasion and a massacre of Protestants. This was a fairly standard belief for Irish Protestants to hold at times of tension or crisis. But the actual outbreak of rebellion in 1798 accentuated Musgrave's conviction, and he soon gave monumental expression to this in his notorious encyclopedic *Memoirs*. Explicitly modeled on Temple's account of 1641, Musgrave's book collated a huge number of Protestant testimonies from the rebellion, largely relating to the atrocities visited on Protestants by Catholic insurgents, and cast them within the interpretive framework of anti-Catholicism.[199] The 1798 revolt was thereby defined as merely the latest installment in the eternal efforts of Roman Catholicism to extirpate Protestant "heresy" in Ireland. Temple had previously made this argument with regard to 1641; Musgrave simply used 1798 to update it. By implication the events he depicted were a universal and unchanging danger and were precisely what any Protestant should expect at Catholic hands, at any time, in any place. Given its publication in a new United Kingdom in which the prospect of Catholic emancipation seemed very real, Musgrave's work had an inevitable and enduring resonance in both islands.[200]

Its reception in Ireland was shaped in part by the fact that even prior to the outbreak of the United Irish rebellion, some Irish Protestants had, amid the heightened sectarian tensions of the 1790s, looked back to 1641 to provide a model for what might yet happen. In this regard the militantly Protestant Lord Chancellor John Fitzgibbon, Earl of Clare, proved a very public weathervane. As early as February 1789 he had reminded the Irish House of Commons that the structural and legal basis of the Protestant interest was "an act of violence, an act palpably subverting the first principles of the common law of England

and Ireland. I speak of the Act of Settlement, passed in this country immediately after the Restoration, which vests the estate of every man who had been dispossessed during the rebellion of 1641 absolutely in the crown, and puts the old proprietors to the necessity of proving that they had not been guilty of high treason."[201] During the same 1793 debate that saw Hume being read into the parliamentary record, Fitzgibbon assured the assembled peers that "religious bigotry produced the rebellion in 1641."[202] By 1796 the continuity between his public stance and his private opinion was indisputable. In February of that year he had assured the lords that "if this session should pass over without the enaction of laws strong enough to meet the smothered rebellion in the country, there will be a revival of the miseries of 1641."[203] In August, writing to the Earl of Camden, he assured him that "a great majority of the giddy people of this country are disaffected to British government. One class is actuated by the restless republican spirit which seems to be inseparable from the Presbyterian church, another by a rooted and hereditary hatred of the British name and nation." But for Fitzgibbon the most dangerous ingredient in this cauldron of discontent was "the natural disaffection of the Irish," and he was convinced that "if the opportunity were to offer, we should see the scenes of 1641 renewed, and the country again desolated by every species of savage enormity."[204]

Fitzgibbon's analysis tallied with broader fears and expectations that could be discerned among at least some Irish Protestants in the months prior to the eruption of rebellion in 1798. Despite the occasional reservations of some loyalists about the whipping up of such expectations, the actual events of the rebellion, especially the atrocities committed at Scullabogue and Wexford bridge, convinced many Protestants—especially in Wexford—that like so many of their ancestors, they were now on the receiving end of a sectarian onslaught that would inevitably result in their destruction.[205]

This was the event that Musgrave presented to the world. He provided a sample of what was to come in a pseudonymous tract printed in January 1799, in which he sought to prove that Catholic doctrine was inherently nefarious and dangerous to Protestants in two ways: in its assumption of spiritual (and by implication temporal) supremacy and in its apparently explicit advocacy of the need to exterminate heretics:

> Doctor Troy says, in his pastoral letter published in 1798, "the religious principles of Roman Catholicism being unchangeable, they are applicable to all times." This position is strictly true, and we find them equally destructive against the Albigenses and Waldenses in the thirteenth century, against the Protestants at Paris in the sixteenth, in the expulsion of the Moors from Spain, in the Irish rebellion of 1641, against the Protestants of

France in 1791, in the massacre on Vinegar-hill, in the barn of Sculla-bogue, on the bridge of Wexford, and in the general carnage of Protestants which took place in that once-peaceful and happy country on which such an indelible stain has been cast by the sanguinary spirit of popery.[206]

This viewpoint was by no means unique. As an iconic instance of bloodthirsty sectarianism, this version of 1798 could easily be substituted for 1641; at the very least it seemed to confirm the unending cycle of danger faced by the ancestors of Ireland's Protestants as much as by themselves.[207] In February 1800 Lord Chancellor Fitzgibbon once again invoked the shadow of 1641 for the benefit of his fellow peers. Speaking in favor of the impending Act of Union, he referred to 1641 and the wars of the 1640s as "a civil war of extermination," his point being that "the rebellion of 1798 would have been a war of extermination if it had not been for the strong and merciful interposition of Great Britain."[208] This newer example was grafted onto the older one: the representation of 1641 offered by writers such as Temple provided the model for that later articulated by Musgrave. And the shadow of 1641 seemed to cast itself over the work of other writers on 1798 as well.

George Taylor was moderate in his loyalism and devout in his Protestantism, but his own account of 1798 in Wexford used rhetoric that would be familiar to readers of Temple. Deeply skeptical of the professed intentions of the United Irishmen, Taylor's suspicions were vindicated when, with the outbreak of their rebellion, "the time arrived when destruction and assassination (before masked in sacerdotal vestment) laid the forsworn robe of deep hypocrisy aside and stepped forth to drench the thirst of diabolical passions in the blood of Protestants!"[209] Taylor painted a portrait of gleeful sectarian butchery being visited upon the Protestants. Take, for example, the rebels of "Ballynamonabeg" (seemingly a townland near Enniscorthy), who, after the retreat of the local yeomanry to Gorey, "began their murders; they went to the house of Samuel Maud near Ballynamonabeg, a fine old man who had attained the great age of 96, [and] piked him in the throat and various parts of the body till they killed him!"[210] Taylor's description of events in Enniscorthy deployed rhetorical flourishes reminiscent of earlier accounts of 1641; it deserves to be quoted at length:

Now parents deserted their children, and children, their parents, husbands, their wives, and wives their husbands, never to meet more [sic]—for many of the yeomen and loyalists who were wounded would probably have recovered, but they were murdered by the merciless pike-men; many more, whom the tender cries of nature caused to cling to their wives and children, hoped for mercy from some one neighbour or other; but alas! there was no such thing! no mercy for any man who bore the name of *Protestant* from the age of 15 and upwards! and some under that age were put to death! The Rev. Samuel Haydon, rector of Ferns, a very old man, was murdered and thrown out to be devoured by swine; Richard Whealy, a lock-smith, near 100 years old, also became a victim to their cruelty. The massacre became general as soon as they got possession of the town . . . many were torn out of the arms of their wives and murdered before them in the most barbarous manner; nor would those women be even permitted to bury their husbands! Here now were hearts torn with sorrow of the deepest kind; many a widow and fatherless orphan wept sore, while smoke and flames, blood and slaughter, shouting and blasphemy, triumphed in the desolation of this town![211]

Afterward, following the eventual rout of the United Irish forces at Vinegar Hill outside Enniscorthy, "the town of Wexford" remarked Taylor, "recovered from popery's persecuting reign . . . ; The shocking acts of barbarity practised during this period would make as many pictures of inhumanity as are to be found in the history of martyrs."[212] The implication was obvious, though it was left to others to integrate 1798 into a pattern of Catholic atrocity that had long encompassed 1641, and to make the connections between the two.[213] The logical conclusion to draw from this linkage was spelled out in a ballad published in 1823 that related the various dangers that Protestants had faced in Ireland:

> Remember the rebellion of the popish Lord Tyrone,
> And, oh!, be ever mindful of the bloody forty-one;
> When at least two hundred thousand Protestants, they write,
> Were by their cruel popish neighbours murder'd in one night.[214]

The Catholic menace did not stop there. Just as Protestants had continued to confront danger in the reign of James II, in 1798, and in Robert Emmet's rebellion of 1803, so they continued to face it in the course of agrarian upheaval and the charged sectarian atmosphere of the 1820s. As this balladeer put it,

> Present times most clearly shew, whatever popery feigns,
> That in the hearts of popish men, old popish feelings reign.[215]

That such continuities were being drawn in the 1820s was understandable: the "Catholic question" had lingered on in the decades after the Act of Union, and the increasing politicization of the Catholic community facilitated a sharpening of sectarian self-awareness. The mounting popular sectarianism of the 1820s had been prompted by a prolonged crisis—a severe economic depression along with the famine and typhus epidemic of 1817—that followed the end of the Napoleonic wars. The hardships that stemmed from these contributed to the rise of the Rockite movement of 1821–24, which exhibited similarities to previous agrarian movements such as the Whiteboys and Rightboys, but which was characterized by "a strain of millenarianism propelled by an anti-Protestant bias more vehement than in any of the earlier outbreaks of agrarian unrest."[216] Latent Protestant fears of a massacre were likely to be exacerbated by the tenor of threatening letters such as this one, found in County Limerick in January 1822: "At Ardpatrick ye shall march, join us as your eyes shall have no pity on the breed of Luther, for he had no pity on us. . . . Every man ye shall find ye shall thrust him through—Their children also shall ye dash to pieces—before their eyes their houses shall be spoiled, and their wives ravished. . . . Lament and mourn ye heretics for the day of your destruction is come, let no man's heart be faint on that day."[217] To judge from another threatening notice issued in the same month, life in Limerick must have presented an appalling vista for Protestants. Headed "General Rock's speech to the men of Ireland," this notice declared: "Now brethren from James the Seconds time to this period you have borne the greatest calamity under affliction, tyranny, slavery and persecution that ever a nation suffered. . . . This year is the year of liberty when the seed of Luther will be locked by Hell's inexorable doors. Those dog teachers, the police, have no mercy on them, for it is no sin to kill heretics. It was never so easy to massacre them as now. There shall be one conflagration made of them, from sea to sea."[218] A key to the vitality of such visceral sectarianism was the popularity of the prophecies of "Signor Pastorini," which had originated as an exegesis of the Book of Revelation contained in the English Catholic cleric Charles Walmesley's *General History of the Christian Church* (1770). The prophecies themselves were widely disseminated as cheap tracts and broadsides, as well as orally, by travelers, peddlers, teachers, and wandering "prophecy men." While deplored by the religious authorities of all denominations, Pastorini's prophecies rapidly secured a foothold in popular belief owing to their simple sectarian appeal: they claimed that Protestantism would be overthrown in or around 1825. There were obvious inferences to be drawn from such ideas; explicit references to a forthcoming massacre of Protestants (at least according to one informer) had emerged in parts of Galway as early as 1817.[219] The "politically conscious" Catholic middle and upper class and clergy often played down or dismissed the embarrassing significance of Pastorini; after all, they were seeking greater political rights for Catholics, and there were occasional dark accusations that the distribution of the prophecies was in fact the work of Protestants. But the prevalence of such sectarianism, augmented as it was by the organized violence of the Rockites, had already prompted the Earl of Rosse to observe that if such things were indeed the prelude to another Catholic rebellion, then "this time will be as memorable for the massacre of Protestants as 1641."[220] The echo was unmistakable.

The egregious bigotry of Pastorini's prophecies (such as continual references to Protestants as "locusts") inevitably elicited ripostes; the "incendiary" prophecies were depicted by some as essentially an incitement to Catholic rebellion. One tract drew the obvious examples from history to illustrate what this threatening calamity would involve. As for its reading of 1641, its author conceded that "a particular statement of the savage and bloody measures which were then pursued would too much shock the reader's humanity; it will be sufficient, however, for my present purpose to state that everything which the most brutal ferocity could suggest, or the most fertile imagination conceive or invent, was put into execution."[221] In the 1820s, as the issue of Catholic emancipation added further fuel to the sectarian atmosphere, it was notable that Protestants should be reminded that "every relaxation of the penal laws has been rewarded by insurrection and the massacre of Protestants."[222] The Brunswick Clubs that mobilized in the face of what was seen to be the threat posed by Daniel O'Connell had planned to give tangible reminders of this perceived connection in the form of monuments to the Protestant victims of 1641 (though little seems to have come of this idea).[223]

Popery remained unchanged; the descendants of those who took part in the original rebellion were "people little better in point of civilization than demi-savages, unrestrained by moral or religious feeling, at a period when they have entered into a conspiracy, the avowed object of which has been proved to be the massacre of Protestants and the subversion of the constitution."[224] The same writer insisted on the continuing relevance of 1641 for Irish Protestants in the 1820s: "A brief survey of the sanguinary transactions of this country during the horrid series of massacres and cruelties which were perpetrated against the Protestants by Popish fury in the memorable year of 1641 will give the reader an impressive lesson of what must be the awful consequences of a civil war breaking out at the present period."[225] This observation was echoed in November 1824 when the *Dublin Evening Post* pointed out with alarm that "the country is converting into an immense theological arena, and polemics are likely for some time to usurp the place of politics, if indeed they will not be mixed together and form that delightful compound, the fermentation of which produced such remarkable consequences in the reign of Charles I."[226]

This simmering sectarianism did not abate. Even as late as October 1836, a notice appearing in one of the Leinster counties declaimed, "Down with the heretics! Heretics, prepare for death, and for the flames of hell after death! We will have Daniel O'Connell and Lord O'Musgrave to our head, and we will murder bloody heretics!"[227] The resonance of 1641 was bound to survive in such circumstances, to be revitalized and made relevant to Irish Protestants who felt endangered. These threats could be seen lurking behind the most unlikely of facades. In June 1832, for example, the arrival of cholera in Ireland (the local manifestation of a global pandemic) prompted an extraordinary phenomenon. An alleged apparition of the Virgin Mary (seemingly in County Cork) revealed that certain tokens could prevent the cholera, and uncoordinated networks suddenly sprung up to distribute such tokens: ashes, stones, burning straws, and burning turf. In less than a week the phenomenon had spread across the country with extraordinary speed. Yet there were reports that Protestants were deliberately excluded from this divine protection on the instructions of the Catholic clergy, as the tokens were withheld from them.[228] The speed with which this happened was interpreted as either the prelude to a rebellion and massacre or merely a trial run for the same.[229] This belief in the prospect of a massacre was not merely the product of popular hysteria; in 1843 it was quite seriously suggested to Arthur Wellesley, Duke of Wellington (and by now a staunch defender of the Protestant interest), that ships could be used as safe havens for isolated Protestants in the event of their being rendered vulnerable by a Catholic rebellion that raised "the fear of a Protestant massacre on a large scale."[230] From the persistence of such inchoate beliefs, linked as they were to the template provided by 1641, it is worth extrapolating inwards to examine how imaginative constructions of Irish history could reveal the particular nature of such perennial fears.

Let us explore how a particular version of 1641 could be depicted in fiction. James Meikle's *Killinchy* was a fictionalized (and markedly religious) account of the life of John Livingston, the Scottish minister of Killinchy in County Down.[231] In this work the outbreak of the rebellion was described thus:

> In the month of October 1641 the long expected day arrived: the tocsin of rebellion was sounded: the shout of death and the cry of extirpation were raised. From the mountain lands of the north the hordes of rebels that had long nursed their wrath amid the wildness and sterility of these retired tracks rushed down, with all the fury of a torrent, on the Protestant population of the plains. They came down, as the wolf comes on his prey: they came to destroy and exterminate. In the work of death every feeling of humanity was disregarded; every trait of civilization obliterated, and every law of nature and God unheeded. The passions of human nature, inflamed to madness; the animosities of many generations, resuscitated, the supposed wrongs of their fathers ringing in their ears and the spirit of religious bigotry, frantic and insatiable, impelled them on to deluge their

path with blood in order to leave the records of their vengeance and their victory in the utter extinction of the Protestant name.[232]

What was notable about *Killinchy* was that it was written from an explicitly Presbyterian perspective; its denominational affiliation was not submerged beneath the umbrella of "Protestant," even if its actual descriptive passages were derived from and resembled the traditionally reductionist Protestant accounts of 1641. It was cast as an account of the martyrdom of Christ's chosen few.[233] The Scottish provenance of its various protagonists was illustrated by the phonetic rendering of the Scots dialect. For example, as one unfortunate victim died a cruel death, "his cries micht ha'e meltet hearts o' stane. His bowels were laid open, an' his vera entrails twint about the big thorn that stan's aboon the mill."[234]

This dramatic narrative ended on a defiant note. The eponymous Livingston, having heard the tale of a boy whose parents had been butchered, implores the youth to remember that "should the enemy again assail the Zion of thy fathers and seek to destroy the glorious fabric of the Reformation in these lands, defend her walls and stand fearlessly on her high towers. When the shout of war shall again be heard as they assail her battlements, think that the spirits of thy martyred kindred call on thee to avenge their blood."[235] To this entreaty the youth gave a reply with another unmistakable echo, "I will never surrender."[236]

But this was not the end. The coda to the story itself was a ballad:

> Oh! Loud was the wail over Cuan's dark water,
> As the breeze, o'er its surface, brought tidings of slaughter;
> When Rome, with her demons, rushed forth like a flood,
> And the green fields of Ulster were deluged with blood![237]

Following this ballad, *Killinchy* was adorned with appendices that served to drive home its central message. The explicit distinction between fiction and history was inevitably blurred, for these appendices consisted of extracts from authors such as the ubiquitous Temple and were prefaced with this observation:

> The Irish rebellion of 1641, or the Popish massacre as it has been called, forms one of the darkest pages in the history of popery and was an event that will long be remembered as an exemplification of the genius and spirit of the "mystery of iniquity." The incidents mentioned in the preceding narrative as occurring in one district of the north of Ireland are but a specimen of the dark and bloody scenes which characterised that dismal period. Historians of various parties have investigated the causes and traced the progress of the rebellion; and yet a plain and satisfactory

account of the massacre is a desideratum which might serve valuable purposes for the Protestant youth of this country.[238]

Should the Protestant youth of Ireland have turned to the *Dublin University Magazine* a year later, they would have found another work of fiction that differed little in its essentials from the Presbyterian sufferings brought to life in *Killinchy*. "A Legend of Ulster in 1641," while serialized anonymously, was apparently the work of the Church of Ireland divine and man of letters James Wills.[239] His tale was centered around the character of one Sir David Fitzowen, an English grantee settled in the wilds of Antrim under the plantations, for "never was a political measure so fully justified, both by its antecedents and its consequences, as the plantation of Ulster. It terminated a period of misery and strife for which no other adequate remedy could be found, and was the commencement of a period of order and tranquility unexampled in the rest of Ireland."[240]

The influence of Temple's idyllic depiction of the early seventeenth century also made itself felt; a running theme in the first chapter was that of the peaceable and harmonious relations between native and newcomer, a subject that recurred in a subsequent discussion about the weather between Fitzowen, the main protagonist, and the steersman of a boat in which he and his family were traveling to Dunluce Castle in 1637:

> "Our weather," said the man, "is like our people, never long quite still; a storm is often brewing; and the fairer and softer the surface, the deeper lies the mischief."
>
> "Do you think so?" said Sir David.

Despite his dark insinuation, the boatman was surprisingly optimistic, telling Sir David that "the whole province of Ulster is become a shining land of peace and plenty; its influence must be felt and must spread amongst even the most inveterate lovers of disturbance."[241] But this happy opinion was cast into stark relief by what followed soon afterward: a breathlessly depicted and appropriately symbolic storm that boldly foreshadowed the fact that, unbeknownst to the protagonists, an Irish rebellion was in the works. Had the Protestants been more attentive, they might have noticed that "there was more in the minds of their neighbours than their common occupations of tilling the ground and rearing their cattle."[242] When it came to what exactly the neighbors had in mind, "The massacre of Saint Bartholomew in France is not better known or authenticated than the inhuman sacrifice of Christian blood throughout Ireland and in the province of Ulster in particular."[243]

The British had been too lenient toward the Irish whom they had defeated. Unlike other conquerors, they had neglected the precautions that should have been taken against them. "It was abhorrent to their British feelings as men and Christians to keep under restraint a people to all appearance so defenceless and abject."[244] Now they paid the price: "Flight or concealment of purpose has been the constant policy of the native Irish, until their enemies, lulled into security by the apparent peace and prosperity around them, might be suddenly overwhelmed by stratagem; and on this occasion they were actuated by the united impulses of superstition and revenge to wreak upon their unsuspecting neighbours the pent up malice of generations, which now burst forth in a flood of cruelty of which the world either before or since has furnished no such terrible example."[245] Massacre overtook the Protestants. The treachery and barbarity of the Irish was revealed in the following exchange, as the rebels proceeded to burn Fitzowen's books after his death and after "Hughes, the good-natured old butler," had fortuitously escaped. As the rebels went about their sanguinary work, one of them took exception to certain matters spiritual:

> "Here goes the Bible and the Englisher's prayers, which they say to the devil in English, being the language he best understands."
>
> "I wish," said another, "we had one of the Englishers themselves to kindle the fire with his own breath! If we had but the old butler when the fire begins to flag, he would make it blaze rarely with his fat sides."
>
> "No, no," said a woman frantic with liquor and the scenes she had been engaged in, "give me the butler; the fat of his carcase will make us candles to light us through many a winter's night, and, if I can catch him, he shall do us that good at any rate."[246]

The butler Hughes eventually came across a surviving child, only to be told by Denny (the token benign Irish simpleton) that "Father O'Marah" had baptized the boy a Catholic: "He told me you may there see the end of the Sassanagh's accursed race."[247] Denny died just as a priest arrived, but not before crying out so as to be overheard by (the now hidden) Hughes that nobody would believe that the child had been baptized if somebody killed the priest.[248]

The story's occasional preoccupation with the afterlife gives credence to its attribution to a clergyman. A recurring theme was that of the sanction to kill "heretics" granted by the Catholic clergy to their flocks (no fear of the afterlife here, for according to one rebel, "they have no more spirits nor souls than one of the calves which you kill every fair"[249]), along with offers of absolution for such killings ("the priest can absolve us if our hands were red with the blood of our own father, and he a heretic"[250]). The untrustworthiness of the Irish was slyly reiterated when Hughes was informed that some Catholics offered succor to Protestants, which only served to remind him of a previous betrayal, and "with this conviction on his mind he could not help advising the speaker to be very cautious."[251] The story ended with the survivors making their way to the appropriately symbolic sanctuary of Derry, and it is very tempting to view both this story and *Killinchy* as reflecting a tendency within post-union Irish fiction to engage with a contested past in an uncertain present—in this case, the period after Catholic emancipation in 1829 and the danger to Protestant Ireland that it seemed to foreshadow.[252] Indeed, aspects of "A Legend of Ulster in 1641," written as it almost certainly was by a member of the Church of Ireland, bear a strong resemblance to the version of 1641 contained in Richard Mant's contemporaneous official history of the Church of Ireland, which basically reiterated the version of Irish history originally formulated by Sir John Temple, namely, that prior to 1641, Ireland was at peace, native and newcomer lived in amity (though the Scots continued to disturb the peace), Catholicism was tolerated, and all was well. But papists took advantage of this happy situation and over some years hatched a plot for the inevitable rebellion and massacre of Protestants. For Mant the primary motivation for 1641 was religious bigotry, as priests had preached that "to kill a heretick was no more sinful than to kill a dog, but that to relieve or protect one would be an unpardonable sin."[253]

The congruence is evident. In Wills's fiction the killing of Protestants was no different from killing a calf; in Mant's history killing Protestants was no different from killing a dog. But when we see that essentially the same point could be stated in two contemporaneous works in two different genres, we gain a tantalizing glimpse of the degree to which the version of 1641 that facilitated such beliefs had become ingrained at the level of plausible imaginative construction— at least on the part of two members of the Church of Ireland. To what extent such convictions reflected the mindsets of the community to which they ministered is, however, much less certain.

Between the outbreak of rebellion in 1641 and the last quarter of the eighteenth century, a version of its events had been created that can effectively be described as the "Protestant" account, one that remained notably static as it made its way from one era to another. Its origins lay in the response of Ireland's Protestants to the eruption of rebellion in the 1640s, and this sectarian interpretation became the canonical version adopted by Protestants in both Britain and Ireland. Given that this Irish rebellion was part of a broader crisis in both islands, the version of it generated in the 1640s became and long remained enshrined in British political culture and popular belief. Indeed, its perpetuation owed a great deal to the fact that it was disseminated in the work of such prominent figures as Hume. This set of British circumstances did, of course, influence the recollection of the events of 1641 in Ireland, as printed works spilled over to (or were re-printed in) the smaller island. In Britain 1641 was subsumed within a more general sectarian discourse as but one example, albeit a close one, of the evils and dangers of Catholicism. But there was a crucial distinction to be made between this British experience and the significance of the rebellion in Ireland. It was in Ireland that the revolt had actually broken out, and Ireland, unlike England or Scotland, had the unique distinction of possessing a Protestant community who were a minority, and one surrounded by members of the religious group whose inherent traits were deemed to have caused the rebellion in the first place.

This special set of conditions had serious implications. While 1641 undoubtedly became a touchstone for an emerging Irish Protestant identity, we must also bear in mind the extent to which it provided both a rationale for the measures intended to safeguard Protestants in Ireland and a cynical pretext by which some members of the nascent Protestant interest sought to exploit their newly secured status in Ireland. The 1641 rebellion was intertwined with both the nature of the seventeenth- and eighteenth-century Irish state and with the mental world of those Protestants who dominated it; they bequeathed an enduring legacy as the Protestant interest of the seventeenth century was slowly transformed into the "ascendancy" of the eighteenth. Over time the Irish Protestant "ascendancy" whose members emerged victorious from the sectarian conflicts of seventeenth-century Ireland formulated an exclusive and sectarian concept of a distinctly Protestant Irish nation, one that had its ideological roots in the cataclysm of 1641. This victory would not be left uncontested by those whom it sought to exclude; and consequently, lessons learned from the horrors of the past were brought to bear on the dangers and perceived needs of the present.

All of this brings us back to where we began: with John Gamble's visit to the inn near Dungiven in the summer of 1812 and to his encounter with the work of Sir John Temple. Gamble remained unconvinced by Temple's wilder claims, not least his estimate of the death toll from 1641 (150,000, "as he says"), and Gamble suggested instead that only 12,000 had been killed. Interestingly, he dismissed the notion that the victims were "English in any other sense than the Irish Protestants of the present day are English. They were the descendants of Englishmen, settled in those lands of which the unfortunate natives were (often perhaps very unjustly) dispossessed."[254] But such speculation led him to reflect further on the ultimate consequences for Irish Catholics of both the beliefs engendered by such works as Temple's and the events that these works had sought to represent. Gamble concluded that "it is impossible, without a sinking of the heart, to think of the fate of these generous and warmhearted, though often misguided and misled people, of their sufferings, their proscriptions, their expulsions, and when actual violence had ceased, of the contempt which unceasingly pursued them—the brutal scorn, the idiot laugh, the pointed finger, which have marked with indelible letters the Catholic character." But Gamble was no bigot and was at pains to dispel any suggestion that he thought "the Catholics are not to be gained by kindness, or that if they were relieved from what they deem the degradation of their present condition, the past would many years longer occupy that strong hold of their imagination which it now assuredly does. Were present grievances removed, ancient ones in a few years would probably only be a subject for tales or ballads." And perhaps if Ireland were to be governed with generosity and wisdom, "some future Catholic genius might find his hero in King William and might deck with all the charms of poetry the battle of the Boyne."[255] But the elusive dream of which Gamble wistfully wrote remained precisely that. The enduring and nightmarish power of the Protestant version of 1641 could hardly permit such a resolution.

2

"The Naked Truth of This Tragical History"

Catholic Interpretations of the Rising, c. 1641–c. 1865

There was of course another perspective on the events of 1641. John Curry was a Catholic physician in Dublin who had arguably entered his profession by default; his grandfather had fought for James II, and the family, who had lost most of their Cavan lands in the 1650s, were stripped of their remaining holdings in the aftermath of the Williamite war. Consequently, Curry's father became a merchant and Curry himself studied medicine in Paris, eventually returning to Dublin where he acquired a good reputation in his chosen profession. But on 23 October 1746, in the grounds of Dublin Castle, he came across a scene that perhaps propelled him into another field of endeavor:

> As he passed through the Castle-yard on the memorial day of the Irish rebellion in 1641, he met two ladies, and a girl of about eight years of age, who stepping on a little before them, turned about suddenly, and, with uplifted hands and horror in her countenance, exclaimed, *Are there any of those bloody papists in Dublin?* This incident, which to a different hearer would be laughable, filled the doctor with anxious reflections. He immediately inferred that the child's terror proceeded from the impression made on her mind by the sermon preached that day in Christ-Church, whence those ladies proceeded; and having procured a copy of the sermon, he

found that his surmise was well founded. In a spirit very different from that of the preacher, he immediately, on returning to his house, sat down to give some check to the hatred and asperity revived in these anniversary invectives from seats set apart for the propagation of truth and benevolence among men.[1]

The result of this, apparently, was the composition of a sequence of works that collectively made up the most formidable attempt at articulating a Catholic perspective on Irish history in general—and 1641 in particular—to be undertaken since the seventeenth century. The account of what prompted this may or may not be true; it was written by Curry's close associate, the antiquary Charles O'Conor, and there are indications in some of Curry's own works that it was in fact the anti-Catholic atmosphere generated by the Jacobite rebellion of 1745 that spurred him into print. But the resonance of the story was strong enough to attract the attention of Walter Love two centuries later. Drafts of Love's unfinished work survive, including the prospective opening: an evocation of 23 October 1746, with Curry's encounter with the frightened young girl as the centerpiece.[2]

Love recognized the symbolism of the encounter. For him it was a moment in which was revealed the dissent of Irish Catholics from a version of history that served to justify their official exclusion from political and social rights in eighteenth-century Ireland. Curry had sought to redress this imbalance through his own historical writings. His eventual corpus of work made up one of the most comprehensive refutations of the assertion that 1641 had been little more than a massacre of Protestants. But he was not the first to have tried to do so.

The Catholic Riposte,
1641–95

The "Protestant" or pro-massacre version of 1641 had been disputed virtually since the outbreak of the rebellion itself. Protestants had not been the only victims; Irish Catholics had also been the victims of a less publicized onslaught.[3] An inevitable reaction to the articulation of a "Protestant" interpretation of 1641 was the formulation of a diametrically opposing "Catholic" version of the rebellion. One tract published in 1642 accepted that there had been a Catholic rebellion in Ireland, and that Catholic rebels were indeed robbing Protestants. But it also went on to refute the allegations of Catholic atrocities against Protestants that had, even at this early stage, become common currency. The authors of such "fabulous pamphlets" simply produced "blubbered writings, making credulous people to believe such things as are contrived from their hellish brains."[4]

There is no way of knowing who wrote this tract, but its authorship is a moot point. Its central argument highlighted what eventually became a recurring theme as Catholics in Ireland, both Irish and Old English, sought to deflect the allegations that were being leveled against them with increasing frequency in the wake of the rebellion. It was immediately obvious in the aftermath that no distinction would be made between the various Catholic communities; all of them were to be accused of complicity in the rebellion. A proclamation issued by the government on 27 October, for example, had referred to the rebellion as having been "raised by a multitude of evil-affected mere Irish papists."[5] While this assertion was clarified on 29 October after a complaint by the Old English that the official declaration made no distinction between them and the "old mere Irish in Ulster," on 8 February 1642 another proclamation indicted "those of the Pale" in the rebellion.[6] Indeed, it was the subsequent assault by the government on the Old English of the Pale that eventually drove them into rebellion. The Confederate Association was formed to represent the disparate strands of Irish Catholicism in the face of the government's onslaught, and its leading members were naturally inclined to challenge allegations of Catholic atrocities (ironically, the same type of allegations were sometimes viewed with approval by contemporary observers in Catholic Europe[7]). The belief that Protestants had been brutally massacred was so extensive that in 1644 the Confederates felt compelled to refute the notion that their campaign was intended "for the extirpating and banishing them out of this kingdom"; an assurance was provided that Protestants would not be attacked, for liberty of conscience and security of estates—key issues in negotiations between the Confederates and Charles I—were guaranteed in exchange for Protestant loyalty to the king and the toleration of Catholicism.[8]

Yet aside from such declarations of intent, a more enduring strategy by which Irish Catholics sought to exonerate themselves was by questioning the received version of events. Another contemporary tract, cast as a discourse whereby an Irish statesman sought to explain Irish affairs to an English counterpart, argued that the rebellion had been provoked, and that the government of Lord Deputy Thomas Wentworth, later Earl of Strafford, had been systematically swindling the Irish (which may also have been shorthand for the Old English) out of their estates in the 1630s. Their grievance was compounded when "their fears of a total subversion of their religion began to have some just ground in the time of the parliament held at Dublin, 1641."[9] These were claims that would be repeated over time (and have largely been confirmed by modern scholarship). Pointedly (and accurately), the unknown author claimed that such mitigating factors were deliberately excluded from the depositions presented to the English parliament by Henry Jones, the better to "stir up this nation against the Irish to an implacable hatred" by stripping the rebels of any justification for their actions.[10] Allegations of atrocities against women, children, and prisoners were repudiated as "inventions" designed to prompt continued support for the war; consequently, Jones and his colleagues "did represent the Irish in as horrid shape as they could imagine, and doubtless far worse than they were, as appears evidently by the liberty they took to comment upon some depositions beyond the sense of the deponents," and by "taking every hearsay for positive proof."[11] Instead, the exploits of figures such as the Lord Justice William Parsons and Sir Charles Coote (whose own career offered rich pickings for polemics) proved that the English were quite capable of the kind of brutality that was being laid at the door of the Irish. Jones himself, in a manuscript copy of the text, disputed this charge. But the effective marginalization of such rebuttals is reflected by the fact that this tract seems never to have been published; only the manuscript survived. Within popular discourse in English (so far as we can tell), the dominant view of the rebellion was that being articulated by such figures as Jones himself; as a consequence some Catholics disputed that view. Sir John Temple stated that the bedrock of his *Irish Rebellion* was the testimony provided by the depositions collected in the aftermath. But he also observed that those depositions were "most commonly decried and held by the Irish as very injurious to their countrymen."[12] As the anonymous riposte to Jones indicates, their polemical value was not lost on contemporaries.

As time passed, more considered and comprehensive Catholic accounts began to elaborate on the rebuttals formulated in the early 1640s. The anonymous author ("R.S.") of the *Aphorismical Discovery of Treasonable Faction* painted an almost idyllic picture of Ireland on the eve of the outbreak of rebellion: the country was "rich in the plenties of a long peace" and was in "fairer terms of happiness and prosperity then ever it had done these 500 years past (being the time that the nation began to decline)."[13] This description was strikingly similar to Temple's, but the author of the *Aphorismical Discovery* had a very different purpose: Catholic writers "wanted to portray the rebellion as an aberration, interrupting an otherwise peaceful coexistence between the various religious and ethnic groups in Ireland," whereas "for Protestants the allegedly undisturbed nature of Ireland prior to 1641 simply exacerbated the enormity of the rebels' crimes."[14] The author of the *Aphorismical Discovery* argued that the uprising was prompted by "the parliament's intended rebellion as well against the crown as against all Catholics of the three kingdoms"—an objective supposedly shared by the lord justices and council in Ireland, intent as they were on exterminating or exiling those Catholic Irish who would not conform to the established church.[15] Consequently, the Irish themselves "begin to be wary and to look about them for the securing of their religion, his majesty's prerogatives, and proper lives and fortunes."[16] In other words, they had simply been prepared to defend their interests—not to mention those of the king—should the necessity arise. Seventy-eight persons were reputedly sworn to secrecy, and each of them was tasked with capturing a town or fort somewhere across Ireland. The conspirators, however, found themselves defeated by "unconstant fortune, grudging as it were, at so great happiness of both king and Irish nation"; the element of surprise was lost in Dublin when "a drunken sot . . . discovered the plot."[17] Nevertheless, Sir Phelim O'Neill struck at Charlemont fort, and the rest was, quite literally, history.

Within this account was the bedrock of the pro-Catholic version of 1641. The conspiracy of the Irish leaders was, in this reading, simply a combination of prudence, self-interest, and loyalty to the crown. Phelim O'Neill himself had apparently given his own reasons for getting involved in the rebellion: "the maintaining of the holy religion, defence of his majesty's prerogatives, and vindication of the free liberty of the Irish nation, the mere destruction and extirpation of whereof was actually intended."[18] This was the stance previously outlined in the "Generall Remonstrance or Declaration of the Catholics of Ireland" of December 1641, which had argued that the English parliament was seeking to usurp royal power and to crush Catholics in Ireland (those in England and Scotland had, it claimed, already been crushed). "That this whole and studied plot was, and is, not only to extinguish religion (by which we altogether live happy) but likewise to supplant us and raze the name of Catholic and Irish out of the whole kingdom" was deemed self-evident.[19] Consequently, the Irish had "taken arms and possessed ourselves of the best and strongest forts of this kingdom to enable us to serve his majesty and defend us from the tyrannous resolution of our enemies."[20] The rebellion was thus a matter of conscience as well as self-defense; it took little to depict the motives of the rebels' opponents as being of a very different nature.

This pro-Catholic historiography was essentially reactionary. A running theme within it was an attempt to demonstrate the consistent loyalty of the Catholic Irish and, by implication, to illuminate the disloyalty of Protestants in Ireland. It was a trope that would occasionally be echoed by Protestant commentators and polemicists in the eighteenth century, and it tended to go hand-in-hand with the suggestion that Ireland prior to 1641 had been a country at peace with itself. But these structural arguments were accompanied by rhetorical strategies of a simpler, more visceral nature.

One way of deflecting attention from allegations of Catholic brutality was to emphasize brutalities inflicted on Catholics instead.[21] For example, the

Aphorismical Discovery of Treasonable Faction dwelled at length on the cruelty of Sir Charles Coote, the MP and landowner who had been appointed military governor of Dublin after the rebellion broke out. The treatment of Coote in the *Aphorismical Discovery* culminated in an account of his activities in Wicklow, "where one of his troopers carried on the point of his spear the head of a little babe which he cut off in the very instant of his delivery, and killed the poor mother, which Coote observing, said that he was mighty pleased with many such frolics."[22] This kind of allegation was by no means unique. Hundreds of innocent Catholics were reportedly murdered by Scottish forces under Captain William Hamilton, who was alleged to have remarked of his sword that it "went as easily through the bodies of little children as through a lump of butter."[23] And while the perpetrators of some atrocities had been held accountable by the Cromwellian regime, many more were "not as much as examined, and much less chastised."[24]

In 1662, after the Restoration, another anonymous "R.S." penned a tract that served as an ironic mirror of the various abstracts of atrocities against Protestants published in the 1640s and 1650s. This author furnished extensive details of similar atrocities committed by Protestant forces against Catholics during the same period.[25] He identified himself as a royalist soldier who had served in both Ireland and England and was outraged at the manner in which he and others had been dispossessed, especially because former Cromwellians had profited despite their disloyalty. The ongoing restatement of the usual Protestant version of 1641 was, this writer asserted, "for no other end than to render all the Catholics there (in all good mens opinions) blasted and unfit to partake of his majesties grace and favour."[26]

The text itself was a reasonably sober account of various brutalities visited on Catholics by Protestants and, later, by parliamentarian forces. But the introduction offered something by way of interpretation. It ridiculed the number of Protestants allegedly killed, doing so on the reasonable grounds that the figures commonly given far exceeded the Protestant population of Ireland. The tract also disputed the veracity of the evidence of massacres collected by the authorities, and, in what proved to be an influential assertion, insisted that the Catholics had been attacked first: this explained their understandable retaliation. According to this writer, the initial Protestant atrocity took place in County Antrim, where "about the beginning of November the English and Scots forces in Carrickfergus murdered in one night all the inhabitants of the territory of Islandmagee, to the number of above 3000 men, women, and children, all innocent persons, in a time when none of the Catholics of that county [*sic*] were in arms or rebellion. Note that this was the first massacre committed in Ireland of either side."[27]

The tract offered a litany of similar stories, itemized county by county. The interpretation of the rebellion that rested on these accounts would certainly be perpetuated. But in the 1660s this was the exception rather than the rule: the tract itself was suppressed and publicly burned in Ireland as the Protestant interpretation of the rebellion monopolized public discourse on the subject.[28] The work of "R.S." had, after all, been published at a particular juncture; in the early years of the Restoration substantial efforts were being made by Catholics to prove their loyalty to the crown and thereby win some measure of redress as Catholic agents lobbied at court for restitution of property.[29] Another tract argued along similar lines that the Old English had been unjustly treated as rebels in the 1640s and sought to prevent the perpetuation of such treatment into the 1660s.[30] These efforts may have carried some weight, as it was the Old English who benefited most from the limited redress offered to Irish Catholics under the terms of the Restoration settlement.[31] But regardless of how they were qualified, these countervailing arguments were themselves disputed. In February 1663 Audley Mervyn, the speaker of the Irish House of Commons, declared that the recently established Protestant interest should not be tampered with, not least because the involvement of Catholics in the rebellion was sufficient to disqualify them from receiving any relief for the dispossession they had suffered. Mervyn emphatically dismissed accounts that "fasten the rise of the rebellion upon the Protestants and [claim] that we drew the first blood."[32]

The Protestant colonial order, confirmed and strengthened after 1660, proved a formidable obstacle to those who would attempt to shift the blame for 1641 from one side to the other. This did not mean, however, that attempts to do so were abandoned. The Old English Richard Bellings, writing in the 1670s, repeated the claim that life in Ireland prior to 1641 was peaceful, prosperous, and harmonious, despite the fact that Catholics had real grievances about the encroachments of the plantations and the existence of penal legislation.[33] In Bellings's account the rebellion was once again prompted by fears that the English parliament had been intent on suppressing Catholicism—fears that were heightened by events in Scotland.[34] But while he seemed to accept the assertion that the *intention* to massacre Protestants was indeed present (this had been flagged in the original testimony of Owen Connolly), Bellings silently passed over attacks on Protestants in his account of the rebellion.[35] He was well aware of the potentially inflammatory nature of his work, which remained unpublished until the nineteenth century.[36]

There was another key argument made by Catholic writers, one that dovetailed with an interpretation of 1641 that viewed Catholics as the innocent victims: that the allegations of atrocities were used in a cynical attempt to justify their dispossession. In 1662 the Catholic cleric John Lynch argued that the desire to maintain the confiscations of the 1650s was the principal reason for inciting hatred against Catholics.[37] According to the Catholic bishop Nicholas French, writing in 1674 and echoing this earlier judgment, "it hath been a principal care and study of some statesmen near the king to oppress and overthrow the Catholics of Ireland, and at the same time to persuade his majesty that we ought to be destroyed by justice and law."[38] The basis for this charge was a combination of genuine fear and naked self-interest that rested on the assumption that in 1641 Catholics had sought to wipe out Protestants in Ireland. Thus Catholics were to be punished in a manner that would safeguard both the nascent Protestant interest and, crucially, the gains that some Protestants had made. Cynicism about the manner in which this strategy was justified after the fact was not confined to the Catholic elite. At the height of the scare over the Popish Plot in late 1678 the incumbent viceroy Ormond was bombarded with missives from the aged and gout-stricken Orrery expounding at length on the threat to Protestants in Munster supposedly posed by the Catholic inhabitants of the province. But Ormond took a very dim view of what he interpreted as little more than reckless and self-interested scaremongering.[39] Writing in a sarcastic vein, Ormond declined to state that "he [Orrery] would be content there should be another rebellion [so] that there may be another distribution of lands, but I am satisfied all he proposes looks very like it."[40] Here was a definite case of Protestant cynicism about the uses to which a version of the 1641 Irish rebellion and a possible sequel was being put.

In these circumstances it was perhaps inevitable that members of the Catholic lay and clerical elites, such as French and James Tuchet, Earl of Castlehaven, continued to state a Catholic case. Castlehaven was an English Catholic peer who had inherited his Irish title after the execution of his father in 1631 for homosexuality and for having facilitated the rape of his wife by a servant. The younger Castlehaven tried to escape his family's unwelcome notoriety and embarked on a military career that eventually brought him back to Ireland to serve in the Confederate forces. For Castlehaven, writing a decade after he had been embroiled in the conflicts of the 1640s, the initial uprising in 1641 had been prompted by legitimate grievances.[41] He maintained that its true nature was being deliberately obscured by the bigotry and rapacity of a newly enriched Protestant interest.[42] His argument followed an increasingly familiar pattern and in doing so raised further questions. For example, while sympathy might be deserved for those Protestants who had suffered, how many had actually been killed? In 1668 French himself claimed that "four hundred English could not be found murdered in Ireland."[43] This assertion was patently ridiculous, but standard accounts of the Protestant death toll (some claims put it as high as 300,000—a number derived from misreading Temple) were equally dubious.[44]

According to one anonymous soldier who had served in Ireland, writing *circa* 1685, "most damnable inhumanity was done by some of the natives by murdering of the British."[45] But, this soldier declared, "that so many were murdered there, as these authors hold forth, is not my opinion, and that they have been misinformed otherwise, as a willing mistake in them; for the most suffered after that manner was in Ulster, as the other provinces say; and the most in Ulster, as the most notorious was at Portadown in the county of Armagh, as all Ulster says; and the most that were there drowned and murdered exceed not *ninety persons*, for which some were hanged, as they well deserved, at the High Court of Justice at Carrickfergus in the year 1653."[46]

This soldier displayed a certain empathy toward his enemies (and was especially dismissive of the writings of Edmund Borlase). He readily conceded that the Irish in many instances were provoked into rebellion. He referred to an attack by English forces on Templepatrick, Co. Antrim, in which eighty men, women, and children were apparently killed in cold blood. According to the author, this slaughter was the reason for the Scottish attack on Islandmagee, which in turn prompted retaliatory attacks such as the infamous massacre at Portadown.[47] And as for the number killed, "the most was committed in Ulster, and it did not exceed through all Ulster above the sixtieth part held forth by those authors I named before" (including Borlase and "one Crawford, a minister").[48]

In any case, the numbers themselves were not the central issue. The essential point being made was that there was a latent groundswell of Catholic discontent that crystallized around the accusations leveled at that community concerning the events of the rebellion. Just as the events of 1641 and their symbolism were contested in print, so too they could be contested in reality, and literally on the street. The ongoing commemorations on 23 October (and indeed the anniversary of the Gunpowder Plot on 5 November) were a regular cause of sectarian conflict, provoking Catholic reactions. The public and raucous nature of the celebrations—complete with bonfires, processions, and enormous quantities of drink—made them perennial flashpoints.[49] This phenomenon intensified under the Jacobite regime after 1685. Take, for example, an incident in Dublin in November 1687, when "the day observed for the Irish rebellion was kept by some as formerly, with making of bonfires and a certain number of soldiers going about and taking upon them to rebuke and chastise the authors were severely beaten about Nicholas Street, but on the Comb [Coombe] the soldiers killed one or two tradesmen, upon which bonfires were forbid this day and for the future."[50]

More ominously, during the attempted Catholic "counterrevolution" of the 1680s Protestants came under a degree of sectarian attack that convinced many of them that a repeat of 1641 would soon befall them. The Jacobite parliament of 1689, just as it sought to undo a settlement legitimized by the Protestant interpretation of 1641, also intended to undo that legitimization by repealing the act that had codified the commemoration—precisely the reason why, almost a century and a half later, Thomas Davis sought to elevate the "patriot parliament" to iconic status in his vision of Irish nationalism.[51] The Williamite victory in 1691 rendered its actual proceedings moot, but in the immediate aftermath of the political and military defeat of Catholic Ireland, the Catholic riposte to 1641 continued to be articulated. This was most evident in a text that would be continually reprinted over much of the next 150 years: Hugh Reily's *Ireland's Case Briefly Stated*.[52]

Reily was a Catholic priest who held a number of official positions under the Jacobite regime. His explicitly Jacobite text, written to vindicate the cause of Irish Catholicism in the wake of the Jacobite defeat, contested Protestant arguments about both the origins and nature of the events of 1641. He began from first principles, with an outright denunciation of Protestant historians and commentators such as William King, whose "interest prompts them to play the devil in God's name."[53] Reily claimed that Charles I, via the Marquis of Antrim, had tried to persuade Ormond to seize control of the Irish government from the lord justices just after the rebellion broke out. The Irish reportedly got wind of this and rose to take advantage of the opportunity it presented. But the spread of the rebellion was blamed on the lord justices, who, argued Reily, provoked it to provide themselves with the perfect excuse to seize the remaining Catholic estates.[54]

It was inevitable that Reily would discuss the massacres. "I think it is very plain," he wrote, "that the Protestants were the first actors upon the stage."[55] Reily justified this assertion by reference to massacres by Protestant forces at "Santry, Clontarf, and Bullock [*sic*]," Islandmagee, and Carrickfergus, not to mention the sanguinary excesses of Broghill and Coote. Consequently, the Irish—or at least the "common soldiers"—who had hitherto been unwilling to harm unarmed Protestants, sought to exact revenge.[56] As for the scale of what had happened, Reily dismissed Temple's "romantic legend," along with what he mistakenly assumed to be Temple's estimated death toll of 300,000 as "not only incredible but most ridiculous and absolutely impossible."[57] Catholics were apparently less likely to live in towns and cities, so presumably their deaths were more likely to be overlooked. Attacks on Protestants had been committed by the "rabble," whereas those on Catholics had been explicitly ordered by such prominent figures as Coote; and the allegedly small number—140 men and women—executed by the Cromwellians at the behest of the "pretended high court of justice" was proof in itself that the Protestant death toll was massively exaggerated, "unless we fancy them so many giants."[58] Reily concluded: "This briefly is the naked truth of this tragical history which has raised so great a clamour in the world. The Catholics suffered in much greater numbers; but dying as it were dumb, like so many sheep brought to the slaughter, their blood made no great noise, at least in England; but the Protestants fell, as I may say, with so many speaking trumpets in their mouths that every individual seemed an hundred."[59]

Having dealt with the events of the rebellion, Reily then examined its causes and consequences. In his view "there never was, under a legal government, any insurrection more necessary for self-preservation, and consequently more excusable, if we except the aforesaid outrages committed by the unruly rabble, than that of 1641."[60] Since this was self-evident, he was scathing of the use to which 1641 was put in the settlements of the 1650s and 1660s. And this perspective provides the key to the enduring popularity of his work, for the preeminent status of Irish Protestants that these settlements had engendered at the expense of Irish Catholics would be greatly solidified in the decades after 1691.

Within Reily's work were the key themes of the Catholic interpretation of 1641, one that was ultimately a reaction to the authorized version that had long been in place. These themes had persisted because of both their enduring relevance and the subaltern vitality of the Catholic community. This vitality was perhaps manifest in the 1725 dispute between the Catholic priest Cornelius Nary and the Anglican cleric Edward Synge (archbishop of Tuam), who was rebuked by his peers for advocating religious tolerance in a sermon preached before the Irish House of Commons on 23 October 1725—the anniversary of 1641 no less. Yet surprisingly, Synge's call for toleration was opposed by Nary on theological grounds—a stance that can arguably, according to James Livesey, be seen as proof of the enduring vibrancy of coherent Catholic intellectual and cultural traditions, maintained despite the exclusion of Catholic Ireland from official life.[61]

Reily's work filled a surprising gap, for its original publication in 1695 marked the end of the first phase in the ongoing assertion of a Catholic version of 1641 that had been stated and restated since the 1640s to contest the Protestant version that traditionally monopolized discourse on the subject (at least in English). As far as Irish Catholics were concerned, the mantle of apocalyptic event was more properly applied to the Cromwellian invasion of 1649. While contemporary poets writing in the 1640s, such as Uilliam Og Mac Uilliam Oig Mheic an Bháird and Pádraigín Haicéad, had sought to justify the Irish (or at least the Irish nobility's) rising in 1641, they did not dwell on the specifics of what had happened.[62] The same was true of the broader overviews of the significance of the seventeenth century contained in the later work of poets such as Dáibhí Ó Bruadair and Aodhagán Ó Rathaille; while infused with the rhetoric of dispossession, references to 1641 took the form of oblique allusion rather than detailed exegesis, if indeed it was mentioned at all.[63] By contrast, Reily's work was markedly different in nature and arguably signaled a break with more traditional Irish perspectives on the recent past. Furthermore, his account was genuinely popular. Unlike the great works of the Catholic clerical and lay elites after the Restoration, it was reprinted in cheap, accessible chapbook editions well into the early nineteenth century; indeed, the fact that it appeared in Irish at least once, in 1772, suggests a demand for its contents outside a purely Anglophone public sphere.[64] Essentially a reaction to Protestant accounts that it sought to combat through a rhetorical triptych of Catholic loyalty, the denial of Catholic atrocities, and the concomitant highlighting of Protestant ones, this alternate perspective on the causes, course, and consequences of 1641 would not be reasserted in a new form until John Curry wandered into Dublin Castle in October 1746.

Curry and the Catholic Counterargument, 1747–80

Curry's first venture into print on the subject of 1641 came in 1747 with the publication of *A Brief Account from the Most Authentic Protestant Writers of the Causes, Motives, and Mischiefs of the Irish Rebellion on the 23rd Day of October 1641.*[65] It seems incongruous that prior to its appearance, despite—or perhaps because of—the continued vitality of Irish Jacobitism and the recurrence of agrarian unrest (often interpreted in starkly sectarian terms), Irish Catholics at home and abroad declined to enter the ranks of formal disputation about the events of 1641. It is more surprising given the occasional flashes of what appeared to be Catholic ripostes to the state-sanctioned commemoration. Walter Love, for example, reinterpreted an ostensibly mundane incident in Daniel Corkery's *The Hidden Ireland* in which Corkery quoted at length from an account by J. M. Caldwell, who described how on the night of 23 October in 1747 "the whole of Galway was illuminated, and . . . there were candles even in the windows of the convents."[66] Caldwell's explanation was shared by Corkery—that this was a celebration of the successful mopping-up operations carried out by the Irish Brigade after the French capture of the fortress of Bergen-op-zoon in Brabant on 16 September 1747. The candles were assumed to be a celebration of victorious Irish arms in the service of England's enemies. But there was no mention whatsoever of the obvious significance of 23 October. Love, on the other hand, made the reasonable suggestion that the scene described may have been a deliberate and symbolic act of collective dissent on the part of Galway Catholics from the official version of 1641 sanctioned by the Protestant state that governed them.

This posture of Catholic dissent is the crucial context in which Curry's literary endeavors must be located. The mid-eighteenth century saw increasing levels of Catholic agitation aimed at altering the confessional nature of the Irish state, most strikingly by arguing for the repeal of the penal laws that underpinned it: here was the rise of the "Catholic question."[67] Activism in its service took a variety of forms. For example, in 1756 Curry and his close associate Charles O'Conor of Belanagare would be founding members of the Catholic Committee. But pamphleteering and propaganda were an integral element of, and a constant accompaniment to, the "Catholic question." Both Curry and O'Conor readily engaged in these paper wars, which arose in part from a heightened interest in the Irish past that developed in the course of the eighteenth century, and which was the province of antiquaries such as O'Conor himself. This new-style antiquarianism was part of a broader trend that was to become manifest across contemporary Europe, but it was inevitably shaped by the particularity of Irish conditions. Antiquarianism may have held out the possibility of uncovering an agreed past with which both Catholics and Protestants could engage, but the practice of dwelling on the glories of native civilization prior to the English conquest naturally posed awkward questions about the superiority (or otherwise) of the culture that had arrived after it. There was a sectarian edge to these antiquarian debates about the nature and origins of the ancient Irish, about whether or not they were "Scandian" [sic] or "Phoenician," northern or southern, barbarous or civilized? Underpinning such seemingly innocuous disputation was a more visceral reality, for as Walter Love noted, "the clash of rival systems of ancient history was also a clash between Protestant and Catholic."[68] If such an essentially sectarian debate could be conducted about the ancient past, it was probably inevitable that it would eventually be extended to more recent events. As the eighteenth century wore on, such debates "were sharpened by the incorporation of the wars and rebellions of the sixteenth and seventeenth centuries into the available narrative."[69] Preeminent among such "wars and rebellions" was that of 1641. Curry's ventures into historical discourse were intended to undermine the role that 1641 played in legitimizing the Protestant state, and thereby to transform the Protestant nature of the state itself.

Perhaps the most eloquent statement of this reality, and of the prospect of contesting it, was made by no less a figure than Edmund Burke, whose interest in Irish history (at least in the early phases of his career) was directly related to the nascent "Catholic question." Indeed, Burke even recommended Curry's

Historical Memoirs to the English writer Tobias Smollett in order to secure a favorable review of the work in London (though as his career progressed in England, he became wary of such open advocacy).[70] Burke's most significant contribution to debates on the Catholic question were the unpublished "Tracts Relating to the Popery Laws" (1765), originally drafted against the backdrop of agrarian unrest in Munster in the 1760s. The repressively sectarian response of the Munster Protestant elite (such as the notorious judicial murder of Nicholas Sheehy, the parish priest of Clogheen, Co. Tipperary, for alleged involvement in Whiteboy activities) made a lasting impression on Burke. He subsequently argued that "the great prop of this whole system is not pretended to be its justice or its utility, but the supposed danger to the state which gave rise to it originally, and which they apprehend would return if this system were overturned. Whilst, say they, the papists of this kingdom were possessed of landed property, and of the influence consequent to such property, their allegiance to the crown of Great Britain was ever insecure; the public peace was ever liable to be broken; and Protestants could never be a moment secure either of their properties or of their lives"; after all, had not the Catholics shown their readiness to rebel? Burke laid out his opposing case with some vehemence:

> Such are the arguments that are used both publicly and privately in every discussion on this point. They are generally full of passion and of error, and built upon facts which in themselves are most false. It cannot, I confess, be denied, that those miserable performances which go about under the names of histories of Ireland do indeed represent those events after this manner. . . . But there is an interior history of Ireland, the genuine voice of its records and monuments, which speaks a very different language from these histories, from Temple and from Clarendon; these restore nature to its just rights, and policy to its proper order. For they even now show to those who have been at the pains to examine them, and they may show one day to all the world, that these rebellions were not produced by toleration but by persecution; that they arose not from just and mild government but from the most unparalleled oppression. These records will be so far from giving the least countenance to a doctrine so repugnant to humanity and good sense as that the security of any establishment, civil or religious, can ever depend upon the misery of those who live under it.[71]

Burke realized that by buttressing the eighteenth-century Irish state, the ideological utility of 1641 rested on a distinct symbolic interpretation. Curry sought to challenge this version with a different one.

Curry's *Brief Account* did not confirm O'Conor's claim about his reaction to the terrified little girl whom he allegedly overheard on 23 October 1746.

According to the preface, it was written instead against the tense backdrop of the Jacobite '45. Curry's authorship was disguised; he cast himself as a member of the Church of Ireland in dialogue with a Protestant Dissenter, and began by stating that "Irish papists" had, for "more than fifty years past," been peaceful and dutiful subjects. "Why, therefore, is the *rebellion* of *forty one*, with so many unjust and unhumane exaggerations, at this time trumped up against them?"[72] The contrasting argument from the ostensible Dissenter was that this quiescence was precisely why 1641 should be remembered, for a similarly misleading veneer of peace had prevailed prior to the horrors of the rebellion.[73] The influence of earlier histories was obvious and undoubtedly deliberate; it facilitated the response, which was that Irish Catholics had been provoked into "that horrid rebellion" by the many and varied excesses of Strafford's "oppressive administration."[74] Curry (in his guise as a member of the established church, successfully winning the Dissenter to his cause) proceeded to argue that despite these provocations, Irish Catholics, unlike some others, had remained loyal to the crown. The eventual outbreak of the rebellion stemmed from the continuation of such oppressive practices and the apprehension of greater trials to come.

The substance of all this was not in itself particularly unusual; it was essentially no different from the pro-Catholic arguments used in the previous century. What was different was the form in which they were expressed. Curry employed the unprecedented rhetorical strategy of using material openly lifted from Protestant writers such as Temple and Borlase to bolster his own case while at the same time turning their arguments against them.[75] Indeed, he even used the words of Charles I himself (from *Eikon Basilike*) to substantiate the claim that Irish Catholics had feared further persecution against the backdrop of the early 1640s in England.[76]

Up to this point Curry had simply restated the standard Catholic version of 1641 originally formulated in the seventeenth century. Yet while the version of events that he outlined may have provided the rationale for the rebellion, it did not, as the Dissenter pointed out, provide one for the massacres that were supposed to have characterized it. Though Curry, in his adopted Anglican garb, readily stated that nothing could justify such massacres, the fundamental point he wanted to make was that these massacres had never happened at all.

A footnote provided the starting point. In it Curry noted the "surprising difference and inconsistency given us of these murders by the enemies of the Irish papists."[77] To challenge the allegations that a massacre had taken place, he used the depositions printed in the works of Temple and Borlase, which, he claimed, mentioned only five killings, and even then only in a generalized way. "There is the strongest presumptive proof that, I think, can be had of anything, that no murders at all, at the least none considerable, were committed by the Irish at their first breaking out."[78] If they had occurred, why were these massacres not mentioned by other witnesses or other contemporaries? After all, he argued, so much else of note had been reported: "I am far from pretending to justify those cruelties (perpetrated by some of the rabble of the Irish during this rebellion), which all the sober and unbigoted Roman Catholics then among them, and now among us, did and do sincerely condemn and abhor. But I must insist upon it that they neither began that tragedy nor committed a murder, at that unhappy juncture, that was not returned upon them at least four fold."[79] To prove the point, he approvingly used the work of "R.S." (the tract burned at the Restoration that had since, perhaps incongruously, been reprinted as an appendix to Clarendon's *History*). Curry now reproduced it in a documentary appendix to his own work and readily adopted one of its key assertions: that 3,000 Catholic men, women, and children had been massacred by English and Scots forces at "Carrickfergus." Presumably, he meant the attack on Island-magee and, taking a cue from "R.S.," Curry claimed that this slaughter had in fact taken place in November 1641.[80]

This date was of fundamental importance to his case. If Islandmagee had seen the first blow struck in 1641, then any Catholic attacks on Protestants were merely retaliation. To dismiss any depositions that could cast doubt on this notion, Curry quoted from some of the more debatable testimonies, particularly those relating to the appearance of the ghosts of Protestants at Portadown. Finally, in an echo of what French and Lynch had argued nearly a century earlier, and in anticipation of what Burke would imply in 1765, Curry maintained that what was now the official version of 1641 had been deliberately and cynically adopted to blacken the name of the Catholic Irish amid the formulation of the land settlement of the 1660s, and thereby used to dispossess them.[81]

This line of argument naturally met with a response. In 1752 the Protestant antiquary Walter Harris published *Fiction Unmasked* as an explicit riposte to Curry's work ("a book supported by a numerous and bold faction").[82] Harris suggested that Curry had written his work not to counter the inflammatory atmosphere that accompanied the '45 but to foment unrest against its back-drop; Curry's literary endeavors were "monstrous," "atrocious," and "destitute of the least foundation of truth."[83] Even worse, they had apparently made an "impression" on many "real and well disposed Protestants."[84]

Fiction Unmasked was virtually a mirror image of Curry's work. In its title Harris rightly pointed out that he was responding to the work of a "popish physician," and in a reversal of Curry's technique he cast his work as a dialogue between a "Protestant" who dismissed Curry's work and a "papist" who con-sidered it a "solid, unanswerable piece."[85] Even aside from this engagement with Curry, *Fiction Unmasked* took the form of a broader discourse about Catholicism (complete with stock allegations about the inherent disloyalty of Catholics and their obligation to extirpate "the *northern heresy*"),[86] sectarianism, and the nature of the Irish state. But Harris inevitably turned from the general back to the particular to impugn Curry's motives: "Surely such books were calculated for some expected season of conspiracy and murder."[87] Much of the text consisted of an intricate attempt to refute any justification or excuse for 1641 in terms of Protestant provocation or persecution of Catholics. It began by questioning whether Clarendon's assessment of Ireland prior to 1641 was accurate—after all, Curry had argued to the contrary. A key strategy used by Harris was the vindication of Protestant writers such as Temple, Borlase, and Clarendon, and just as Curry had pitted such writers against one another, so Harris used Catholic historians in the same way.

Harris claimed that Curry's use of a dialogue was little more than sophistry intended to bolster his argument. But this accusation did not dissuade Harris from using one himself. In rhetorical terms it was highly disingenuous: his "papist" was usually no match for his "Protestant." For instance, a discussion of the aftermath of the Nine Years' War ended with the Protestant asking, out of the blue, if "I suppose you think it reasonable that some light punishment should be inflicted on these rebellious children":

PAP: Yes, I think they should be punished as offending children, but not
    extirpated.
PROT: Nor were they extirpated, as evidently appears from their being able
    to carry out the cruelest rebellion that ever happened in Ireland.[88]

According to the Protestant, that "there may be a few *Roman Catholicks* unbigoted is possible, but in my conversation through a long life I must profess to you I have met with very few under that denomination."[89] Supporting this contention was the notion that "all *unsuperstitious papists*, both then and now, did and do condemn and abhor such cruelties. But where are such to be found? Perhaps to look for them would be to hunt after a black swan."[90] The implication was obvious. Harris concluded: "I have answered in the best manner I could from the several histories of the times contemporary with the actions, which must carry the strongest weight of authority; and now I submit all I have said to the judgement and censure of the publick. So, sir, I wish you a good night."[91]

Such a challenge did little to discourage Curry; on the contrary, it stiffened his resolve and prompted a fuller response in the form of his *Historical Memoirs of the Irish Rebellion in the Year 1641.*[92] In a deliberate rebuttal of *Fiction Unmasked*, Curry accused Harris of attempting "a shameful and (it is to be hoped) an impotent design to spread hates, perpetuate rancour, and oppress the living by the abuse of the dead."[93] Curry's new book began with a fascinating attempt to unshackle religion from "civil principles"; by extension he sought to remove religion from his interpretation of the rebellion more generally, presumably to further undermine assumptions about its sectarian character.[94] In the actual text he adopted a more prosaic strategy, beginning with the origins of the original account that had prompted Harris's ire.

Though the *Historical Memoirs* was composed as a specific response to Harris, there was considerable continuity between it and Curry's earlier work. He had certainly been alarmed by the revived fears of 1641 that he felt were encouraged in the anti-Catholic atmosphere that accompanied the Jacobite rebellion in 1745. But "as there were no *Roman-Catholic* authors, that he knew of, who *professedly* treated of that insurrection, he carefully turned over the *Protestant* writers on that subject."[95] In his preface Curry had singled out Clarendon and David Hume for perpetuating the notion of 1641 as Catholic massacre. (Hume was still alive and could potentially have mended his ways; Curry later expended considerable energy in an attempt to persuade him to do so).[96] But in the text itself he focused once more on the triptych of Temple, Borlase, and Clarendon. The parliamentarian Temple and the royalist Clarendon wrote from opposing political perspectives, while Borlase "has botched up what he calls an history from pilfered parcels out of *both*."[97] Having comprehensively dismissed one set of authors, he sought to vindicate one of the few writers to articulate a pro-Catholic perspective: Curry returned to the defense of "R.S." and the events at Islandmagee, all of which had been contested by Harris.[98]

Curry did not substantively deviate from the model established in *A Brief Account*. The *Historical Memoirs* simply provided a far more substantial and forensic account, one that was given pointed relevance as an explicit intervention in the debate with Harris. Curry had devoted considerable space to refuting Harris's assertions that the rebellion had not been provoked.[99] This led, in turn, to the raising of two weighty questions that others had already asked. Was the rebellion justified? And had it consisted of a massacre?

Certainly, Curry tried to show that the answer to the first question was in the affirmative; he dwelled at length on the provocative brutality of lord justices Borlase and Parsons.[100] More novel was the manner in which he sought to answer the second, for he used the depositions to ensure that the answer would be "no." Curry shrewdly questioned their specific details once again. He now claimed that dates had deliberately been removed from the depositions that had appeared in print, thereby making it more difficult to disprove them.[101] This line of attack indicated that while he knew of the depositions, he was aware only of the tiny fraction that had actually made their way into print. Curry did not consult the originals and had indeed declined the opportunity to do so.[102]

But with remarkable effrontery he accused Harris of ignoring them as well; he claimed that Harris had merely taken advantage of those depositions printed by Temple and Borlase.[103] Curry had already used the accounts of Peter Walsh and Castlehaven to reduce the level of casualties by a rhetorical sleight of hand, though he advanced no alternative to the wilder figures put forth by Temple or Milton.[104]

Curry pressed a wider attack on the depositions. He questioned whether the deponents had even been literate, and suggested as he did so that they had been open to manipulation. Hearsay and exaggeration, he noted, had been recorded in the depositions alongside the most outlandish allegations; indeed, some deponents had supposedly refuted them afterward.[105] His final flourish invoked the case of the Irish émigré Jesuit Conor O'Mahony, whose enormously controversial *Disputatio Apologetica* (1645) had argued, among other things, that Irish Catholics owed no allegiance to a heretical king and should continue to exterminate heretics as best they could (a stance that prompted the Confederates to publicly burn it in Kilkenny in 1647). But according to Curry, "One *popish incendiary* writer, living at *Lisbon* during *the whole time* of this rebellion, has related upon *mere hearsay* that in the *first four years* of it the same number of *English* were cut off by the *Irish* in battle or otherwise, which *Temple* and his numerous followers have impudently asserted to have been massacred *in cold blood*, and in the *first two months of it only!*"[106] The contradiction seemed to illustrate Curry's point. No doubt with the intent of infusing his arguments with greater force, Curry attached an extensive documentary appendix to his new work as he had to its predecessor.

The actual reception of such works remains hard to discern. One reviewer was somewhat skeptical of Curry's desire to blame the Dublin government and the English parliament for the rebellion, though he admitted that there was a grain of truth in this interpretation. As for whether there had been wholesale exaggeration of the numbers killed in the "murders and massacres," this reviewer harked back to the Jacobite '45 and concluded that "when facts are seen through the medium of *fear*, they appear of course magnified beyond the bounds of truth."[107] But on the whole the reviewer found Curry's case to be persuasive. Aside from the immediate political context in which Curry operated, it is worth considering the intellectual milieu that facilitated the reception of his work. Part of that milieu was the ongoing interest in antiquarianism and the Irish past that characterized Irish intellectual life in the latter half of the eighteenth century. Often underpinning this interest (as Walter Love later discerned) were sectarian considerations. Yet the very fact that Curry began to write about 1641 after the failure of the '45 was a tacit admission that the lot of Irish Catholics was not going to be changed by the victorious return of the Stuarts. Consequently, different strategies would be required to improve the conditions of Irish Catholics. Such intellectual activism did not always meet with success or encouragement. Some members of the Catholic Committee were not enthusiastic about the publication of the *Historical Memoirs* in 1758, and even his close associate O'Conor expressed occasional reservations about Curry's unwillingness to concede that Catholics had been at fault in the past.[108] But the manner in which Curry went about his project was unprecedented. And part of that ongoing project was to encourage others to write about the historical controversy that so exercised him.

Paradigm Shifts?
The Influence of the Catholic Version of 1641

By the middle of the eighteenth century the iconic status of 1641 had become a symbol that defined both political belief and sectarian allegiance. In the course of his campaign in the contentious Dublin by-election of 1748–49 the "patriot" Charles Lucas (who was less prejudiced toward Catholics than is often assumed) controversially adopted a more temperate (and familiar) line on 1641. While a "general massacre" of Protestants had indeed been on the cards, the Irish, according to Lucas, had simply sought to defend themselves from the depredations of Strafford's regime.[109] "But as they destroyed many thousands [of] *Protestants* by various cruel deaths, so the government cut off, without quarter, as many of the native *Irish* as could be found, so that it is hard to say whose party lost most lives; only the *Roman Catholics* will not allow of 200,000 *Protestants* slain because there were not so many in the island."[110]

English misgovernment in Ireland was a key theme of Lucas's campaign; he endorsed the suggestion that Catholics had sought to defend themselves, and in doing so became the victims of atrocities as much as the perpetrators. But his vignette hinted at a dialectic: the possibility that the arguments of Catholic writers, articulated since the 1640s, were crossing Ireland's denominational barriers and might yet modify the official Protestant version of 1641. It was impossible to fully unshackle the meaning of the rebellion from unresolved contemporary issues. But as the eighteenth century advanced, attempts were made to analyze the events of the rebellion in a scholarly and judicious manner that might prove sufficient to defuse its polemical power. One of the more significant contributors to these efforts was Ferdinando Warner.

Warner was a native of Tewkesbury and the Church of England rector of Barnes in Surrey. He was also a prolific author on matters theological and, in later life, historical (albeit to a lesser extent). In the early 1760s he had embarked on a history of Ireland, only one volume of which was ever published.[111] Warner was unable to secure financial backing to complete his project, but in the process of his research he had worked on various manuscripts in Dublin. These became the basis for the more modest work that came from his hands in 1767: *The History of the Rebellion and Civil War in Ireland.*[112]

In the preface he rapidly came to the essential point about 1641: "Though the business of the massacre hath made as much noise, and been as much the subject of dispute and crimination [*sic*], as any point of history in the world, it hath never yet been fully nor fairly represented."[113] Warner was fully aware of the partiality of such writers as Temple and Borlase; he was especially dismissive of Richard Cox, the former lord chancellor of Ireland whose *Hibernia Anglicana* (1689) simply regurgitated their accounts, augmenting them with newspapers and pamphlets, and whose work "in no part deserves the name of a history."[114] On the other hand, he was wary of such figures as the Confederate Ulick Burke, Marquis of Clanricarde, and of Castlehaven, even though he judged these two to have been the only worthwhile Catholic writers on the topic. But the former could write with authority only about his own locality, while the latter wrote at so great a chronological distance that his account was inevitably flawed.[115] According to Warner, the only English writers to have produced substantive treatments of 1641—Clarendon and Thomas Carte—were compromised by their loyalty to the Stuarts, and most English accounts of events in Ireland had taken their cue from them.[116]

Warner, like any writer, was firmly rooted in his time and place. By the 1760s one could make a case that international Catholicism was perhaps not as powerful or sinister as had traditionally been assumed, but Warner remained concerned about the prospect of Jesuits swarming into England and favored some legal attempts to prevent the "increase of popery" (though he was opposed to repeating the excesses of previous centuries).[117] He saw himself as occupying a middle ground between extremes. He insisted that he had "no apprehension . . . of having the crime of partiality laid to his charge—and a great crime it is: for he believes he is more likely to give offence to all sides." Warner did concede that by not damning Catholics, he could be perceived as favoring them. But he concluded by suggesting that his history should persuade Irish Catholics to seek lawful toleration rather than "those measures which brought their ancestors to ruin"; and as for Irish Protestants, his work "should incline them to the repeal of those severe and vindictive statutes against their fellow-subjects in the reign of Anne which are as contrary to sound policy as to true religion."[118]

This deliberate and instructive polemical purpose was nothing new; its form may have been unprecedented, but its essential nature was not. Warner's text seemed to synthesize the differing accounts of the rebellion that had been produced in previous generations. He conceded the validity of key motivations for the rebellion: Catholic resentment at dispossession and religious subjugation, especially in the form of a desire to restore Catholicism to what was deemed to be its rightful place. These grievances explained "the design of a general insurrection."[119] He located the immediate cause of its outbreak in the crisis of the early 1640s, the machinations of Strafford, and the Irish Catholic fear of a Puritan parliament. But he leavened his account with a good deal of skepticism about the justifications for the rebellion traditionally advanced by Catholic polemicists, and he did not doubt that the rebellion was intended to "root out and destroy all the British and Protestants that were settled in Ireland."[120] Nor did Warner question the assumption that appalling cruelty had characterized the rebellion, though unlike so many who had preceded him, he declined to provide a detailed account of its supposed events.[121]

Yet his account was, on the face of it, far more judicious than many of its predecessors. For example, Warner accepted that there probably had been a massacre of Catholics at Islandmagee, but he argued that given the geography of the narrow peninsula, it was physically impossible that there had been enough people on it to permit the killing of three thousand people; he suggested three hundred as a more likely death toll and deliberately refuted various other accounts as he did so.[122] Warner's approach may have been influenced in part by his recourse to source material: the depositions, Clanricarde's memoirs, the correspondence printed by Thomas Carte in his biography of Ormond, and even a manuscript copy of the *Commentarius Rinnuccinianus* obtained by the Earl of Leicester.[123] It was this raw material that enabled Warner to write the most striking section of his work—his actual assessment of the evidence of a "massacre" contained in the depositions.[124] Vouching for his own dedication to ferreting out the truth, Warner said of the value of these documents: "As a great stress hath been laid upon this collection in print and conversation among the Protestants of that kingdom, and the whole evidence of the massacre turns upon it, I took a great deal of pains and spent a great deal of time in examining these books; and I am sorry to say that they have been made the foundation of much more clamour and resentment than can be warranted by truth and reason."[125]

Warner noted—as apparently nobody had before him—that while the depositions were supposed to have been taken on oath, the words "being duly sworn" were often struck out; much of the collection could be disregarded as "parole evidence," composed in terror and in the heat of the moment. Take, for example, the reported appearance of ghosts at Portadown, previously ridiculed by Curry: Warner now invoked this as an example of a ludicrous allegation, illustrating how untrustworthy the depositions actually were. Furthermore, he noted that it was only the sworn accounts that were replicated in another manuscript in his possession, a duplicate of which was to be found in "the museum" (presumably the British Museum). This manuscript, he deduced, had been intended for presentation to the king and to parliament in England. He could hardly overestimate its importance: "Here then it is only that we can expect the most authentic account of the Irish massacre."[126]

Warner's curiosity about the depositions arose from a perennial question: How many were killed in the rebellion? While it was impossible to come up with a precise death toll, it was "easy enough from hence to demonstrate the falsehood of the relation of every Protestant historian of the rebellion."[127] Ireland had not been sufficiently settled to support the impossibly high death tolls suggested by such writers as Clarendon, and some of those alleged by Temple to have been killed were supposedly still alive decades after the event. Therefore, such figures were "impossible to be credited by men of sense."[128] Having effectively dismissed the depositions as useless, Warner based his own estimate of the numbers killed in the rebellion on the manuscript he had seen in "the museum," which was an unpublished sequel to Henry Jones's *Remonstrance* of 1642. Using "positive evidence" for the two years following the rebellion, the accounts of other Protestants, and those of the rebels themselves, he arrived at a death toll of 4,028 (with further indications, "on the report of others," that another 8,000 had died through "ill-usage"). These figures were apparently consistent with a letter from the parliamentary commissioners in Ireland to parliament in 1652, stating that 848 families and 6,052 individuals had been killed.[129] Though it might appear that Warner had provided a levelheaded and scrupulous estimate of the numbers killed in the rebellion of 1641, he had not done so.

The distinguishing feature of Warner's book was its ostensible attempt to analyze the evidence. The problem was that he did so in a completely erroneous way. His estimate of *circa* 4,000 dead has silently been adopted by scholars in search of a judicious estimate ever since, but beneath Warner's veneer of scholarship was a highly disingenuous approach. He mistrusted the depositions because he was confused about what precisely they were. He was unable to make sense of them and instead based his assessment of 1641 on the selection of extracts contained in the unpublished sequel to Jones's *Remonstrance*. This egregious shortcut meant that his figures were no more trustworthy than any others that had been thrust forth into the light.[130] It might also indicate that Warner was simply hedging his bets when he stated that "the truth is, the soldiers and common people were very savage on both sides," and that while the Irish were the "first aggressors," "both sides will do well to guard against or to extinguish those unchristian animosities which led the way to every species of barbarity and ended in desolation, pestilence, and famine."[131]

This discussion brings us once again to the material from which accounts of 1641 were traditionally drawn. The selective reproduction of contemporary accounts of the rebellion has always been a feature of its contested historiography. Since the 1640s primary source material had been placed in the public domain, if only in a limited and tendentious way. Indeed, as previously noted, Curry had attached major documentary appendices to his works, and the antiquarianism of the eighteenth century did not always restrict itself to the ancient past. In 1772 a collection of documents published in Dublin included a number of texts that implicitly (and perhaps unintentionally) exonerated Catholics from complicity in the outbreak of the rebellion by stating the grievances that had prompted them to rebel in the first place.[132] But alongside such publicly available source material, which naturally allowed prospective readers to make up their own minds, there was arguably a necessity for a new interpretative framework within which to cast the rebellion. Given that a minister of the Church of England had now provided a crucial (if flawed) evidentiary analysis, it was appropriate that the task of formulating this new framework for discussion should fall to a minister of the Church of Ireland—Thomas Leland.

In a manner akin to what Hume had attempted in his history of Britain, Leland intended to write a "philosophical" history of Ireland that would rise above the traditional limitations of sectarian factionalism. O'Conor and Curry both encouraged his project and were themselves heartened by a sermon given by Leland on 23 October 1771 that was a radical departure from the norm; it placed a measure of responsibility for the rebellion squarely upon the Protestants (a stance that naturally proved unpopular).[133] But Curry and O'Conor were bitterly disappointed at the eventual work that emerged from Leland's pen. For despite his ambitions, he simply reiterated a standard Protestant version of 1641.

This was probably unsurprising to many, since Leland's distaste for popery in general and priests in particular was obvious from an early stage.[134] His depiction of the atrocities committed in 1641 followed a standard model, though perhaps with a certain additional moderation; it was by no means as lurid as previous accounts of the rebellion, and was dismissive of the wilder rumors and allegations. Like Curry, Leland accepted the role played by such rumors in fostering the belief that a massacre had indeed taken place. Crucially, in light of the significance accorded to it by Curry, Leland's work contained a swingeing rebuttal of atrocity charges relating to Islandmagee, where, he stated, only thirty families had been killed, but "as if the incident were not sufficiently hideous, popish writers have represented it with shocking aggravation."[135] And while questioning the scale of the slaughter, Leland also queried the timing. He argued that the depositions proved that the attack had happened in January 1642 rather than November 1641, and therefore could not have been "the first massacre in Ulster."[136] A traditional version of 1641 was reinvigorated rather than replaced.

One immediate consequence was that Leland received a rap on the knuckles, so to speak, in the form of an anonymous tract penned by an apparently incensed John Curry, who took issue with three aspects of Leland's work: the imputation of disloyalty on the part of the Catholic Irish; the suggestion that Catholic doctrine had been a crucial element in the rebellion; and finally and perhaps most significantly, the treatment of Islandmagee. The death toll, Curry contended, was bound to be much higher than Leland had suggested, for the population of Islandmagee had been swollen with refugees at the time of the assault. Curry also refuted the changing of the timing of the attack to January by insinuating that the depositions were not to be trusted. Warner was invoked to prove this point. Curry included a list of the more debatable extracts from the depositions (relating yet again to the ghosts at Portadown) to strengthen his case. In an ironic postscript he then thanked Warner for his offer to help find a bookseller for Curry's imminent *Historical and Critical Review*.[137]

Given his background, it was probably unreasonable to have expected more from Leland; he had altered the Protestant version of the rebellion perhaps as far as his instincts permitted. But the episode illustrated two things: the extent to which that "Protestant" version of 1641 had been deeply assimilated within the Protestant community; and the opposing fact that by the final decades of the eighteenth century there were writers—and one above all—who could be relied on to contest this interpretation. Curry's final statement on the events of 1641 came in 1775 with the publication of *An Historical and Critical Review of the Civil Wars in Ireland*.[138] This had a much broader sweep than its predecessors, effectively ranging from the twelfth century to the end of the eighteenth, and was explicitly located within the ongoing discourse of the "Catholic question." It was of a piece with Curry's earlier works in both purpose and method; the key difference was that he now tackled later—even living— authors such as Hume, Leland, and Warner. He placed particular emphasis on refuting allegations that the Catholic clergy were intimately involved in the rebellion, and he dwelled once again on the events at Islandmagee.[139] Curry's discussion of the depositions approvingly quoted Warner's assessment of them, but unlike Warner, he made no exceptions and explicitly dismissed all of them as worthless.[140] Curry's techniques were the same as they always had been, namely, to use Warner against himself by exploiting the caveats and ambiguities in his arguments; Curry applied the same device once again to Borlase and Carte among others. But there was little new ground broken here. The 1775 book was merely an expansion and elaboration of what Curry had essentially stated nearly thirty years before.

It made an impression, however, on at least one reviewer: "The evidences have been re-examined; the facts newly *stated* on the most approved *authorities*; and additional lights have appeared. We now see that much may be justly said in extenuation of the guilt of the papists, and that the Protestants were in many instances even more blameable [*sic*]."[141] As for the author himself, said this reviewer, "he appears to be a moderate, sensible, and philosophic inquirer after truth, though not destitute of zeal for that church in behalf of which he has employed his researches and his pen."[142] But it would be fairer to say that Curry's varied activities were on behalf of the Catholic community more broadly. His decision to articulate an alternative perspective on the events of 1641 was consistent with this wider scope of action. It was not without precedent, but the energy that Curry brought to his task during a specific historical moment reinvigorated that Catholic perspective and reclaimed its place in public discourse. As yet another Catholic polemicist asserted in 1778, "the history of the bloody transactions of 1641 in Ireland is written by the enemies of the Irish."[143] In a notable nod to balance he observed that "if the Irish had their Sir Phelim O'Neill, the English can produce Sir Frederick Hamilton and Sir Charles Coote," and furthermore, "the whole might have been quelled with great facility in the first six weeks if it had not been the wish of the infamous Sir William Parsons . . . to continue the rebellion in order to create forfeitures." There were several lessons for Catholics: "It is too clear that the usurpations begun upon your civil and religious rights before that time are intended to be justified by the histories published of the conduct of the Irish at that period, and that the same accounts are to plead excuse for the enacting since, and continuing in force, a code of penal laws disgraceful to the times in which we live, as they are ruinous to the country we inhabit."[144]

Curry had sought to rectify this pernicious syndrome. In doing so, he became the fulcrum of one of the relatively few attempts yet made, albeit in a deliberately charged and deeply flawed manner, to determine what had actually happened in 1641. The traditional and opposing versions of the rebellion generated in the 1640s had simply been regurgitated in a rather static fashion by generations of opposing writers and polemicists (indeed, the same thing would happen again within a generation). For all the flaws in the work of Curry and those in his orbit, no genuinely critical attempt to examine the realities of 1641 would be made until the latter half of the nineteenth century. In the meantime Curry's work laid the foundation for a key strand of Irish nationalism that would emerge during the course of the nineteenth century in an Ireland then undergoing changes that he and his peers could scarcely have imagined.

Perhaps surprisingly, the structural and rhetorical techniques pioneered by Curry—the accumulation, interrogation, and presentation of masses of documentary evidence aimed at refuting Protestant accounts of 1641—made only rare appearances in the decades after his death. This scarcity may have stemmed in part from a desire not to reinvent the wheel. Curry's works were extensively republished, and there seemed little reason for other Catholic polemicists to follow in his footsteps. Thus, while such figures as the radical Dublin journalist Walter ("Watty") Cox might take the occasional swipe at writers like the "lying and bigotted Sir John Temple," there seemed little inclination to build on Curry's foundations by writing a more extensive exegesis of the documentary record.[145] Besides, circumstances had changed because the repeal of most of the penal laws by the 1790s had rendered Curry's particular purpose redundant. Nevertheless, his literary enterprise would have a greater, if more nebulous, resonance. Curry had tried to replace one version of 1641 with another, and with the crystallization of Irish nationalism in the nineteenth century the alternative that he had propounded became assimilated into a broader nationalist analysis of Irish history; his works seemed sufficient to that task. It was presumably for these reasons that one of the only attempts to follow in Curry's literary footsteps was written and published not in Ireland but in America.

To be precise, it was published in Philadelphia. Mathew Carey was born in 1760 into a middling Catholic family in Dublin.[146] A printer by trade, he left Ireland after writing a number of anonymous (but contentious) pro-Catholic pamphlets, and went in 1779 to France, where he began to work for no less a figure than Benjamin Franklin. Returning to Ireland to work on the *Freeman's Journal*, he formed associations with the Volunteer movement that landed him in trouble with the authorities, and in 1784 he emigrated to Philadelphia, where he became active and prominent in both the publishing trade and Irish émigré circles. Given the scale of Irish emigration to Philadelphia (perhaps as many as 3,000 arrived in the 1790s alone, many of whom were United Irishmen), such circles were inevitably politicized. Carey became accustomed to venturing into print on behalf of both his country of origin and his countrymen, and in this regard his most significant work was the labyrinthine *Vindiciae Hibernicae*.[147] It took its title from James Mackintosh's *Vindiciae Gallicae* (1791), itself a riposte to Edmund Burke's denunciation of the French Revolution. Carey's work, on the other hand, was apparently prompted by the North American success of the

English radical William Godwin's *Mandeville* (1817)—the first fictional depiction of the events of 1641.[148]

Let us glance at that work for a moment. While mostly set in England during the civil wars of the 1640s, *Mandeville* began in Ireland with the birth of its eponymous narrator in Charlemont fort in 1638 as the son of a soldier serving there. Readers were soon presented with Sir Phelim O'Neill's duplicitous visit to the fort, during which he told the governor, Caulfield, that "we meditate no injury" but also that "we will have our rights."[149] Mandeville's father was captured, and in Godwin's version of the fall of the fort, the brutality of the Irish soon emerged as they fell prey to the wiles of their priests. Godwin adopted a traditional interpretation of such atrocities; he pointed to Portadown as the scene of a particularly brutal incident, where 180 Protestants were killed after the bridge was broken in two and they were forced into the river. Those who did not drown were callously finished off, and the notorious ghosts eventually made their appearance.[150]

Godwin's unprecedented fictional account of 1641 was not automatically anti-Irish (like Voltaire, Godwin had a broader distaste for organized religion, and *Mandeville* itself was dedicated to the liberal Irish Whig John Philpot Curran). But his work encapsulated a traditionally unflattering Protestant depiction of 1641 and its prelude.[151] As the rebellion wore on, it soon degenerated "into a scene of cruelty and massacre such as had rarely occurred in the annals of the world."[152] O'Neill was depicted as especially savage, ordering the execution of the prisoners at Charlemont, including the parents of the infant narrator (who still managed to weave an impressionistic account of what happened, comparing the rebel assault to the sack of Rome). The three-year-old Mandeville was the only survivor, and he was spirited to safety by Judith, a kindly Irish nurse (complete with dubious brogue) who saved his life by claiming that he was her own child. One of the rebels was unconvinced and intended to finish him off, but Judith deterred him: "'Begone,' said the would-be murderer sternly, drawing back his skein, 'and mix no more with this dunghill of Protestant dogs.'"[153] She declined to follow this advice and instead brought Mandeville to Kells, where the chaplain of the Charlemont garrison (who detested Catholics) took the baby from her against her protestations. She was expelled from both town and story as the clergyman spirited Mandeville to England, there to embark upon the rest of his adventures.

To judge from the contents of *Vindiciae Hibernicae*, Carey was not overly concerned with the rest of Godwin's novel; it was the opening that attracted his ire. After two somewhat fulsome dedications[154] (and two pages of quotations from Edmund Burke on the iniquity of Protestant ascendancy), Carey came straight to the point. *Vindiciae Hibernicae* was an enormous and sustained

Title page of Mathew Carey, *Vindiciae Hibernicae*, Philadelphia, 1819. (courtesy of the National Library of Ireland)

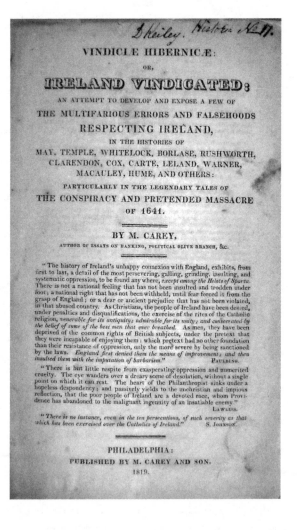

VINDICIÆ HIBERNICÆ:

OR,

IRELAND VINDICATED:

AN ATTEMPT TO DEVELOP AND EXPOSE A FEW OF

THE MULTIFARIOUS ERRORS AND FALSEHOODS

RESPECTING IRELAND,

IN THE HISTORIES OF

MAY, TEMPLE, WHITELOCK, BORLASE, RUSHWORTH, CLARENDON, COX, CARTE, LELAND, WARNER, MACAULEY, HUME, AND OTHERS:

PARTICULARLY IN THE LEGENDARY TALES OF

THE CONSPIRACY AND PRETENDED MASSACRE

OF 1641.

BY M. CAREY,

AUTHOR OF ESSAYS ON BANKING, POLITICAL OLIVE BRANCH, &c.

"The history of Ireland's unhappy connexion with England, exhibits, from first to last, a detail of the most persevering, galling, grinding, insulting, and systematic oppression, to be found any where, *except among the Helots of Sparta.* There is not a national feeling that has not been insulted and trodden under foot; a national right that has not been withheld, until fear forced it from the grasp of England; or a dear or ancient prejudice that has not been violated, in that abused country. As Christians, the people of Ireland have been denied, under penalties and disqualifications, the exercise of the rites of the Catholic religion, *venerable for its antiquity; admirable for its unity; and consecrated by the belief of some of the best men that ever breathed.* As men, they have been deprived of the common rights of British subjects, under the pretext that they were incapable of enjoying them; which pretext had no other foundation than their resistance of oppression, only the more severe by being sanctioned by the laws. *England first denied them the means of improvement; and then insulted them with the imputation of barbarism."*   PAULDING.

"There is but little respite from exasperating oppression and unmerited cruelty. The eye wanders over a dreary scene of desolation, without a single point on which it can rest. The heart of the Philanthropist sinks under a hopeless despondency; and passively yields to the unchristian and impious reflection, that the poor people of Ireland are a devoted race, whom Providence has abandoned to the malignant ingenuity of an insatiable enemy."   LAWLESS.

"*There is no instance, even in the ten persecutions, of such severity as that which has been exercised over the Catholics of Ireland."*   S. JOHNSON.

PHILADELPHIA:

PUBLISHED BY M. CAREY AND SON.

1819.

refutation of the Protestant version of 1641, as articulated by virtually every Protestant writer who had ever addressed the subject.

The reasons why were straightforward enough. "The history of Ireland, as stated and proved in the body of this work," declared Carey, "is almost one solid mass of falsehood and imposture, erected, particularly during the seventeenth century, on the basis of fraud and perjury." The prejudices arising from this Protestant version of history had apparently been transplanted to America. And in the new world, far from an ascendancy "whose power is built on the pestiferous basis of fraud, perjury, and misrepresentation," there was no obvious reason to uphold the version of 1641 that had for so long damned Irish Catholics.[155] "The frauds and falsehoods I have undertaken to expose and refute," argued Carey, "have unfortunately survived the causes which gave them birth; become engrafted in history; taken complete possession of the public mind; and are almost as thoroughly believed as the best established fact in the annals of the world."[156] Hence his mammoth attempt to refute those same falsehoods. Indeed, *Vindiciae Hibernicae* "is among the most thoroughly researched and most strongly argued of nationalist histories written in the early decades of the nineteenth century."[157] Its broad thrust can now be summarized.

Despite what Sir John Temple and so many others had claimed, in the forty years prior to 1641 Ireland was far from at peace. Catholics dwelled in continual uncertainty of being robbed of their lands. The informer Owen Connolly was a liar; there was neither a conspiracy nor a massacre, except for those perpetrated against the Irish on the orders of the Dublin administration (the deeds authorized by its leaders were deemed to have been "as ferocious, as brutal, and as bloody as the horrible feats of Cortes or Pizarro, Attila or Genghis Khan").[158] Those deeds had been meant to facilitate the confiscation of Irish land by provoking a response (and if the Irish had been rebels in 1641, so too had the English in 1688, the Americans in 1776, and the French in 1789). The alleged contradictions of most historians of the 1640s rendered them "utterly unworthy of credit"; and finally, all of this oppression and subterfuge had culminated in the tyranny of the penal laws, "covered by as base a cloak of hypocrisy as the annals of the world can produce."[159]

Carey explicitly followed Curry's lead. The Philadelphia printer based his work on an extensive trawl through those of Protestant writers and shaped it as a massive forensic commentary that turned the works of those same writers against themselves.[160] And he did so with tremendous invective. The standard story of 1641 was a "foul, bloated mass of fraud and perjury," and anyone who would give credence to it "ought to be confined for life to the edifying perusal of the voyages and travels of Sir John Mandeville, of Baron Munchausen, and their illustrious compeer, Sir John Temple."[161] When it came to the most contentious issue of all—the estimates of the number of Protestants killed—Carey neatly dissected and discarded the various death tolls, concluding that "the writers on this subject are so haunted by the idea of a massacre that although it rests on the sandy foundation of forgery and perjury, as shall be fully proved . . . , their minds cannot be divested of the terrific object."[162]

This is merely one instance of his slashing rhetoric. When it came to revealing where Carey's sympathies lay—assuming that there was any lingering doubt—then the index said it all:

Carte, fraudulent statement of
Carte, gross inconsistency of
Carte, obliquity of
Carte, imbecile views of

Historians of Irish affairs, vile views of

Inconsistency, gross, of Carte, Warner, and Leland

Leland, gross inconsistency of
Leland, gross errors of
Leland, obliquity of
Leland, ridiculous absurdity of

Temple, Sir John, a legendist of the first order
Temple's statement of the pretended conspiracy
Temple's legendary tales, analysis of
Temple, ashamed of his legend, endeavours to suppress it
Temple's legend, attempts to bolster up
Temple, a cheat and imposter[163]

Carey's book met with some success; it was revised and reprinted twice. The 1823 edition was enlarged and rearranged, not least with two pages of congratulatory comments (including those of former U.S. presidents John Adams and James Madison) and a lengthy list of subscribers. Carey's essential point seems to have struck a chord in at least some quarters. In March 1833 a number of Irish Catholic clerics (headed by the bishop of Philadelphia) recommended that their congregations subscribe to an abstract of Carey's key points, the better to refute the version of 1641 "scattered throughout the United States" in such works as Foxe's *Acts and Monuments*.[164] But in his preface to the third (1837) edition of the *Vindiciae*, Carey claimed that his work had met with indifference from Catholic luminaries in Ireland like Daniel O'Connell and Daniel Murray, the archbishop of Dublin; without success Carey had sought to enlist the support of both men to drum up subscriptions (he had apparently suffered losses on the first two editions). Carey was disappointed at such neglect from within the "British dominions, where such a work is incomparably more necessary than in the United States."[165] He was particularly irked by "the deplorable apathy and indifference of those to whom it might naturally have looked for support. . . . The author, a layman, by no means particularly interested in the subject, had for years prodigally lavished his money, devoted his leisure hours, impaired his sight, and on the verge of eternity, at 76, once more entered the list on behalf of his and their country."[166] It was ironic, then, that in less than six years Daniel

O'Connell himself followed in the footsteps of Curry and Carey by producing a work in a similar vein. In the course of his campaigns for Catholic emancipation and repeal of the union, O'Connell increasingly seemed to articulate the aspirations of a historically dispossessed Catholic community.[167] His rhetorical recourse to the experience of that community found literary expression in his *Memoir on Ireland Native and Saxon*, published in 1843 and dedicated to Queen Victoria. O'Connell explained his reasons for writing it at the outset:

> Is none of the spirit of Coote or of Parsons to be found (in a mitigated form) in those who refuse to the Catholic people of Ireland their just share of elective or municipal franchises, and who insist that the Irish shall remain an inferior and a degraded caste, deprived of that perfect equality of civil and religious liberty, of franchises and privileges— which equality could alone constitute a union or render a union tolerable?
>
> I wish to arouse the attention of the sovereign and of the honest portion of the English people to the wrongs which Ireland *has* suffered, and which Ireland *is* suffering, from British misrule.[168]

O'Connell's work offered a sweeping summary of Irish history for the benefit of an English audience. But the fact that he invoked Coote and Parsons at the beginning showed the extent to which, in a Catholic version of Irish history, the received Catholic version of 1641 could stand as an indictment of the cruelty, injustice, and iniquity of English rule in Ireland. In his discussion of 1641 O'Connell pulled no punches: "There were *two* objects to be gratified by the English Protestant rulers of the day. The first was the increase of plunder to themselves in the confiscation of the estates of the Catholics. The second was the indiscriminate slaughter of those Catholics without any distinction of age, sex, rank, or condition."[169]

To prove this O'Connell, like Curry and Carey, deployed a huge array of sources to reveal the litany of Protestant and English atrocities inflicted on the Catholic Irish during and after 1641, and up to the Cromwellian invasion: Warner, Leland, Carte, Borlase, Clarendon, "R.S.," and many more were invoked.[170] Sir Charles Coote featured prominently for obvious reasons, with O'Connell comparing him to the notorious French revolutionaries Robespierre and Carrier, the better to evoke a sense of "the demoniacal means by which Protestantism and English power achieved their ascendancy in Ireland."[171] But O'Connell was especially determined to show that the prolonged period of Catholic suffering in the wake of 1641 stemmed largely from calculated and gross Protestant misrepresentations of Catholic conduct during the rebellion:

It was not sufficient for the English party to commit those most horrible
atrocities of which I have collected a small portion of instances. They carried
their malignity further, and they accused the Irish of those very crimes
which they themselves committed upon that unhappy people. . . . What
Clarendon and Temple originally asserted has been of course taken up by
that infidel falsifier of history, Hume; and the Catholics of Ireland for more
than a century were persecuted to the loss of their lives and properties; and
(what was still more grievous and afflicting) by the loss of their reputation
for that conduct which, while it really merited the applause of all good
men, was converted into the imputation of foul and horrible slaughter.[172]

As for the death tolls provided by such Protestant writers as Temple and
Milton, O'Connell was totally dismissive. Instead, he tepidly accepted the
estimates of Warner (without actually endorsing them), whose status as a
Protestant cleric (and worse, "a fellow, by the bye, of the Protestant University
of Dublin!"—a mistaken notion) rendered him the more reliable.[173] O'Connell's
legal background was perhaps revealed in the following piece of sophistry: if
Coote, Borlase, and Parsons were intent on exterminating the Irish, he reasoned, then "these villains had therefore the deepest interest in falsely accusing
the Irish of cruelty. It is manifest that nothing could gratify them more than
being able to substantiate against the Irish the charges of massacre or murder.
The absence of any such charge is indeed a trumpet-tongued acquittal."[174]
The showmanship typical of O'Connell in the courtroom was probably reflected
in the rhetorical flourish with which he concluded, namely, by quoting in
full capitals Ferdinando Warner's statement about how easy it was "TO
DEMONSTRATE THE FALSEHOOD OF THE RELATION OF
EVERY PROTESTANT HISTORIAN OF THIS REBELLION."[175]

For nearly a century Catholic and pro-Catholic writers from Curry to Carey
and O'Connell engaged in an intermittent pseudo-scholarly "debate," the
purpose of which was the destruction of the received and "Protestant" interpretation of 1641 and its replacement with another. The progress of such disputations
is relatively easy to track, and in the later decades of the nineteenth century this
form of argument would be reinvigorated. But these debates occurred at a
rather elevated social level, though they may have had hard-to-detect repercus-
sions lower down the social ladder. What of popular beliefs "on the ground"?
These are perhaps what Burke had in mind when he wrote of the "interior
history" of Ireland in the 1760s—a stratum of popular beliefs and assumptions
about the nature of 1641 that, while perhaps not wholly divorced from more
cerebral disputations, remained nonetheless distinct. Alongside the more rarefied

disquisitions was another level of conviction at which a pro-Catholic version of 1641 was actually believed.

Interior Histories:
1641 and the Shaping of Irish Nationalism

The crisis that emerged in Ireland in the late eighteenth century and culminated in the eruption of 1798 has been used as a window through which the fragmentary surviving evidence of popular political beliefs, especially as expressed in Irish, can be identified and drawn together into something resembling a coherent whole.[176] The persistence throughout the eighteenth century of rhetorical tropes of dispossession (at least on the part of the Irish literati), and of its eventual or imminent undoing, naturally implied a link between those beliefs and the 1641 rebellion that was increasingly interpreted as the pretext for that dispossession.

There were of course occasional flashes of Catholic popular attitudes toward the symbolic meaning of 1641, or at least toward the official version of it. These flashes included the riot in Dublin in 1688, the note on the flyleaf of the 1724 edition of Temple's *Irish Rebellion* retained in Marsh's Library, and the candles in Galway's windows in 1746. It was obvious that opposing versions of 1641 found an audience at subaltern levels in accordance with its sectarian relevance. One observer of the sectarian disturbances in County Armagh in 1787 bemoaned the riotous inclinations of the "lower order of inhabitants," especially in such an "enlightened period,"[177] and made explicit reference to the circulation of stories about 1641:

> There is not wanting at present amongst us a set of vipers, or I may say snakes in the grass, that are poisoning the mind of the unwary peasant with the dregs of the forty-one rebellion; even admitting it all to be true, is it not an unchristian piece of policy in a modern divine to revive such obsolete writings among a set of ignorant peasants that are already too much inflamed by the ill-timed writings of such spurious fabricators? Would it not be much more honor to the sacred character of a minister of the gospel of peace to enforce as much as possible that great commandment, to love God above all things and thy neighbour as thyself?[178]

This was a pregnant observation, one that strongly suggests how reflections on the past remained near to hand in Irish popular culture. Nor was such recourse to history hidebound by religious affiliation. The explosion of 1798 prompted Protestant writers like Musgrave to reach toward a particular version of 1641. But the opposing interpretation articulated by generations of Catholic writers retained its valency, even if it seemed to fade from prominence. The gradual dismantling of the penal laws arguably rendered a Catholic refutation of 1641 (à la Curry) redundant; Carey's massive work of 1819 was published in America rather than in Ireland. And while debates over 1641 had marked the early stages of Catholic activism for emancipation, the government's default in not granting full emancipation in the aftermath of the Act of Union prompted Catholic writers and polemicists to shift their focus to other events in Irish history, for example, the Treaty of Limerick and, perhaps more pertinently, its violation.[179]

Yet just because 1641 was overshadowed did not mean that it was forgotten. On the contrary, the Catholic version of the rebellion survived and was disseminated. A hint of its persistence can be found in a small primer on Irish history seemingly intended as a schoolbook. In it the bare bones of the traditional Catholic analysis was evident:

> What was the conduct of the English towards the natives?
>
> It was marked by every species of dissimulation and oppression that disgraces human nature; nor does it appear that they [Protestant settlers and English soldiers] for some time pursued a different line of conduct. For from this period a deluge of woes poured in upon Ireland; her subsequent annals are written in characters of blood and are but the records of division and persecution.[180]

True to the Catholic tradition, Parson and Borlase were blamed for provoking the rebellion to profit from the forfeitures that might follow:

> Did not the northern rebellion break out by a general cold-blooded massacre of all the Protestants that could be found?
>
> So we are told by the vilifiers of Catholicity and of Ireland, but if we may credit Lord Clarendon and other authors of respectability, the first massacre was committed by the English and Scotch troops, not by the Irish.[181]

The reference was presumably to Islandmagee.

The consistency with which such allegations were restated suggests how a particular version of Irish history—the "interior history"—might gradually have come to underpin a sense of identity or self-definition—in this case an Irish Catholic identity that in the course of the nineteenth century would play a crucial role in the evolution of a distinct version of Irish nationalism. Thomas Crofton Croker's 1824 pen portrait of the archetypal hedge-school master depicted him as the propagator of an historical consciousness characterized by firm belief in the existence of British oppression, the strength of Irish patriotism (apart from occasional traitors), and the utter rejection of the legitimacy of

British rule in Ireland from Brian Boru to Robert Emmet; he was "frequently the promoter of insurrectionary tumults" to boot.[182] This perspective was enshrined in works by a diverse variety of writers and had arguably been a key feature of "an indigenous tradition of historical writing that originated in the mid-seventeenth century."[183] It was also present in a notable work published in the early nineteenth century that came from an unlikely pen.

The contemporary fame of the Dublin-born Thomas Moore arose from his contribution to music rather than literature; he is still best known for his hugely popular and influential *Irish Melodies*, originally published in 1808. But he could also turn his hand to caustic satire, and having done so throughout his early career, he was prompted to return to the genre by the destabilizing sectarianism and widespread agrarian disturbances of the early 1820s. The title of his *Memoirs of Captain Rock* (1824) deliberately echoed the traditional pseudonym to which the agrarian insurgents were so attached.[184] His work was framed within the experience of a naïve English evangelist who, despite his profound ignorance of Ireland, felt compelled to go there to facilitate "the conversion and illumination of the poor benighted Irish."[185] Having endeavored to redress his ignorance by reading various works on Irish history (such as Musgrave's), on a coach journey to Limerick he met an outlandishly dressed, yet intriguing stranger: the eponymous Captain Rock. Soon afterward, the missionary met him again by chance after stumbling across a huge nocturnal assembly of his followers, and there he received from the Captain's hands a manuscript divided into two sections. These made up the remainder of the book.

One can easily locate *Memoirs of Captain Rock* within the polemical debates that accompanied the demands for Catholic emancipation that intensified under O'Connell's leadership in the 1820s (though Moore was no fan of O'Connell). In the figure of Captain Rock, Moore sought to personify the grievances of the Catholic Irish and to encapsulate their historical experience within the message that the Captain and his adherents sought to present to the world. The first part of Rock's putative manuscript was a history of Ireland up to 1763; the second was a memoir of the Captain's own life and times. The former seemed to take its cue from Curry as it very deliberately relied on "English authorities"[186] for its interpretation of Irish history. Its central argument was that the rapaciousness, brutality, and sectarianism of Ireland's English and Protestant rulers were the reasons for the violence of the Irish themselves. Rather than having been inherently brutal, degenerate, and unworthy of political rights, throughout their history the Irish had simply been forced to strike the second blow, as it were—an expansive analysis that echoed the traditional Catholic version of the specifics of 1641.[187] Within these broad-brush strokes, two years were singled out for particular attention.

The first part of *Memoirs of Captain Rock* was subdivided into chapters that each covered a number of years. But there were two exceptions: 1641 and 1649. The significance of 1649 was obvious enough; the Cromwellian invasion of that year seemed for Irish Catholics to have been accorded an apocalyptic significance similar to that granted to 1641 by Protestants; Moore was thus obliged to engage with its prelude in 1641. He fixed the rebellion within his broader argument in the form of a diary purportedly written by one of Captain Rock's ancestors, which provided "an insight into the process by which great rebellions have always been got up in Ireland. The same drama, a little modernized, was acted over again in 1798; and the prompters' book and stage directions are still at hand in the archives of Dublin Castle whenever an able Orange manager shall be found to preside over a renewal of the spectacle."[188]

The account of 1641 consisted of a series of brief extracts (containing "the concentrated essence of Irish history"[189]), which collectively told a tale that would surely be familiar to readers of Curry's work. The simmering resentments of the Irish had been deliberately fanned into outright rebellion by the lord justices ("rebellion is a goose that layeth golden eggs, and they, at least, will not be the ones to kill it"[190]), with threats of a massacre and the actual killings at Islandmagee finally combining to provoke outright rebellion in a deliberate attempt to justify further forfeitures. So far, Moore's story is familiar. For good measure, the Protestant version of 1641 contained in the depositions was implicitly rejected *in toto* by the dismissal of the notorious accounts of ghosts appearing at Portadown.[191] Moore's account was notably hostile to that of David Hume and, by extension, those of Temple and Musgrave, both of whom he yoked together while giving an approving mention to Mathew Carey.[192]

At bottom there was nothing unusual about such an interpretation. What was distinctive was the manner in which it was now very consciously assimilated into a broader (if facetious) narrative. As if to link the micronarrative of Captain Rock's life with the macronarrative of Irish history to which it was appended, the Captain revealed that he had been born on the same day that Father Nicholas Sheehy had been executed in Tipperary; the link to this notorious act of egregious bigotry left little to the imagination.[193] Indeed, toward the end of Captain Rock's own account, 1641 and 1798 were explicitly linked; the parallels between them were reiterated, especially in terms of their sectarian legacies: "Both born in the perfidy of the government, and both nurtured into strength by its cruelties, they each ran the same career of blood, and each, in expiring, left its unburied corpse, to poison the two parties that still sullenly contended over it."[194] Once again, the symbolic value of 1641 was not to be underestimated.

Memoirs of Captain Rock was a fiction. But it was a fiction created for a purpose, one that sought to encapsulate Irish history from the perspective of the Irish and, by doing so, to substitute a voice of some sort in place of silence—at least in print and in English. The enduring contentiousness of 1641 within such a discourse emerged again when subaltern "memory" encountered a new organ of the state—the great Ordnance Survey.

Alongside its ambitious plan to map the entire country, the Ordnance Survey project of the 1830s "also involved the memoir scheme, an in-depth ethnographical and historical survey . . . of the Irish people, their culture, folklore, religious practices, oral histories, and social structures in the first half of the nineteenth century."[195] The memoirs were intended to complement the maps produced by the survey (an initiative attributable to its assistant director Thomas Larcom, who had overseen the cartography). The plan was indicative of nineteenth-century conceptions of "scientific" history, not to mention post-Enlightenment notions of improvement and reform, which in turn had to be based on accurate and comprehensive information. In an Irish context it was hoped that such "improvement" might also incorporate reconciliation. Ironically, this aim may have led to the assumption by those involved in the memoir scheme that early modern colonization had itself been a principal part of the process of improvement. The writers of the memoirs often made distinctions between descendants of "settlers" and "natives"; stereotypes of the ignorant, lazy, and uncivilized Catholic natives, as opposed to the industrious, civilized, and virtuous descendants of Protestant English or Scottish planters, made themselves felt.[196] Assumptions about the cultural superiority of the planters were in some instances all too evident.

What made the memoir project distinctive was that the official collectors found themselves heavily reliant on oral information as they arrived in localities. Initially, local elites and prominent members of society provided contacts and introductions that gradually enabled the collectors to work their way down the social scale. But perspectives on the past naturally differed among the ethnoreligious groupings from which these were taken, and differed even among those employed by the survey. With regard to 1641, one man's "civil war" was another's "war of extermination."[197]

The implications of such divergence dogged the scheme from the outset. While the first published memoir (1837) dealing with Templemore, Co. Londonderry, was favorably received, in April 1838 Thomas Spring-Rice, the chancellor of the exchequer, outlined a number of objections to continuing with the memoir project: "A government can scarcely sanction such a publication without making itself responsible for opinion. With mere facts we may deal, but giving the history of Derry and the history of Limerick, the siege of one and the treaty of the other, open all the debatable questions in Irish party division."[198] Consequently, the memoirs project was discontinued in July 1840. Despite later attempts to revive it and public support for doing so, it was never completed. Yet it provides a means of accessing, admittedly through the mediating influence of the collectors, some of the otherwise lost oral history of prefamine Ireland, including the traditions relating to the vexing question of what had actually happened at Islandmagee in 1641–42. After all, according to James Boyle, the author of the relevant memoir in April 1840, one of the only notable events to have survived in local tradition there was "the alleged massacre of the Roman Catholics by a part of the Protestant garrison of Carrickfergus on the 8th of January 1641 [*recte* 1642]."[199]

Accounts of the Islandmagee tragedy in the early decades of the nineteenth century often had recourse to "tradition," and the Ordnance Survey was no exception.[200] The memoir provided a brief description of the massacre, "of which so many very conflicting, contradictory statements have appeared in the different historical publications, not merely local, but of the entire kingdom, not one of which is entitled to the least credit."[201] The memoir also noted that the casualty estimates allegedly ranged from six to three thousand, "at which the humanity of historians has allowed them to remain."[202]

The killings were said to have been carried out by Scottish troops from Ballymena in retaliation for the "horrible butcheries" of Protestants in neighboring parishes, including women and children. Forty to fifty Catholics were killed in retaliation, women and children included; one child was supposedly "stabbed in its mother's arms," while another woman threw herself over a cliff (an incident that was usually among those greatly exaggerated).[203] Interestingly, according to a local tradition, some Catholics were saved by a Protestant named Hill, who apparently owned a ship manned by his relatives from Islandmagee. Having put into Westport, Co. Mayo, the crew was treated with great courtesy on account of Hill's willingness to hide Catholics during the "massacre of 1641"; the crews of subsequent ships from Islandmagee carrying potatoes to Galway and Mayo reportedly passed themselves off as "Hill" to secure the same treatment.[204]

It is tempting to speculate that a more complex historical experience lay behind this conciliatory vignette. Perhaps 180 men from the overwhelmingly Presbyterian population of Islandmagee turned out as United Irishmen in 1798. Might this event have influenced such an ecumenical tale?[205] Yet the memory of Presbyterian involvement in the radicalism of the 1790s became a victim of the sectarianism of the nineteenth century and of 1798 itself. The harmonious story of Hill's ship was presumably the exception rather than the rule.[206] Larcom himself had been aware that sensitivity would be required when asking about the massacre, for the subject "looks like a party question."[207]

A more revealing insight into Catholic mentalities toward the events of 1641 had been found in 1836 in the County Londonderry parish of Dungiven. An unnamed gentleman had reportedly thrown out a number of books, all of which were burned apart from one—an edition of a work attributed to Castlehaven and entitled *Secret Memoirs of the Rebellion of 1641*, apparently written in exile and dated 1648. Its actual contents were uncertain, but it supposedly claimed that the papal nuncio Rinuccini had instigated the rebellion. Having been passed from hand to hand among the peasantry, the book was eventually traded to two peddlers for a number of other books (mostly on astrology and the "magic art"), one of which was a more recent (ten- year-old) edition of Castlehaven's work that differed markedly from the book with which it had swapped places: "Lord Castlehaven relates in this edition the wrongs of his country, the oppression, the hard, grinding tyranny, and how all *this* produced the rebellion. A diminutive account of the great massacre is given, and a retaliation is made of equal barbarities on the opposite party. The book is in large print, and the editor in his preface considers the republication as a means of giving a true and just idea of those times."[208]

Does this account suggest recollection or reconstruction? The absence of a direct link to the past was no impediment to perpetuating a particular version of it. The manner in which versions of 1641 in general (and Islandmagee in particular) seeped into public discourse was also exemplified in ballads and poetry. There was at least some overlap between otherwise obscure popular traditions and an emergent print culture offering a more formalized and self-conscious rhetoric and symbolism that could exert its own influence on Irish nationalism.[209]

Admittedly, the self-conscious shift from the vernacular evident in anthologies such as Charles Gavan Duffy's *Ballad Poetry of Ireland*—an enormously successful anthology that went through thirty-eight editions, selling 76,000 copies in twenty years[210]—makes them a questionable source.[211] But the creative process of selection permitted the inclusion of "Rory O'Moore," a work by the highly prominent radical Presbyterian and United Irishman William Drennan, which, while hardly indicative of a strictly Catholic perspective, does indicate a degree of empathy on Drennan's part with Irish Catholics.

> Do you ask why the beacon and banner of war
> On the mountains of Ulster are seen from afar?

'Tis the signal our rights to regain and secure,
Through God and our Lady and Rory O'Moore.

For the merciless Scots, with their creed and their swords,
With war in their bosoms, and peace in their words,
Have sworn the bright light of our faith to obscure,
But our hope is in God and in Rory O'Moore.[212]

Gavan Duffy, a Young Irelander, had written another ballad explicitly recalling the Catholic version of the attack on Islandmagee, and this song would remain a stalwart of anthologies well into the twentieth century. "The Muster of the North" concerned itself with the desire for revenge on the part of those Ulster Catholics who had suffered at the hands of the lord justices:

Pity! No, no, you dare not, priest—not you, our father, dare,
Preach to us now that godless creed—the murderer's blood to spare.
To spare his blood, while tombless still our slaughter'd kin implore.
"Graves and revenge" from Gobbin Cliffs and Carrick's bloody shore![213]

The "Gobbens" were cliffs at Islandmagee over which Catholics had supposedly been driven to their deaths in 1641. That such details were not spelled out seems revealing in itself. Was it because the image was sufficiently well known?

Even if it was, the literary representation of the Catholic version of 1641 was being transformed. Instead of the blunt refutations and voluminous documentary expositions that had previously characterized this tradition, the Catholic version of 1641 that had been articulated from the 1640s to the 1770s was now being given a form of imaginative life in genres other than history. In the same year (1843) that O'Connell published his triumphant assertion of "the falsehood of every Protestant historian of this rebellion," the version of 1641 that he wanted to replace found further expression in fiction. James French's *Clongibbon*, an undistinguished tale of the 1640s that adopted the trick of footnoting writers such as Carte and Leland, depicted 1641 as an act of self-defense by loyal Irish Catholics faced with the treasonous and venal inclinations of Borlase and Parsons. Their villainy knew no bounds as they dedicated themselves to exterminating Catholics and seizing their lands. According to the fictional Parsons, "we may, by a little judicious hanging, get rid at once of those troublesome papists, render an infinite benefit to our king and country, and convey the forfeitures to those of our friends most deserving of them."[214] Any displays of humanity by the Irish stood little chance in the face of such unscrupulous perfidy, for "so trifling were the encroachments made at this time by the Irish party on the settlements of the English in Ulster, which were chiefly confined to carrying off their cattle, and they having issued a proclamation to their followers to draw as little blood as possible, the lord-justices saw that it would never answer their ends were they not to exasperate the Irish by sending armed forces into the three other provinces of the kingdom to commit depredations on the poor and exasperate the rich!"[215]

The assumptions within such fiction were mirrored in historical writing a year later when C. P. Meehan published *The Confederation of Kilkenny* (1846), which basically glossed over any aspect of 1641 that might have proved awkward for Irish Catholics (perhaps unsurprisingly, it was dedicated to Charles Gavan Duffy). Here the rebellion was once more portrayed as a direct result of the provocative actions of Strafford and the "odious tyranny" of the lord justices.[216] But Meehan still found time to dwell on the excesses of Borlase, Parsons, and Coote; the former merrily tortured Palesmen on the rack in Dublin Castle, while the story of Coote's delight at seeing a baby impaled on a pike was repeated yet again.[217] In the version of Irish history represented by such works, there could be no question as to who had been the victims.

In the overlaps between conscious polemic, folklore, and imaginative reconstructions, a common thread can be discerned. The Catholic (or pro-Catholic) account of 1641 that had crystallized by the early decades of the nineteenth century ultimately did not diverge from the response to the rebellion that had been formulated by Catholics in the seventeenth century. The plot lines were essentially the same. The rebellion had been provoked by greedy and rapacious British Protestant colonists and it had been necessary for Catholic self-defense. Protestants had deliberately exaggerated the extent to which they had been attacked and killed, while at the same time playing down the extent of the atrocities they had visited on the Catholics. Since all of this gross misrepresentation was meant to justify the expropriation and dispossession of Catholics, it was imperative that this version of 1641 be disputed.

A Protestant interpretation of 1641 had been used to justify the maintenance of the eighteenth-century Protestant state. A Catholic interpretation had been used in a prolonged attempt to counter this. It should not be forgotten that the energy devoted by John Curry to formulating and giving written expression to that Catholic version of 1641 was harnessed in support of the "Catholic question." O'Connell's memoir was also an historicist tract in support of the repeal of the union. Both Curry and O'Connell had written for specific purposes, which may explain why Carey's work was, to his chagrin, seemingly ignored. Even aside from its publication on the other side of the Atlantic, his timing meant that it fell between the two stools of the two great Catholic political campaigns of late eighteenth- and early nineteenth-century Ireland. These works were part of a conscious, quasi-scholarly articulation of an alternative version of 1641; they were deliberate responses to the manner in which Protestant writers had engaged in a similar process. Yet such relatively highbrow endeavors, emanating from both ends of the denominational spectrum, could become intermeshed with popular patterns of belief. They dovetailed with the assumptions and mentalities underpinning corresponding and contrasting versions of Irish history in general. In the belief system of Irish Catholics this congruence assumed great significance as an increasingly unified version of Irish nationalist history began to be reflected in a variety of forms.[218] Irish nationalism can perhaps be categorized in two distinct ways: in terms of a "civic" or "territorial" nationalism in which the category of nationality could be extended as an umbrella encompassing a plurality of peoples or creeds; or in terms of a more visceral "ethnic" or "cultural" nationalism in which nationality was defined in exclusivist terms by virtue of cultural origin or, more potently, religion.[219] These concepts were polar opposites, but as we shall see, the version of 1641 that has been the subject of this chapter could accommodate itself to both. With regard to the singular depiction of 1641 as an uprising, perhaps the fullest exemplar of this perspective to emerge in mid-nineteenth-century Ireland was found in a work of fiction that internalized these assumptions to bring them to a wider audience.

The Confederate Chieftains (1864) was seemingly written in New York by Mrs. J. Sadlier (the pen name of the prolific Cavan-born Mary Anne Madden). Here was a romantic tale set amid the tumults of the 1640s and written, as its author declared, to reclaim Irish history and bring it to life in order to "ennoble our country and give her that place amongst the nations to which the glory of her sons entitles her."[220] In doing so, she cast 1641 as a strike against oppression: "the newly awakened thirst for freedom increased from day to day,"[221] as 23 October 1641 was "fixed on for striking a grand and simultaneous blow in the cause of civil and religious freedom."[222] And soon, as bonfires blazed forth over Ulster, "the voice of a newly-awakened people could be heard."[223]

Her story soon came to the crux of the matter: "Had the Catholic people of Ulster been what their enemies delight to represent them, few Protestants would have lived next day among its hills and valleys to tell the tale of retributive justice. As it was, not one single murder stained their hands throughout that general insurrection."[224] Assuming that this point might well be lost on prospective readers, she added a footnote helpfully stating that "all Protestant historians admit that during the first week of the rebellion—that is to say, in the first glowing outburst of recovered liberty—not one individual was put to death by the Irish. It was only when murders and massacres perpetrated on themselves drove them to it that they adopted a system of retaliation."[225] Indeed, she claimed, "by a strange anomaly characteristic . . . of the Irish people, there was comparatively little blood shed during that first memorable week even in

Fermanagh."[226] In Leitrim Owen O'Rourke captured a number of Protestant prisoners, but rather than slaughter them he entertained them "with that princely hospitality which became his noble ancestry."[227] While his prisoners were initially fearful, they were soon made to feel welcome by the "polite attentions" of his family and the soothing music provided by his harpist; as a result, "the prisoners—at least the female portion of them—almost forgot their captivity and learned to love the chains which the chivalrous O'Rourke contrived to interweave with flowers."[228]

This portrait of Irish chivalry stood in stark contrast to the dastardly figure of the Scottish planter Sir Frederick Hamilton, whose "swarthy face" and "great black eyes" oversaw the killing of Tiernan O'Rourke, bound and flung to his death from the parapets of Hamilton's castle in Leitrim in full view of his brother Manus, who refused to kill his own Protestant prisoners in revenge; indeed, he released them unmolested.[229] Equally, the gallantry of the Irish was a world apart from the depredations of the Scots, who bayoneted an old woman in the throat at Islandmagee with "shouts of fiendish laughter," thereby becoming "marked like Cain with the murdered brand stamped in the blood of their victims," and providing a thoroughly understandable excuse for the cruel retaliation of the Irish in the aftermath.[230] The innocent Catholics of Islandmagee were vulnerable to a terrible Protestant atrocity: "Of all the gallant chieftains who were then in arms with their legions of brave followers to repel the aggressions of bigotry and legalized rapine, not one was near in that dark hour to save the unoffending peasantry of Island Magee from the exterminating sword of fanatical ruffians. . . . They were far, far away, little dreaming of the foul butchery which on that night commenced the work of slaughter in the northern province."[231]

In a curious text whose prose was redolent of the popular historical writing of its time (and which was virtually a compilation of the worst anti-Catholic atrocities reported from the 1640s), it was perhaps inevitable that Mary Anne Madden would paint the greatest villain in the blackest colors. *The Confederate Chieftains* pilloried Sir Charles Coote and his soldiers as ghoulish fiends. As he oversaw the attack on the O'Byrnes in Wicklow, "babes were torn from the arms of their shrieking mothers and tossed on the points of spears or bayonets from one to another of the soldiers, amidst shouts of laughter and yells of delight."[232] The climax was reached as his soldiers smoked women and children out of a cave to their doom, to the ringing accompaniment of "a chorus of fiendish laughter."[233]

A debate about the true nature of the rebellion—or rising—of 1641 had raged ever since its outbreak. If nothing else, *The Confederate Chieftains* was perhaps the apotheosis of one side of the argument, an argument made consistently over the centuries, insisting that the historic community of Irish Catholicism had been the victim of the most grievous wrongs. In the nineteenth century such a vision of Irish history underpinned the rise of Irish nationalism by providing it with a "vocabulary and cultural map" to serve as a template for the present.[234] As Joep Leerssen has observed: "History was revived to inspire the present. Not only that, but the reviving of history was performed time and again, by writer after writer, each of them telling the old story afresh, like a needle stuck in the groove, in an uncanny, obsessive recycling process of the past, of the old familiar, oft-told story of the past."[235] History by its nature was continually grafted onto the present. By the time that *The Confederate Chieftains* was published, the Great Famine of the 1840s had become the latest event to assume an apocalyptic significance for Irish nationalists.[236] Yet 1641 remained a touchstone for those who felt that they had ended up on the wrong side of the course of Irish history. Although there were other markers of this mentality among Catholics, 1641 was perhaps the most fundamental, for all that came afterward had flowed from it—or seemed to do so. What figures like John Curry or the unknown "R.S." did was to pose a set of questions of great importance and enduring relevance: Who were the real victims of Irish history? How was their experience to be weighed in the balance? How were the historic wrongs visited upon them to be righted? And from these questions flowed another, simpler one. To paraphrase the great German historian Leopold von Ranke, what had actually happened in 1641?

3

"Historical Facts" and "Stupendous Falsehoods"

An Irish Insurrection at the Limits of Scholarship, c. 1865–c. 1965

Eminent Victorians?

Toward the end of the nineteenth century, in the twilight of his life, the renowned Dublin lawyer John Patrick Prendergast reflected on the times in which he had lived and wrote a memoir that, among other things, contained an account of what he termed his "literary work and experiences." The memoir marked a new departure for him, as his "literary work" had until then been historical in nature. His interest in Irish history had originally been prompted by his involvement in a chancery case in the 1840s that had touched on aspects of the eighteenth-century penal laws. To satisfy his burgeoning curiosity he began to dig through the copious pamphlet holdings of the library of King's Inns and slowly began, as he put it, to "perceive the importance of the land settlement" of the 1650s.[1] Since nobody seemed to know anything about this particular subject, by September 1848 Prendergast was poring over the Commonwealth documents held in Dublin Castle, "and here I found the record of a nation's woes."[2] His enthusiasm intensified as he "ransacked other depositories."[3] Through the opportunities provided by his travels on the legal circuit and through various connections and acquaintances, he accumulated more and more material until he eventually concluded that "all the information that could be hoped for had now been obtained; and if not brought forth, the subject might sleep for another period as long as the last." Furthermore, he remarked, "much of it had been collected with the view of being able some time or other to treat the subject of the settlement of landed property in Ireland historically considered before the bar of Ireland."[4] This is what Prendergast eventually did; the fruit of his labors was the publication in 1865 of *The Cromwellian Settlement of Ireland.*

Prendergast is not easily pigeonholed. A member of the Church of Ireland (an ancestor conformed in the eighteenth century) who in later life was vehemently opposed to Home Rule, he was nonetheless a nationalist whose experience as the administrator of the Clifden estates made him a strong proponent of tenant right. Prendergast's opinions on contemporary events, however, were by no means divorced from his scholarly preoccupations; rather, the two went hand in hand, and this could be said for virtually all who sought to engage with the Irish past amid the tumultuous upheavals of the later nineteenth century.

The book that established Prendergast's scholarly credentials corresponded to a Catholic interpretation of Irish history. Indeed, the composition of *The Cromwellian Settlement* was prompted by contemporary concerns, for the eponymous settlement, having allegedly been designed "rather to extinguish a nation than to suppress a religion,"[5] was quite simply "the foundation of the present settlement of Ireland."[6] To reach this point Prendergast had some preliminary ground to cover, and within that compass 1641 loomed large.

The preface to *The Cromwellian Settlement* stated that it was "needless here to recapitulate the long-continued injuries and insults by which the ancient English of Ireland were forced into the same ranks with the Irish in defence of the king's cause in 1641."[7] Having thus declared his intention, Prendergast went on to do the opposite. His actual account of 1641 (a necessary prelude to his fuller treatment of the land settlement) began by disputing the argument that the rebellion had been preceded by four decades of harmony.[8] Prendergast's sympathy with those who were subsequently dispossessed was evident in such statements as the following: "There was peace, but it was the peace of despair because there remained no hope except in arms, and their arms were taken from them."[9] The logical outcome of this situation came on 23 October 1641, when "the English power was overthrown in three-fourths of Ireland in a night."[10] Prendergast then refuted the notion of Catholic atrocities: "It has been represented that there was a general massacre surpassing the horrors of the Sicilian Vespers, the Parisian Nuptials, and Matins of the Valtelline, but nothing is more false . . . ; The Irish, to use the words of an old divine, have ever lacked gall to supply a wholesome animosity to the eternal enemies and revilers of their name and nation."[11]

Prendergast argued that Protestant propagandists confused the expectation of a massacre with the reality. He also described the atrocities committed by government forces; the massacres committed by the Irish were thereby recast as retaliations.[12] For as he asserted, "The subsequent cruelties were not on one side only, and were magnified to render the Irish detestable, so as to make it utterly impossible for the king to seek their aid without ruining his cause utterly in England. The story of the massacre, invented to serve the politics of the hour, has been since kept up for the purposes of interest. No inventions could be too monstrous that served to strengthen the possession of Irish confiscated lands."[13] In a nutshell this was Prendergast's basic point.

There was little new in it. Unsurprisingly, for some reviewers it was a perfectly sensible assessment of 1641, and one with enduring contemporary relevance. Perhaps this circumstance aided its popularity. In 1871 Prendergast distributed copies of the second edition to reading societies in answer to demands for a cheaper edition.[14] One favorable reviewer of the first edition observed: "It is a characteristic of the English nation that whenever a rebellion arises in any district of the empire, their first disposition . . . is to stigmatise the recalcitrant race with the guilt of every conceivable form of inhuman and unnatural atrocity."[15] But again, there was no new departure here: one gets the sense that Prendergast simply confirmed what this reviewer believed in the first place. Where he did break new ground was in his extensive use of original and hitherto unfamiliar documents—"the true materials for Irish history," as one hostile reviewer put it.[16]

A key trend in the nineteenth-century "professionalization" of the study and writing of history was a renewed emphasis on original documentary sources—precisely the material that Prendergast had pored over. It is debatable whether such trends influenced his work; he was after all a lawyer by profession. But his knowledge of primary sources was later recognized when he was employed to catalog the enormous Carte collection retained in the Bodleian Library at Oxford in conjunction with the Catholic priest and scholar Charles William Russell, the president of Saint Patrick's College, Maynooth. (Russell was apparently included to provide denominational balance, though according to Prendergast's memoir they became cordial and firm collaborators.) Prendergast had become something of an expert in this new field. Yet such empiricism did not mean that the furious polemical potential of Irish history was in any way dissipated. In his memoir Prendergast recalled an incident in which an unnamed friend had upbraided him outside Leinster House one night by telling him, "I never knew anyone who seemed to have more knowledge of Irish history than you. But will you do me a kindness? Will you promise to give it up? It is a dangerous and unprofitable study."[17] Prendergast could have been in no doubt about its potential for sowing discord. Perhaps his strongest testament to the persistence of such vituperation was indirect: the conspicuous absence from his memoir of any account of his dealings with James Anthony Froude.

Froude remains at the center of what is arguably still Ireland's most notorious historiographical controversy. Since it arose from his depiction of the Irish in what were, to say the least, uncharitable terms, those scholars who have examined it in detail tend to comment on the paradox that in the course of his turbulent life Froude had actually been quite familiar with Ireland. The son of a Church of England parson from Devon, Froude originally seemed destined for the clergy himself, but a restless mind dragged him away from this path as he carved out a career as a popular, if often contentious, man of letters. He had visited and worked in Ireland at regular intervals since the early 1840s and had even come to regard it with a certain fondness.[18]

The contradiction between this fondness and the eventual ferocity of his invective toward the Irish themselves can be explained by his polemical purpose. For Donal McCartney, Froude wrote as a committed imperialist and opponent of Home Rule; for Ciaran Brady, the Englishman's invective was prompted by a higher moral purpose, as Froude embarked on a rhetorical exercise aimed at the moral regeneration of an English audience. There was no contradiction between these positions—quite the opposite. If Froude's writing on Ireland and the Irish could be seen as a "protest against the movement for Irish self-government and its threat of disruption of the empire,"[19] then his exposition of what he deemed the deficiencies of the Irish was intended to be "a continuing reflection of the failure of the English themselves."[20]

The storm that broke over Froude's views first emerged in the course of an American lecture tour undertaken in late 1872 to counter a series of lectures by the Fenian Jeremiah O'Donovan Rossa; the tour was cut short thanks to the reaction Froude provoked. He "had been insulted at railway stations, his life was threatened, and a special guard had been provided for him. In hotels and homes where Froude stayed, Irish servants staged what was known as the strike of the Noras and Biddys," refusing to deal with their increasingly unwelcome guest.[21] Such pervasive outrage was intensified by unprecedented newspaper coverage of the controversy on both sides of the Atlantic, as Froude ("a phenomenon of history who had insulted American intelligence"[22]) was pursued by—among others—the Galway-born Dominican preacher Thomas Burke, who in 1869 had presided over the reinterment of Daniel O'Connell's remains in Glasnevin and who had been invited to the United States to present a set of lectures by way of riposte.[23] In Ireland Prendergast himself was spurred into print. He had apparently put his unrivaled knowledge of Irish archives at Froude's disposal, and having done so in good faith, he was incensed at the consequences. He contributed a series of apoplectic letters to the *Freeman's Journal* aimed at dismissing Froude's view of Irish history in general ("his language is that of the hypocrite, and there is poison under that tongue") and of 1641 in particular, for as Prendergast put it, "there was no massacre. It was not a rising of the Catholics upon Protestants, but of an oppressed nation against the tyrants in the interest of the rightful king."[24] Prendergast's condensed conclusion was, however, mild in comparison to what came afterward. When he wrote his first letter, he had been aware only of the content of the lectures. What prompted him to write a second was that he had read the book from which they were drawn. And having done so, he concluded, "I would withdraw the term cold-blooded hypocrite and substitute bloodthirsty fanatic."[25]

The one mention of Froude in Prendergast's autobiography was itself an echo of his sustained jeremiad: a recollection of Father Russell upbraiding him outside the library of Trinity College and urging Prendergast to prudence, given his "violence against Froude."[26] But Prendergast's "violence" was applauded in other quarters; it even prompted a versified tribute in *The Nation*:

> When Froude, with bigot fury blind,
> To strike at Ireland felt inclined,
> He wrote a book, to ease his mind,
> Crammed full of lies of every kind. . . .
>
> 'Tis false and foul as book can be
> 'Tis black with spite and enmity
> But every lie, as all may see
> Is caught and smashed by John PP
>
> Hurrah for John P. Prendergast,
> He nails his colours to the mast,
> He strikes for Ireland hard and fast,
> So here's to John P. Prendergast.[27]

In the columns of the *Freeman's Journal* Prendergast made his argument about 1641 by using the time-honored technique of Curry and Carey—that of deploying writers against themselves and augmenting his own rhetoric with documents held in the Irish Public Record Office.[28] Given the ferocity of Prendergast's reaction, it is worth turning now to the notorious work against which he was reacting: Froude's epic *The English in Ireland*.

The notoriety of Froude's assault on the Irish justifies discussing it at some length. His contentious treatment of 1641 was placed within an overarching view of Irish history that Froude helpfully outlined in the preface. He began with a discourse on the inherent inequalities found among the various components of humankind, resulting in the conclusion—from which, helpfully enough, it had proceeded—that might was right: "The superior part has a natural right to govern; the inferior part has a natural right to be governed; and a rude but adequate test of superiority and inferiority is provided in the relative strength of the different orders of human beings."[29]

Having set out his stall, Froude then moved from the general to the particular—Ireland, "the last of the three countries of which England's interest demanded the annexation."[30] The conquest of Ireland had been apparently a far more difficult proposition than the "annexation" of Scotland and Wales, given the impassability of the Irish terrain and the courage of the natives. Yet something had gone wrong in the course of this great struggle for Ireland, for "in a successful struggle for freedom, she would have developed qualities which would have made her worthy of possessing it."[31] But it was not to be: "Ireland would neither resist courageously nor would she honourably submit . . . ; Their insurrections, which might have deserved sympathy had they been honourable efforts to shake off an alien yoke, were disfigured with crimes which, on one memorable occasion at least, brought shame on their cause and name."[32] Froude reached his dubious conclusion:

> Nations are not permitted to achieve independence on these terms. Unhappily, though unable to shake off the authority of England, they were able to irritate her into severities which gave their accusations some show of colour. Everything which she most valued for herself—her laws and liberties, her orderly and settled government, the most ample security for person and property—England's first desire was to give to Ireland in fullest measure. The temper in which she was met exasperated her into harshness and at times to cruelty; and so followed in succession alternations of revolt and punishment, severity provoked by rebellion, and breeding in turn fresh cause for mutiny till it seemed at last as if no solution of the problem was possible save the expulsion or destruction of a race which appeared incurable.[33]

There had been slivers of hope prior to this denouement. The Irish, on the eve of the Norman invasion, "had some human traits": singing and a devout faith, not to mention "pretensions to learning" among the clergy.[34] But these were exceptions rather than the rule, for "when Giraldus Cambrensis was sent by Henry the Second to report on Ireland, their chief characteristics were treachery, thirst for blood, unbridled licentiousness, and inveterate detestation of order and rule. To such a people, needing bit and bridle, liberty was only mischievous, and the Normans came to take direction of them."[35] Their arrival was a good thing; the Irish were "essentially unfit" for "English liberty";[36] even "if they possess some real virtues, they possess the counterfeits of a hundred more."[37]

Froude's text was deeply and openly racist; the presumed negative characteristics of the Celt were a running theme ("The Irish are the spendthrift sister of the Arian [sic] race"), though this prejudice was tempered slightly by some extraordinarily patronizing appreciations of their occasional virtues.[38] But on the whole he cleaved to the view that the Irish were a savage, turbulent, and violent people who needed to be kept in check and brought to English civilization. The question was how best to achieve this feat, and the implication was that the fault for failure lay with the English for not going about it successfully; something had gone wrong. The Tudor monarchs escaped censure; during their reigns, "when England showed strength and resolution, Ireland became immediately submissive."[39] But had England always acted in such a resolute way? And was the lack of resolve the principal problem faced by those who would govern Ireland? Admittedly, Froude was critical of the depredations of the Elizabethan soldiery, who "were little better than banditti themselves" and regarded "the Irish peasantry as unpossessed of the common rights of human beings and shot and strangled them like foxes or jackals."[40] But he also affirmed that "the worst cruelties of the garrisons were but the occasional copies of the treatment of the Irish universally by one another"; and thus "the best and only hope for the country was the extension of English influence over it."[41] The unionist undertone was obvious.

So too was the militant Protestantism. Catholicism was indicted here as an evil and subversive doctrine that inevitably redounded to the detriment of its professors.[42] Froude glossed over the Ulster plantation, except to observe that the maintenance of some Irish on their estates and in government offices could be explained as a gradualist attempt at assimilation to English mores. Yet once again the natives were found wanting, since "experience was to show that the Irish did not understand forbearance, that they interpreted lenity into fear and respected only an authority which they dared not trifle with."[43]

Froude's work had a lengthy gestation, and its particular nature reflected both the specific circumstances of its composition and a more general view of the world. *The English in Ireland* was undoubtedly composed, at least in part, to draw an extended argument from history against granting any form of "Home Rule" to Ireland, lest this have dangerous implications for the empire as a whole—a stance that was by no means unusual among contemporary English intellectuals.[44] Froude's almost metaphysical outlook on human nature, seemingly influenced by a lengthy association with Thomas Carlyle, was reflected in his view of the Irish as an inferior people who required molding by a superior power. If the manifest deficiencies of the Irish were indeed "a continuing reflection of the failure of the English themselves," then Froude's outrageously offensive tone becomes eminently explicable.[45] Fond memories of Ireland and the Irish counted for little within his grand design. It is curious to see how Froude's treatment of 1641 attracted the ire of hostile reviewers, given that it occupied a relatively small amount of his three volumes. But what his treatment symbolized was of crucial importance; it was to be the exemplar of the unrivaled degeneracy of the Irish.

Froude was undoubtedly a skilled and vivid writer with a gift for rhetoric. In discussing 1641, he now had a subject that encouraged him to give his gift free rein:

> The gravest event in Irish history, the turning point on which all later controversies between England and Ireland hinge. The facts, real or alleged, are all before us; for the excitement created was so terrible that the most minute particulars were searched into with agonized curiosity. Forty volumes of depositions are preserved in the library of Trinity College, which tell the tale with perfect distinctness; and as the witnesses relate one consistent story, they are dismissed by those who are offended by their testimony as imaginary beings, forgers, liars, and calumniators. The eagerness to discredit the charge is a tacit confession how tremendous is the guilt if it can be proved; the most certain facts can be made doubtful if they are stoutly and repeatedly denied; and not evidence but sympathy or inclination determines the historical beliefs of most of us. Those who choose to think that the massacre of 1641 was a dream will not change their opinion. Those who see in that massacre the explanation and the defence of the subsequent treatment of Ireland, however unwilling to revive the memory of scenes which rivalled in carnage the horrors of Saint Bartholomew, are compelled to repeat the evidence once held to be unanswerable.[46]

There was, however, a concession of sorts to his opponents: "That a rebellion should have broken out at that particular time was in itself so natural that a looker-on might have predicted it with certainty."[47] Froude accurately noted that Irish *perceptions* of plantation prior to 1641 had indeed been of a heretical tyranny; whether this was actually the case was another story entirely. He also noted the rumors and unrest evident throughout the country in the years prior to the outbreak of the rebellion, and he conceded that the majority of the Irish leadership was opposed to exterminating Protestants, not least out of loyalty to the king.[48] Froude had previously shown an awareness of the distinction between Old English and Irish, and later approved of the loyalty shown by the

Old English to the crown owing apparently to their ethnic heritage.[49] But all of this was a prelude to his characterization of the slaughter of Protestants by Catholics:

> It does not fall within the purpose of the present history to relate circumstantially the scenes which followed. Inasmuch, however, as Catholic historians either deny their reality altogether, slur them over as enormously exaggerated, or lay the blame on the Protestants as the first beginners of violence; and inasmuch as the justification of the subsequent policy of England towards Ireland depends upon the truth of events of which the recollection was kept alive for a century by a solemn annual commemoration, it is necessary to relate briefly the outline of those events as recorded by eyewitnesses, who were examined in Dublin, fresh from the scenes which they had witnessed, before commissioners "of known integrity," men of all stations and of both nations, whose evidence is the eternal witness of blood which the Irish Catholics have from that time to this been vainly trying to wash away.[50]

His footnotes contained a running commentary on the trustworthiness of the depositions (which he took at face value), along with refutations of Catholic accounts written by figures like Curry and Nicholas French and an uncritical acceptance of Protestant commentators. With regard to Temple's work, "the circumstantial minuteness of the picture," declared Froude, "is itself a guarantee of its fidelity."[51] His adherence to that assessment was reflected at another point in his text: "Murder, the Irish writers say, was begun only in retaliation. The first blood, they affirm, was shed at Islandmagee early in November, when three thousand Catholics were killed by the garrison of Carrickfergus. Were this story true, there is something naïve in the complaint that soldiers appointed to keep the peace should have used strong measures when the country was in the hands of bands of robbers who were confessedly plundering the entire province."[52] Froude dismissed this accusation, claiming instead that only thirty Catholics had been killed at Islandmagee by both the Carrickfergus garrison and a number of settlers in a retaliatory attack. His desire to set the record straight—at least from his somewhat fevered perspective—prompted him to a more general imprecation: "When will the Irish Catholics, when will the Roman Catholics, learn that wounds will never heal which are skinned with lying? Not til they have done penance, all of them, by frank confession and humiliation—the Irish for their crimes in their own island, the Catholics generally for their yet greater crimes throughout the civilised world—can the past be forgotten, and their lawful claims on the conscience of mankind be equitably considered."[53]

Froude used extraordinary rhetoric in his description of the rebellion. Protestant refugees were hunted down, for example, by "starved jackals." Protestants seeking shelter from Catholics were apparently slaughtered without mercy, prompting the claim that "fugitives admitted to shelter are sacred in the Arab tent or the Indian wigwam."[54] His comparison was hardly meant to flatter. Back in Ireland, children were tortured by other children. Such scenes were "witnessed daily through all parts of Ulster,"[55] as "the distinction between Scots and English soon vanished. Religion was made the new dividing line, and the one crime was to be Protestant."[56]

The lurid tone intensified as Froude recited a litany of horrors reputedly visited on those Protestants. Refugees were stripped of their paltry rags in the depths of winter, and pregnant women were left to die in the snow at the instigation of Catholic priests. "Some were driven into rivers and drowned, some hanged, some mutilated, some ripped with knives . . . ; They flung babies into boiling pots or tossed them into the ditches to the pigs. They put out grown men's eyes, turned them adrift to wander, and starved them to death. . . . ; A lad was heard swearing that his arm was so tired with killing that he could scarce lift his hand above his head."[57]

When it came to the number killed by all of these atrocities, Froude opted for an initial estimate of 200,000 Protestants murdered in six months; he credited this figure allegedly because it had supposedly been mentioned by Catholic priests taking pride in their handiwork. He took his cue from the official report by the lord justices in 1643 stating that the rebellion had cost the lives of 154,000 victims; these officials claimed that this death toll had been confirmed "by the priests appointed to collect the numbers."[58] Froude considered Temple's estimate of 300,000 dead before moving down the scale to William Petty's suggestion of 37,000 victims. Seemingly oblivious to his contradictory standards, Froude now entered a caveat about the uncertainty of such contemporary estimates, but he confidently asserted that "the evidence proves no more than that atrocities had been committed on a scale too vast to be exactly comprehended, while the judgement was still further confounded by the fiendish malignity of the details."[59]

Froude then considered other contentious matters. He exonerated Sir Charles Coote, simply referring to his "free use . . . of shot and halter"[60] in County Wicklow, while stating that his "severities" had been used by the Old English as an excuse to join the rebellion. As for the English reaction, "the bitterest invectives of the Puritans against the scarlet woman and her maintainers seemed justified by their new Saint Bartholomew."[61] The logical outcome of such sentiments came with the Cromwellian conquest—a conquest made all the easier by the servile nature of the Irish. For "had Irish patriotism been more than a name, the conquest would have been impossible."[62] Even this result and its facilitating circumstance had a consequence that he sought to counter: "History, ever eloquent in favour of the losing cause—history, which has permitted the massacre of 1641 to be forgotten, or palliated, or denied—has held up the storming of Drogheda to eternal execration."[63] By contrast, Froude's cursory account of the Cromwellian assault on Drogheda was devoid of the rhetorical flourishes and details used in his account of 1641. Discussing the fate of Wexford, he prefaced his equally sanitized version of these events with the claim that "the Catholic inhabitants had lately distinguished themselves by special acts of cruelty and ferocity" inflicted on their Protestant prisoners.[64] He thus found reason to eulogize the failed experiment of the protectorate. Cromwell, he observed, "meant to rule Ireland for Ireland's good, and all testimony agrees that Ireland never prospered as she prospered in the years of the protectorate."[65] To govern the Irish required a tough-minded regime: "In concession they see only fear, and those that fear them they hate and despise. Coercion succeeds better; they respect a master hand, though it be a hard and cruel one. But let authority be just as well as strong: give an Irishman a just master and he will follow him to the world's end. Cromwell alone, of all Irish governors, understood this central principle of Irish management."[66] Consequently, the English failure to fully implement the Cromwellian conquest represented a missed opportunity.

Froude ended on a surprisingly wistful note. If Ireland had indeed been turned into a little England (which was the clear implication of his notion of a missed opportunity), "the lines of difference between the two countries, now as marked as ever, and almost as threatening, would have long ago disappeared."[67] And there would then be no basis, during the era in which he wrote, for the dangerous demand that was Home Rule.

The English in Ireland is perhaps best seen as a contribution to contemporary politics. When it came to scholarly matters, Froude seemed not to advance the discussion of 1641 to any significant extent. One reviewer, assessing the author's account of the rebellion, declared flatly that "there is no evidence for the view of Mr. Froude. Its only support is in the lying tales of panic-mongers, who wanted an excuse for robbery and murder,"[68] before dismissing Froude's book as the product of "the cruellest and most malignant mischief."[69] Another reviewer, however, warmly recommended his account of 1641 to prospective readers, given that the interpretation of 1641 as "a deliberate, wide-spread, and well-organised conspiracy to exterminate all Protestant and English settlers" was by this time "established beyond all doubt."[70]

The enraged responses to Froude's sanguinary vision broke no new ground. Father Burke simply resorted to the venerable technique of using such Protestant writers as Borlase and Warner to refute Froude's account of 1641, while John Mitchel (who felt that Burke had let Froude off the hook) aimed his scornful rhetoric squarely at the integrity of the depositions themselves.[71] In doing so, he was merely following another time-honored tradition. Thus it is noteworthy that the most significant response to Froude came not from polemicists but from the historian W. E. H. Lecky.

Lecky was perhaps the epitome of the Victorian gentleman scholar. Born in Dublin, he spent much of his life based in London (he sat as MP for Trinity College from 1895 to 1902), and his friendly acquaintance with Froude provides an ironic backdrop to his self-conscious refutation of him and, by extension, of the received view of so many other English writers on the subject of 1641.[72] Lecky's initial engagement with Froude's work came in a forthright review of *The English in Ireland*.[73] Here he came straight to the point by telling prospective readers: "This book belongs to the class of histories which are written not for the purpose of giving a simple and impartial narrative of events, but clearly and most avowedly for the purpose of enforcing certain political doctrines."[74] The proof of this criticism was to be seen in the contradiction between the rhetoric of *The English in Ireland* and Froude's earlier accounts of the sixteenth century. Lecky conceded that Froude's account of 1641 was "elaborated with great pains, with great skill, and with great detail."[75] But Froude's emphasis in dealing with 1641 was misplaced. Lecky normalized 1641 as merely one in a succession of such bloodlettings in Irish history ("its magnitude has been greatly exaggerated") and stressed that the balance of terror was not confined to atrocities against Protestants. *The English in Ireland* was, said Lecky, "a work which we believe can hardly fail to injure the reputation of its author . . . ; With a recklessness of consequences that cannot be too deeply deplored, with a studied offensiveness of language that can only be intended to irritate and insult, he has thrown a new brand of discord into the smouldering embers of Irish discontent."[76]

This last phrase was deeply suggestive. One of Lecky's key criticisms was that Froude's work inadvertently and imprudently provided ammunition for "rebels" in Ireland and England's enemies further afield—a point lost on those Irish nationalists who later came to view Lecky as the upholder of Ireland's honor. Lecky, like Froude, was a committed unionist.[77] His deep distrust of Irish nationalism was intertwined with a distrust of democracy, especially in its expanding Irish manifestation (along with his innate conservatism, this bias was perhaps more obvious in his later life). But Lecky offered a version of Irish history that treated the fraught relations between Britain and Ireland in a manner that was the polar opposite of Froude's almost hysterical excesses.

Lecky's hugely influential interpretation of Irish history was originally part of his *History of England* (1878–90) before five volumes were extracted and published as a stand-alone work in 1892. The motivation for arranging for separate publication stemmed from Lecky's having "to deal with a history which has been very imperfectly written, and usually under the influence of the most furious partisanship."[78] This problem obliged Lecky (as he saw it) to return to the original sources and to write a much fuller account than might have been expected. Given that Froude was the most obvious candidate for the accusation of "furious partisanship," it was perhaps unsurprising that Lecky's work provided a counternarrative; his interpretation of 1641 and its prelude differed on almost every key point from that of Froude. According to Lecky, Catholic political demands in the late 1630s were relatively moderate; furthermore, he suggested that irrespective of what had happened in other countries, the history of Ireland did not suggest that its Catholics would have demanded a political ascendancy.[79] On the other hand, he maintained that Protestants had proven to be intolerant and hostile toward Catholics and Catholicism. The same was true of Britain in the early 1640s, as anti-Catholic rhetoric was readily expressed in both the English parliament and the Covenanters' uprising in Scotland. Lecky argued that Catholics had faced an aggregation of provocative measures and gestures prior to the outbreak of rebellion in Ireland.[80] Consequently, 1641 became less of a bolt from the blue and was brought back within the compass of the explicable: "The rebellion was not . . . due to any single cause but represented the accumulated wrongs and animosities of two generations."[81] More important, Lecky insisted on tying the stories about Catholic atrocities to Protestant designs on Catholic estates: "It is tolerably certain that the constant fear lest the Catholics, by coming to terms with the government, should save their estates from confiscation, lay at the root of an immense part of the exaggerated and fantastic accounts of Irish crimes that were invented and diffused."[82]

Lecky offered the pregnant observation that the rebellion had been confined to Ulster for six weeks, and with the exception of a rising in Wicklow by the O'Byrnes (who had been "so recently and flagitiously robbed of their property"[83]), the bulk of the Catholic gentry in Munster and Connacht had remained loyal to the crown. He followed Thomas Carte's argument—itself based on earlier Catholic narratives—that their subsequent gravitation toward the rebellion was prompted by the actions of the lord justices, especially William Parsons. But Lecky drew a distinction between a "defensive religious war"[84] in the remainder of the country and events in Ulster. Those in the north, he admitted, were "speedily disgraced by crimes which, though they have been grossly, absurdly, and mendaciously exaggerated, were both numerous and horrible."[85]

Lecky dismissed the wilder death tolls (such as Temple's misconstrued estimate of 300,000) and "boldly asserted" that there had been no "general and
organised massacre"; such a suggestion was "utterly and absolutely untrue."[86]
He used a sequence of appropriate quotations from various contemporaries to
illustrate that the insurgents had acted with a degree of restraint and accepted
that the wintry elements would also have had fatal consequences.[87] Coming to
the lord justices, Lecky concluded that their reports were "intended to paint it
[the rebellion] in the blackest colours" but that "their language is certainly not
that which would have been employed in describing a general massacre."[88]
These considerations and others, he maintained,

> are sufficient to show that . . . [the massacre] has been exaggerated in
> popular histories almost beyond any other tragedy on record. It has,
> unfortunately, long since passed into the repertory of religious controversy,
> and although more than 230 years have elapsed since it occurred, this page
> of Irish history is still the favourite field of writers who desire to excite
> sectarian or national animosity. English historians have commonly
> bestowed only the most casual and superficial attention upon Irish history,
> and Irish writers have very often injured their cause by overstatement,
> either absurdly denying the misdeeds of their countrymen or adopting the
> dishonest and disingenuous method of recounting only the crimes of their
> enemies. There can, however, be no real question that the rebellion in
> Ulster was extremely horrible and was accompanied by great numbers of
> atrocious murders.[89]

Lecky took the view that in the tumultuous context of the early 1640s "a popular
and undisciplined rising of men in a very low stage of civilisation could hardly
fail to be extremely ferocious."[90] His contemptuous tone was revealing, but it
extended to the victors as well as the vanquished: "A ruling caste never admits
any parity or comparison between the slaughter of its own members and the
slaughter of a subject race."[91] He dismissed the more lurid allegations of a
massacre, but he fully accepted that "murders occurred on a large scale, with
appalling frequency, and often with atrocious circumstances of aggravation."
Portadown was a case in point.[92]

Lecky, like Ferdinando Warner (whom he praised as "the best historian of
the rebellion"[93]), was wary of evidence that amounted to little more than hearsay and was especially aware of the power of rumor and bias in amplifying the
contradictory reports that had found their way to London.[94] This wariness may
explain why he proved so dismissive of the depositions, which he viewed as
largely untrustworthy. In this regard Warner seems to have influenced him,
and Lecky noted with approval Thomas Carte's distrust of the depositions

while at the same time he tried to discredit the iconic account of Sir John Temple—the writer who in Lecky's view bore more responsibility than any other for propagating the notion of a massacre.[95] Lecky also exhibited an ironclad confidence in his own abilities and assured prospective readers: "What I have written will be sufficient to enable the reader to form his own judgement of those writers who, by the systematic suppression of incontestable facts, have represented the insurrection of 1641 as nothing more than an exhibition of the unprovoked and unparalleled ferocity of the Irish people. The truth is that the struggle on both sides was very savage."[96] The slaughters at Islandmagee and Drogheda testified to this twin reality.

But there was one very considerable flaw in an account that has usually been praised for its judicious, if olympian, tone. Despite his veneer of scientific methodology, Lecky "didn't look at the depositions any more than Froude did."[97] His arguments, influential as they proved to be, rested on an analysis of the depositions strikingly similar to the approach of Curry and Carey, for Lecky too had declined to examine the originals.[98] Though he was not alone in this grievous omission, Lecky had less excuse than his predecessors, given the times in which he lived and worked. If historians in the nineteenth century had learned anything, it was the value of returning to their sources. In the case of 1641 the depositions loomed above all other records.

The Return to the Source?

It is worth pausing at this juncture to take stock of the context in which such books were being written. Froude, Lecky, and Prendergast had all composed their works with contemporary concerns in mind; the present cast a shadow on them all. And they were not alone in this. Take, for example, the case of the Irish Quaker Alfred Webb. Born in Dublin and a printer by trade, he came from a liberal and prosperous Quaker background. His parents were active antislavery campaigners, and throughout the course of his life Webb found it easy to sympathize with the wretched of the earth wherever they might be found. A youthful sojourn in Australia on health grounds prompted his solidarity with the Aboriginal population, and back in Ireland, Webb came to support a variety of progressive causes: disestablishment, women's suffrage, and even the public opening of Saint Stephen's Green. Crucially, he also possessed a latent sympathy with the plight of Irish Catholics—a solidarity born of a sense of common suffering between Catholic and Dissenter at the hands of the Anglican establishment. Webb was particularly scathing about an Irish Protestant elite which in his view had "set itself resolutely against all the record of the past 50 years," at least until the Fenians and British liberals had begun to force the pace of events.[99] In later life he was modest when recalling his contribution to Irish nationalist politics, despite acknowledging that since 1865 it had become "one of the chief factors in my life."[100] Webb's commitment to Home Rule was inspired by the example of Isaac Butt and suffering of the Fenian prisoners after 1865 and 1867. He became honorary treasurer of the Home Rule League on its foundation in 1873 and remained politically active in a multitude of Home Rule organizations over the course of his political life.

One of these bodies was the Irish Protestant Home Rule Association (IPHRA), which he helped to found in Belfast in 1886. Irish Protestants were generally unsympathetic toward Home Rule, but there were a handful of exceptions.[101] Given its religious composition, the political commitment of the IPHRA was driven by factors other than nationalism; many members viewed the prospect of Home Rule as simply another liberal reform for better government. Alongside this attitude could be found a desire to see a stable and prosperous Ireland within the empire, devoid of sectarian animosity.

In the early years of the proceedings of the IPHRA, Webb was moved on two occasions to venture into print to win Protestants to its banner. His first pamphlet on the subject was intended to dispel fears of "Rome rule" by publishing answers to the following question: "Have you during your experience of life in Ireland observed any instances of intolerance amongst your Catholic friends and neighbours such as would lead you to fear for your liberty and safety under an Irish constitution such as that sketched out in Mr. Gladstone's bill?"[102] Fifty-two respondents from the urban Protestant middle classes (at least in the second edition) all answered "no," but this was somewhat misleading. The majority of Irish Protestants remained deeply suspicious of Home Rule for reasons that were best encapsulated in a phrase associated with a later era: Home Rule was or would be Rome rule.

The privileged position of Protestants in Ireland had become increasingly eroded in the decades since the famine. By the beginning of 1866, only a matter of months after the publication of Prendergast's work, two issues were coming to dominate Irish public affairs. One was the thorny question of religious education in the National School system, especially the unwelcome prospect of its domination by the Catholic church. The other major concern centered on the activities of the Irish Republican Brotherhood, or the Fenians. The American Civil War had ended in April 1865, and in its aftermath the Fenians, as both a perceived and an actual threat, were at their zenith. But even though their subsequent rebellion in 1867 fizzled out, the disestablishment of the Church of Ireland in 1869 was considered in Irish Anglican quarters as a British surrender in the face of the Fenian threat—a menace made the more worrisome to Irish

Protestants by the fact that the Irish Republican Brotherhood was viewed by some as little more than "an army of papists."[103] The twin bogeys of Fenianism and disestablishment were soon joined by the perennial problem of agrarian insurgency, this time on an unprecedented scale in the form of the Land War of 1879–82 and especially the social revolution that accompanied it. The waning of the Protestant "ascendancy," whose members had previously dominated Irish society, was accompanied by the growth of an ideology—unionism—that greatly helped to define Irish politics in the decades prior to partition and independence. As Home Rule became an integral part of the Irish political landscape from the 1870s, Protestants increasingly feared the possibility of domination and discrimination at the hands of an inevitable Catholic majority in a Home Rule Ireland. Such concerns seeped into more scholarly pursuits. At a time when the Protestant establishment in church and state that had existed since the seventeenth century was effectively in its death throes, the history of Ireland in the seventeenth century became an obvious subject of study. Irish history began to be mined for material with which to answer an increasingly significant question: Should self-government of some kind be granted to Ireland?[104] This issue naturally raised another question: Were the Catholic Irish actually capable of self-government? History could offer an answer to this question as well.

In the era of Home Rule the relevance of a traditional Protestant interpretation of the 1641 rebellion was obvious. It was historical proof that the Catholic Irish were bigoted, bloodthirsty, and by extension, thoroughly unfit to govern themselves. In other words, the received version of 1641 could be deployed as an argument against Home Rule; this was precisely what Froude had done. The reviewer of a slew of recently published works on seventeenth-century Ireland concluded in 1880 that: "We have been informed by high authority amongst the partisans of Home Rule that their ultimate object is an Irish parliament which would [not] be . . . , like the Irish parliament of 1782, a Protestant body." Instead, it would be "an assembly four-fifths Roman Catholic." This reviewer then revealed his worst fears: "It is needless to point out the consequence of a Catholic House of Commons in Ireland opposed to a Protestant House of Peers and a Protestant British parliament. Such a House of Commons would be in great measure returned by the priests and subservient to them, as they are subservient to their church. Home Rule therefore means simply Catholic rule in Ireland."[105]

But Webb intended to rebut and banish such assumptions. He had little time for antiquarian debate for its own sake: "My interests lie in the fate and fortunes of our people and in the politics and future of Ireland."[106] Prompted by these political concerns, he intervened in a debate with enormous ramifications for his own times by publishing in 1887 *The Alleged Massacre of 1641*. His purpose was clear from the outset: "Nothing can be more unfair than the attempt now made to prove from history that the Irish people are unfit for self-government . . . ; It has suited one party in Ireland, and a great many parties out of it, to lend themselves for generations to the task of traducing the Irish . . . ; To prove our innate wickedness, to show that religious toleration and respect for other peoples' opinions are foreign to Irish thought and impossible of development in an Irish atmosphere, no one event is oftener referred to than the 'massacre of 1641.'"[107]

Webb wrote after the rejection of the 1886 Home Rule bill. He seemed to do so for an English audience as much as an Irish one; in a footnote he quoted a tract issued during the recent Cheshire by-election claiming that the Irish had possessed Home Rule before, in 1641, and as a consequence had murdered 150,000 Protestant men, women, and children at the behest of their priests.[108] To parry such notions, Webb fashioned an account of the iniquities of English rule in Ireland encompassing the Nine Years' War and the plantation of Ulster ("an outrage upon common honesty"), and concluded that "a general policy of spoliation, repression, and religious intolerance was maintained up to the breaking out of the insurrection in 1641."[109] In such circumstances, he argued, rebellion was the Catholics' "duty," but "there is absolutely no evidence of a general massacre, preconcerted or other, by the Irish."[110]

Webb took his cue from Lecky's judgment that the depositions used by Froude did not actually prove that a massacre had happened (he also used Froude himself to illustrate the same point). Webb then swiftly turned his attention to the most prominent source for these notions: Temple's *Irish Rebellion*, a work that was apparently "treasured and studied in Puritan households throughout the length and breadth of Great Britain and Ireland," and "wherever English speaking peoples have emigrated, it was regarded as an almost infallible witness against Catholicism. Well do I remember the horror with which in my childhood I hung over its pages and feasted on the unimaginable cruelties depicted on the frontispiece. This is the 'undefiled well' from which succeeding generations and historians have drawn their ideas of the 'massacre of 1641.'"[111]

Webb was healthily skeptical of Temple's book and dismissed both its death tolls and its more exaggerated allegations—for example, that the ghosts of Protestants killed at Portadown had returned to demand vengeance. It must be said that Webb did not completely dismiss the depositions themselves. But just as he had done with Froude, Webb turned Temple against himself, arguing that his reluctance to sanction a second edition of *The Irish Rebellion* in 1674 proved that he had disowned it. Webb explicitly yoked together Temple and Froude as the key polemicists who had perpetuated the massacre allegations. Here was implicit proof of the enduring power of Temple's version of the rebellion. Froude was merely the latest writer to repeat it, and Webb tackled him with the aid of Lecky's judgment that such a massacre was inconsistent with the true nature of the Irish. Webb then concluded: "Were the worst true— had our Irish Catholic fellow-countrymen two hundred and forty years ago committed the full number of murders assigned to them—it would not alter my views regarding present Irish politics. If ever there were a justifiable rising for all that men hold dear, against tyranny and oppression, it was the war of 1641."[112] But the implication underpinning Webb's polemic was that Home Rule would finally resolve the enmities that were the fruits of these ancient events; Protestant fears of the Catholic Irish, he was insisting, were groundless. Why should Protestants fear something that had never happened? Or had the worst occurred after all?

It should be borne in mind that accounts of 1641 did not automatically equate to the extremities of the interpretations outlined so far. Other writers occasionally sought to steer a path between these polarities, the better to come to an assessment of something akin to the truth.[113] According to the anonymous correspondent of a Washington newspaper in 1859, "Terrible tales of the massacre of 1641 formed a large part of tradition amongst Protestants . . . ; Such tales as these, either fictitious or highly exaggerated, formed the conversation of many a winter evening. No doubt among Roman Catholics stories about the oppression and cruelty of Protestants were recited with similar effect. All tended to keep up an unhappy feud between two races which otherwise would have 'mingled into one.'"[114] But if neither one side nor the other was right, how could the reality of the events of the 1641 rebellion be determined? This question brings us back to depositions.

The professionalization of history in the nineteenth century went hand in hand with an increasing proliferation of published editions of source material.[115] The Irish Public Record Office was established only in 1867 (this tardiness arose from a wariness about granting access to its holdings), but the publication of historical documents in the pre-1922 United Kingdom was largely (though not exclusively) the province of the English Historical Manuscripts Commission (HMC) founded in 1869. The HMC did not ignore Irish materials; on the contrary, it examined and published a great deal of such records. It was perhaps inevitable that sooner or later it would devote some attention to the massive corpus of the depositions.

The ways in which authors like Temple, Curry, Walter Harris, Ferdinando Warner, or Matthew Carey had used (and abused) them was succinctly assessed in 1881 by John T. Gilbert, the librarian of the Royal Irish Academy, who reported on the depositions for the HMC with an eye to their publication.[116] Surely, to place all this evidence in the public domain was the best way of resolving the enduring debate over the nature of the rebellion. This attitude now seemed especially legitimate, given that the great questions in Anglo-Irish relations in the latter decades of the nineteenth century—the privileged position of the Church of Ireland and the "ascendancy," not to mention Home Rule and landownership—could be interpreted more fully with reference to the past from which these questions had emerged.[117] The depositions appeared to hold the key to understanding what had actually happened in 1641; thus they lay at the heart of its totemic utility, even if they had rarely been examined in themselves. The whole issue of access to them was becoming more pressing. While various depositions had appeared in print since the 1640s, and would continue to surface in various publications in the second half of the nineteenth century,[118] the most extensive published selection of them appeared in 1884, and this certainly was not the work of the HMC.

Mary Hickson was a Kerry Protestant of modest means whose main contribution to Irish history was her mammoth *Ireland in the Seventeenth Century*.[119] The title was misleading, for her work was essentially a calendar of depositions, selected and presented to the public on an unprecedented scale. But selection was the operative word; the texts chosen related mainly to allegations of the massacre of Protestants, indexed under a range of lurid categories ("murders of children," or "mangling of the bodies of Protestants"). This approach naturally met with approval in some quarters; Froude contributed a glowing and fulsome preface to her work on the grounds that it "may bring about a solution of a most important historical question."[120] What went unsaid was that Hickson's work earned his approval precisely because it seemed to validate the existence of a massacre. Hickson was more fair-minded than such an endorsement might suggest; she was dismissive of such authors as Borlase and Temple, and testimonies relating to Islandmagee were included. But 1641 signified sectarian positions that were perhaps too entrenched to be dislodged, and she published her selection of depositions precisely because she believed that at least some of them could be trusted.

This trenchant restatement of the belief in a massacre of Protestants was arguably her response to the apparent twilight of Protestant Ireland. One favorable reviewer of her work responded to it by noting a perceived continuity between past and present:

> It is impossible to understand the political condition of Ireland at the present hour without a thorough insight into the events of the seventeenth century. The key to the history of the Catholics and the Protestants in their present relations to each other lies in the miserable chaos of this period. It was in the midst of the bloody struggles of the seventeenth century that the

176   THE IRISH MASSACRES OF 1641.

did so they only acted as the Irish had done some days and weeks before. The father of an infant, or a little girl or boy who had been thrown over the bridge with Mrs. Price's five children, and Thomas Taylor's three sisters, was not likely to measure out much mercy to the children and sisters of the Irish a few days after. No reasonable and impartial person will deny that those who committed horrible murders in Ulster and elsewhere between October 22nd and November 22nd were the responsible parties for Coote's severities after the latter date. It was not in human nature that his soldiers,[1] the relatives of the massacred in Ulster, should have refrained from those severities when they had arms in their hands. We cannot excuse those severities any more than the crimes which provoked them, but it is only fair to state the provocation.

X.

ELIZABETH, wife of CAPTAIN ROSE PRICE, late of the parish and county of Armagh, duly sworn and examined, deposeth and saith, That about All Hallowtide 1641, this deponent's husband and she at Turkarry, in the parish and county aforesaid, were deprived, robbed, and otherwise despoiled of their goods, chattels, and estate, consisting of cows, young beasts, horses, corn, hay, sheep, plate, household stuff, jewels, rings, ready money, and other goods and chattels worth (illegible) thousand nine hundred and seven pounds at least, by the grand and wicked rebel, Sir Phelim O'Neil, from whom her husband bought his land within the county of Armagh, worth 100l., and the said Sir Phelim forcibly repossessing himself of the same, taking the profits thereof, which her husband and she are sure to be deprived of and lose until a peace be established. And the other rebels that so robbed and despoiled her are those that are hereafter named, viz. Turlogh Oge O'Neil, brother to the said Sir Phelim, Captain Boy O'Neil, and divers of the sept of the O'Neils, and others whose names she cannot express, their soldiers and accomplices, amounting to a very great number; which said rebels and others of their stock and confederation also robbed all the Protestants in the country thereabouts, and committed divers bloody, barbarous, and devilish cruelties upon and against the persons of a multitude of Protestants there.

[1] 'Sir Charles Coote had a commission for a regiment of the poor stripped English : so likewise had the Lord Lambert.'—Borlase, pp. 29, 38.

DEPOSITIONS.   177

And amongst others their cruelties, they took and seized on her this deponent and five of her children, and above threescore more Protestants at that time in the church of Armagh, and having stripped them of all their clothes, cast them all into prison. About a fortnight after that, the rebels, especially the said Sir Phelim, proposed and offered to send away some of the prisoners into England, and to give them safe conduct for that purpose, which offer being embraced, then the rebels declared that they would suffer the children and those that had no means left to go, but as for the rest, and such as had hidden or conveyed away any money from them, those they stayed, and in particular they stayed there in prison, under the said Sir Phelim, the Lady Caulfield and her children, the Lord Caulfield, whom afterwards they murdered ; Mrs. Taylor and her son, whom they afterwards hanged ; and her this deponent, Mr. Robert (illegible), whom they afterwards murdered and mangled his corpse, and his wife's ; Pierse Newberry, whom they also afterwards murdered, and Henry Newberry ; one Richard Stubb, Richard Warren, whom they also murdered ; Richard Roe and William Warren, whom they hacked all to pieces, and divers others.

But as to this deponent's five children, and about forty more, young and poor prisoners, these were sent away with passes from the said Sir Phelim, together with about threescore and fifteen more Protestants, from other places, within the parishes of Armagh and Loughgall, who were all promised they would be safely conveyed and sent over to their friends in England ; their commander or conductor for that purpose being, as he afterwards proved to be, a most bloody and accursed rebel, by name Captain Manus O'Cane ; and his soldiers having brought or rather driven like sheep or beasts to a market those poor prisoners, being about one hundred and fifteen, to the bridge of Portadown, the said captain and rebels then and there forced and drove all those prisoners, and amongst them this deponent's five children, by name Adam, John, Anne, Mary, and Jane Price, off the bridge into the water, and then and there instantly and most barbarously drowned the most of them. And those that could swim and came to the shore they knocked on the head, and so after drowned them, or else shot them to death in the water. And one of them that was a Scottish minister, swimming below the bridge, to or near the land of one Mr. Blackett, the rebels pursued so far, and then and there shot him to death.

And as for this deponent and many others that were stayed behind, divers tortures were used upon them, to make them confess
VOL. I.   N

Deposition of Elizabeth Price, 1642, from Mary Hickson, *Ireland in the Seventeenth Century; or, the Irish massacres of 1641–2*, London, 1884. (courtesy of the National Library of Ireland)

structure of Irish society was fixed immutably upon its present foundations. . . . Nobody denies that a civil war broke out in Ireland in the autumn of 1641, mainly provoked by the agrarian rapacity and the religious bigotry of the English; but unhappily for historic truth, efforts have been made, principally by Roman Catholic writers, to deny or excuse or ignore some of the worst excesses of that desperate struggle. The war of opinion has succeeded to the war of conquest, making impartiality almost hopeless in the attempt of each side to enhance the guilt of its adversary and to withhold all evidence of its own.[121]

Unfortunately, these seemingly ecumenical sentiments were rapidly undermined by this reviewer's assertion that "Protestant writers with hardly an exception tell the actual truth."[122] The reviewer was in no doubt as to the relevance of the debate into which he had stepped, for "worse than all, the events of 1641 still act with a living force upon the political relations of Irishmen and are the true explanation of the deep and apparently incurable animosity which animates alike the nationalists and Orangemen of the country."[123]

Here was the fundamental issue at stake. Hence the significance of the question of whether or not the depositions ("hearsay reports detailed by the lowest dregs of the Puritan faction," in the words of a Catholic writer[124]) could be trusted. Soon after the publication of her opus, Hickson and the English historian Robert Dunlop debated the point in the rarefied pages of the *English Historical Review*. For Dunlop (who gave Hickson some credit but felt that she had simply fled from one extreme to another), there were three schools of thought about the value of the depositions: "that which looks upon them as little better than mere fabrications and wholly untrustworthy; . . . that which considers them in the main perfectly reliable and the incidents narrated in them to be historical facts with only a slight and perfectly explicable admixture of exaggeration; and . . . that which, while not regarding them as altogether mere fabrications, considers the circumstances under which they were taken as too suspicious to allow much faith to be placed in them."[125] Dunlop was firmly in the third camp, for "it is impossible to make any historical use of them without making very considerable deductions owing to the circumstances under which they were taken."[126] Previous attempts to use (or misuse) the depositions were contradictions in terms, for they had focused on the tiny proportion that had been published over the centuries and paid no heed to the original documents. Even Lecky took the view that they were so untrustworthy, having been untested, that any attempt to examine them was bound to be "quite superfluous"; he claimed instead that the most authentic source was to be found in the selection of extracts published in the *Remonstrance* of 1642, given that it was the report of the commissioners who had actually collected them.[127] Hickson, on the other hand, compared this approach to a performance of Hamlet without the prince. As one of the first to actually examine the depositions in detail, she had a far more sophisticated sense of the garbled nature of the collection, of the manner in which testimony had been authenticated (the issue that had been the erroneous bedrock of Warner's case), and crucially, of the distinction between eyewitness accounts and hearsay.[128] Thus, while Hickson came to agree that Protestants had been massacred, she also concluded that "there is nothing in the MS depositions of 1641–1654 to support the ultra-English and ultra-Protestant view of the events of those years, nor yet the ultra-Roman Catholic and ultra-Irish view."[129]

She responded to Dunlop's challenge by stoutly defending her use of the depositions on the grounds that "I reject the mere hearsay, but I accept facts as related by eye-witnesses."[130] This was a fundamental distinction, to which Dunlop responded by wondering how she had concluded that 25,000 Protestants had been murdered.[131] But she had not done so; instead, Hickson *estimated* that 27,000 had been killed by reworking Sir William Petty's seventeenth-century computation of 37,000 deaths.[132] Dunlop had not read her with sufficient care. This "debate" remained inconclusive but had lost none of its vituperation. Witness the exasperation of Prendergast, who informed Lecky that "this devil Froude and this hell born fury—this she devil—Miss Hickson, are intolerable to me . . . , the only persons I hate on earth!"[133]

But if the documentary record could be distorted to bolster one traditional interpretation, it could also be distorted to bolster the other. Witness, for example, the work of the Catholic writer Thomas Fitzpatrick, who was intent on using the depositions themselves to refute the "'stupendous falsehoods' of the 'Temple-Froude' school of writers."[134] For Fitzpatrick the depositions had been collected by commissioners who were "by race, religion, and calling hostile to the natives" (though he anticipated later historians with his shrewd awareness of their value as a source for subjects other than massacres).[135] According to one enthusiastic reviewer, Fitzpatrick's major work, *The Bloody Bridge* (1903), dispelled "the charge of 'massacre' in any sense in which the word is tolerable."[136] He did so by sifting "the evidence furnished by the depositions" and thereby disposed of "the proofs of Irish villainy which Mr. Froude accepted without question."[137] But this is precisely what he had set out to do in the first place; it is unsurprising that he succeeded. Yet Fitzpatrick did demonstrate how the depositions could be used to reconstruct (or deconstruct) particular episodes, even if he followed his own prejudices in this matter. On this occasion, as on so many others, little had changed.

The rise of "scientific" history in the nineteenth century held out the possibility of determining what had actually happened in 1641. But the contrasting writings of those who debated the point toward the end of that century suggest that the inflammatory utility of 1641 was far too potent to be dismissed so easily. This barrier posed its own problems, for as Walter Love later put it, "the professionals have not been able to solve the problem well enough so as to make the extreme versions fall into [the] realm of legend completely. Nor have they solved it well enough to make it easy for the writer of watered-down history to know how to present it."[138] Love suggested that the obvious solution would be to examine the actual evidence from the rebellion itself in the form of the depositions—an enterprise that he viewed "not as a hopeless task, but as one never properly done."[139]

The question was: Why was it never properly done? Hickson and Fitzpatrick were the first writers to make use of the original manuscript depositions since they had been collected in the seventeenth century; even Ferdinando Warner had ultimately recoiled from them in confusion. The dispute between Froude and Lecky prompted a determination by a few to examine the originals (the impulse behind the endeavors of Hickson and Fitzpatrick), but this resolve proved short-lived, possibly (and perhaps ironically) because Lecky seemed to have conveniently provided the last word on the matter. The depositions remained too difficult and complex a source.[140] Even the circumstances in which they had been collected was as great an obstacle to understanding what really happened in 1641 as were the prejudices of those, such as Hickson or Fitzpatrick, who later made use of them. As Dunlop put it in 1913, while reflecting on his earlier career, "the depositions were very explicit and apparently incontrovertible; but I was living in Dublin at a time when the power of the Land League was at its height, and I could not help asking what value depositions taken by a body of Orange magistrates as to nationalist outrages were likely to possess for an impartial estimate of the state of Ireland during the government of Earl Spencer. Was the state of affairs in 1642 more favourable for an impartial inquiry than it was in 1882?"[141] The continuity with his earlier stance was obvious. But ultimately, such considerations were largely a moot point as the depositions receded from public debate and returned to the shadows of Trinity's library. And there they would remain.

There was, however, a coda of sorts. In October 1933 Robert Dudley Edwards of University College Dublin presented the fledgling Irish Manuscripts Commission—the post-independence Irish equivalent of the HMC—with a proposal to publish the depositions in their entirety (he too was aware of their significance for social and economic history). But a general unfamiliarity with the originals meant that the technical problems that they presented came to light only as the project proceeded. By December 1934 its spiraling size and cost were being queried, not least on the somewhat questionable grounds that the originals were "easily legible."[142] Publication was nearly halted in 1935 because of official wariness about their potentially inflammatory contents. But in January 1936, in an attempt to justify the project to increasingly skeptical civil servants, Edwards argued that this was precisely why they should be published—to refute, as he put it, the "inaccuracy of the Hickson view."[143] There was perhaps a note of desperation in this recourse to the countering of sectarianism. Even so, it was too little, too late.

By the autumn of 1938 three volumes existed in typescript; some segments had even gone to galley proofs. But the project was suspended during the Second World War as the originals were removed from Trinity for safekeeping, and it was eventually abandoned in 1946 (there was a desultory attempt to revive it in the 1950s). This was an inauspicious end to a running debate about 1641 that had rested on the depositions and that for a brief moment at the end of the nineteenth century had looked as if it might find a resolution. The failure to do so was perhaps inevitable, for the sectarianism reflected in the differing and enduring accounts of 1641 had reached its own unexpected resolutions in the meantime. Not for the first time or indeed the last, scholarship had been overtaken by events.

Regressions

After these scholarly (and pseudo-scholarly) interludes, normal service, so to speak, was resumed as "the two traditions went right on, and they have continued, bombast and all, into the present day."[144] This was Walter Love's conclusion in 1965; the truth of his observation was to be seen in the late nineteenth century and the early years of the twentieth when the traditional accounts of 1641 found expression in newer garb.

In truth, the old accounts had never been displaced. In 1883, in a work of over five hundred pages that began with the Celts, the French-born and American-based Jesuit Augustine J. Thébaud devoted a single sentence to "the famous rising of 1641, when in one night Ireland, with the exception of a few cities, freed herself from the oppressor."[145] On the other hand, the Methodist minister George R. Wedgwood, writing in 1891, stated that in 1641 "a fearful massacre of Protestants was perpetrated in the north . . . , the Hibernian Saint Bartholomew. No wonder that reprisals followed."[146] According to J. P. Mahaffy, the notoriously waspish provost of Trinity College, "There is no passage in modern history which affords us a closer parallel to this Irish rebellion than the outbreak of the great mutiny in India, where the contrasts of religion and of race were not unlike those of Ireland in 1641, and where the half-civilised majority of subjects wreaked horrid vengeance upon the minority of masters, excusing to themselves every brutality under the cloak of devotion to religion and of ardent patriotism."[147]

But Mahaffy could be countered by a summary of 1641 such as this one:

1. The rebellion broke out after ninety years of untold wrongs and miseries inflicted on the native race;
2. It took place in that part of the world which, thirty years before, had been the scene of wholesale confiscations;
3. The original intention of the rebels was to drive out the English settlers and to recover the lands from which the native population had been dispossessed;
4. Murders and outrages began when a war of extermination was waged against the Irish;

5. The outrages committed by the Irish were committed by a "tumultuary rabble";

6. The outrages committed by the English were committed by disciplined armies, stimulated by authoritative commanders and provoked or sanctioned by the English government;

7. Finally, all the Irish officers laboured to give the war a character of humanity; all the English officers laboured to give the war a character of inhumanity.[148]

Even a senior member of the Irish parliamentary party such as Justin McCarthy (in a work that began by welcoming "the dawn of a new day in the history of the partnership between Great Britain and Ireland, into a day of mutual understanding, respect, and in the end affection"[149]) went on to dismiss any notion of a massacre having taken place in 1641, "unless we regard any rebellion against constituted authority, no matter how the authority may have been constituted, as a wanton massacre."[150] Both sides carried out atrocities; this was simply the norm at the time, so the Catholic insurgents were no worse than their Protestant adversaries.

Though McCarthy's conclusion was scarcely novel, its reiteration at this juncture pointed yet again to the possibility that a synthesis of the differing interpretations might yet be possible. For the liberal unionist Richard Bagwell, having weighed up the various death tolls that over the course of nearly three centuries had veered between 8,000 and 300,000, both camps had been guilty of widespread slaughter: "The conclusion of the whole matter is that several thousand Protestants were massacred, that the murders were not confined to one province or county but occurred in almost every part of the island, that the retaliation was very savage, innocent persons often suffering for the guilty, and that great atrocities were committed on both sides."[151] But it remained the case that a simmering paper war continued, more often than not by drawing its ammunition (or its targets) from among the usual suspects from the past: Temple, Clarendon, Carte, Curry, Warner, and subsequent writers, including Prendergast, Froude, and Lecky.[152] As the twentieth century moved into its second decade, war and revolution soon made themselves felt.

The decade of upheaval that began with the "Ulster crisis" of 1912–14 and culminated in the war of independence, partition, and civil war of 1919–23 was ultimately molded by the same forces that shaped the versions of Irish history analyzed in this book. Sectarian division underpinned both the Irish revolution and the two states that emerged from it. This is not to suggest that the revolutionary upheaval of those years was prompted by interpretations of history—far from it. But since historical developments could signify broader patterns of belief, it should come as no surprise that the "Protestant" interpretation of 1641 (as bemoaned by Frederick MacNiece) continued to find expression in both Britain and Ireland prior to the outbreak of the First World War.[153] Indeed, during a debate on the third Home Rule bill in January 1913, the nationalist MP T. P. O'Connor told the House of Commons of recent speeches that were little more than "appeals to religious bigotry . . . ; The Protestants of Ulster were told that the wholesale massacres . . . of Protestants by Catholics which are alleged to have taken place in 1641 would be repeated if the Home Rule bill were carried."[154] Equally, the lineage of nationalist rebellion ("six times during the past three hundred years") enshrined in the Easter 1916 proclamation implicitly began with the version of 1641 that was the subject of chapter 2. Even as late as 1920, Catholic periodicals were still publishing articles that, through rhetorical sleight of hand and the time-honored tactic of deploying selective evidence from various sources—such as "R.S." and the acquittals issued by the High Courts of Justice—came to the unsurprising conclusion that "the rulers of the time did *not* believe in the massacres."[155]

This certainty was not shared by southern unionists in the cauldron of revolution, some of whom, like previous generations, reached back into the past to make sense of their contemporary predicament.[156] The killings of Protestants in the Bandon valley of County Cork in April 1922 prompted alarmist reports from loyalists to the British government: 1641 and 1798 were disinterred as historical parallels for another potential massacre of Protestants. According to John Gretton in June 1922, an imminent Franciscan pilgrimage to Multyfarnham Abbey in Westmeath was deemed especially sinister, for such a gathering at the same venue was precisely where the massacre of Protestants had reputedly been planned in 1641 (an accusation first made in the 1640s by Henry Jones and later noted by Froude and Lecky).[157] Indeed, in October 1922 a delegation of southern unionists submitted a report to the British Colonial Office about the danger facing Protestants and many others in Ireland: "The destruction of the last few months is simply staggering. . . . We have to go back to 1641 to find anything like a parallel. Throughout the 26 southern counties of Ireland murder, pillage, rapine, and arson stalk unchallenged. The full force of the cyclone fell on the loyalists first. It has now swept beyond them and threatens to submerge all who have anything to lose."[158]

Such sentiments also lurked in more rarefied settings. One example involved the published musings of the Irish unionist Hugh O'Grady in 1923:

> Imagine Ireland with no government at all, the religious question at full blaze, the land question again in the melting pot, great men bragging of great support from across the water, priests preaching angry jehads, and finally as a bait to the submerged tenth, the land of Ulster, imagine all this

and the wonder is not that the massacre [of 1641] was so terrible, but that all Ireland did not in twenty four hours revert to the age of the cave dwellers. No juggling with figures can minimise the slaughter that ensued, the furies, miseries, savageries, and rapacity . . . ; The incident stands out as one of the most terrible examples in history of what follows when the zeal of men for their "particular ends" tempts them to overthrow the status quo by appeals to force, forgetting that all communities from empires to village communes depend on the mutual trust that each man has in his neighbour.[159]

The patronizing reference to "cave dwellers" was scarcely flattering to the Catholic Irish, while his reference to "juggling with figures" suggested that O'Grady's prejudices were firmly set. He painted an appalling vista; yet forty years later, Walter Love noted O'Grady's rhetorical abhorrence of rebellion and mulled over the fact that he had been writing in the midst of the Civil War: "Does this reflect 1922, when he wrote the intro[duction]?"[160] An echo of contemporary concerns could also be found in the work of another Irish unionist, Lord Ernest Hamilton, who, in a history of 1641 published in 1920, observed that "the 1641 massacres are no greater slur on the Irish nation than the Reign of Terror is on the French nation or Bolshevism on Russia as a whole. All three represent the temporary ascendancy of the brute element."[161] The past may have cast a shadow on the present, but on occasion the two positions could be reversed.

Parallels between the 1640s and the 1920s were probably inevitable, at least for some people in Ireland. Indeed, in the 1920s the British state found itself recording statements from loyalists who had suffered in the course of the revolution, many of whom were Protestants and all of whom sought compensation; an obvious parallel with the 1640s could still be drawn.[162] The rebellion of 1641 was easily invoked during the years 1912–23, for it remained for numerous unionists the exemplar of the danger that Irish Protestants were believed to have faced for centuries. It continued to have relevance for them even as it faded from the horizon of Irish nationalism, since nationalists now identified with a state that looked to other events for its historic legitimacy.[163] If 1641 was sometimes a touchstone for Protestants during the Irish revolution, it could also be a touchstone for the rather beleaguered statelet that came into existence in 1920.

The creation of Northern Ireland reflected a deeper sectarian reality; its essential purpose was to serve as a Protestant enclave, and even before its birth there were those who had sought to harness history to secure its foundation. Ernest Hamilton was the seventh son of the Duke of Abercorn, who had served as lord lieutenant briefly in the late 1860s. Uninterested in politics despite a short period as Unionist MP for Tyrone, he turned to journalism (and in later life gravitated toward fascism). In writing *The Soul of Ulster* (1917), Hamilton, like many others, essentially sought to legitimize the existence of Protestant Ulster and, by implication, unionism as well.[164] He provided a potted history of Ulster since the plantation, incorporating a standard Protestant account of 1641 (based largely on Sir John Temple's) as he did so. Hamilton followed Temple in his musings about how such an atrocious event could even have occurred, given the peaceable, kind, and noble disposition of the planters. But their behavior had made no difference: "The crime of the Protestants . . . was not unneighbourly conduct, but the fact of their presence in a foreign land. They were aliens, and the elimination of aliens has always been the first item on the official nationalist programme."[165] Hamilton tended toward extremities. In his juggling of enormous death tolls he came to no concrete conclusion as to which one was correct, but by providing estimates ranging from 110,000 to 1,200,000, he implied that the true figure lay at the higher end of the scale.[166] He branded 1641 as "the first systematic attempt to exterminate the English in Ireland since the rising of the natives against the very early settlers in 1230," and he came to a very gloomy verdict: "The 1641 massacre may unhesitatingly be put down as the most disastrous occurrence in the history of the island, for—apart from its own intrinsic horrors—it laid the seeds of an undying distrust among future generations of colonists."[167] The lesson to be drawn from this verdict was that "the modern Ulster question may be said to have germinated on the 23rd of October, 1641."[168] Hamilton's narrative, replete with racist and sectarian overtones, dwelled on moments of crisis (1689–91, 1798) en route to its contemporary polemical relevance; his interpretation of Irish history, he assured his readers, "broadly explains the political attitude of the two sections of the population in that little understood province."[169]

Hamilton was at pains to stress that the distinction about which he wrote was racial rather than religious, yet he insisted that "the religion marks the race."[170] This stance might explain both his overt racism and his startling conclusion that Sinn Féin, as a secular organization, might still prove an effective vehicle for removing religion from Irish affairs and thereby nullifying Home Rule.[171] As matters stood, the Irish demand for Home Rule, as articulated from the 1870s onward, was little more than a reflection of Catholic ignorance. Among its manifest malignancies was the fact that it would slowly but surely provide the pretext for the dispossession (at the very least) of the Protestants of Ulster. For this and other reasons Hamilton glumly observed: "It is a pity that English politicians, who think to settle the Irish question with smirks and smiles, do not in the first instance make study of the historical facts which govern the situation. Through these they might then get not only a truer sense of values but an illuminating glimpse into the soul of the Irish people. They might ultimately arrive at the great truth that the soul of the native Irish has not at the present day changed by the width of a hair from what it was in 1641 and again in 1798."[172]

He expanded on this basic point in *The Irish Rebellion of 1641* (1920), a substantial account of 1641 that gave full expression to a litany of horrors and atrocities along very familiar lines.[173] Unsurprisingly, the reviewer for the *Catholic Bulletin* was suitably unimpressed:

> Though this is a book that will detract from the reputation of the firm of John Murray as a producer of solidly valuable works, it is not therefore without its value as an addition to the historian's library. It affords evidence of the type of apologetic history that it was still possible to write towards the close of the first quarter of the twentieth century, and that too by a man who vigorously disclaims all intention of writing apologetically . . . ; The balance of rights and wrongs must be restored by British writers showing more zeal, and Irish writers showing less, in substantiating and denouncing all atrocities committed by the other side. That is the keynote of the book.[174]

Though the *Catholic Bulletin* often displayed a sectarian historical bias, this reviewer made a reasonable point.

Hamilton's book was perhaps the last major work to articulate an account of 1641 that corresponded to the Protestant polemics that were such a dominant presence in the recurrent debates over the rebellion since the seventeenth century. (Hamilton later gave further expression to this perspective in fictional form.)[175] But such polemics had proven persuasive at some level. Perhaps inevitably, the crisis that accompanied the creation of the two Irish states saw the specter of 1641 being conjured in the chambers of the Northern Ireland parliament. The assassination of Sir Henry Wilson in May 1922 was interpreted as conclusive proof that the Provisional Government of the Free State was engaged in "a conspiracy against the Northern government." The unionist politician who made this accusation easily mined the distant past for political ammunition in present dangers: "Since 1641 Ulster has never been confronted with such a serious difficulty (Hon. Members: Hear, hear.) And the spirit that underlay the attack made on the Protestants of Ulster in 1641 is the spirit that animates the attack that is being made on Ulster to-day."[176] But nationalists could respond in kind. There was another tradition of remembrance, and it had not gone away either. During the course of a heated debate in the Belfast parliament on the Boundary Commission in 1925, the unionist members were castigated for the insincere and "conditional" nature of their loyalism. A Catholic nationalist representative took exception to a newspaper article suggesting that in 1641 "the Catholic people were proposing to extirpate the loyalists of Northern Ireland." He firmly contradicted this interpretation: "The editor, or the writer of that article, has quite evidently forgotten the fact that towards the close of the sixteenth century or at the beginning of the seventeenth century these people or their forefathers were dispossessed of the soil of Northern Ireland, and in 1641 all that the people were endeavouring to do was to attempt to regain possession of the soil of which they had been forcibly dispossessed."[177]

Such polarities long persisted. Perhaps the most eloquent commentary on the fixity of these beliefs is the fact that in 1936 (the same year in which Dudley Edwards hoped to save the projected publication of the depositions from the cost-cutting mandarins of the Department of Finance), John Milton's seventeenth-century assertion that 600,000 Protestants had been massacred in 1641 was repeated afresh and without qualification.[178] An indirect testament to the continuing vitality of such attitudes came when J. C. Beckett of Queen's University, Belfast, published a general history of Ireland in 1966. He skimmed over 1641 in a single equivocal passage and thereby dodged the debate; "great brutalities were committed," he wrote, but "popular propaganda" exaggerated them.[179] Thus, when just a year earlier Walter Love had made his acerbic observation about the two traditions continuing into the present day ("bombast and all"), he was hardly guilty of hyperbole. Indeed, if anyone was in a position to make such a pronouncement, Love was the person. He had chosen not to enter the ranks of disputation over what had or had not happened in 1641, and for a very simple reason: he had decided instead to examine how these interminable disputations might have some significance in and of themselves.

Walter Love's "Bloody Massacre"

Walter Love began work in earnest on his study of the historiography of 1641 in early 1964. The American Philosophical Society funded his research in Dublin. By his own admission Love could have seen virtually all of what he required in New York, Chicago, and the Huntington Library in California, but he assumed that a trip to Dublin would be "simpler and much more pleasant (I thought)," though he left no indication of what difficulties (if any) he may have encountered.[180] He seems to have ploughed a solitary furrow but was industrious in doing so; by the time of his death Love was confident that he had read virtually everything of significance to his project.[181]

With one exception, the few publications that emerged from Love's research covered broadly similar ground—Irish historical writing and antiquarianism in the latter half of the eighteenth century.[182] He seems to have arrived at this topic via Edmund Burke, whose own interest in Irish history was driven by an awareness that the Irish past was usually interpreted in polemical, sectarian terms.[183] Love's new scholarly trajectory saw him publish two articles on Irish antiquarianism in the late eighteenth century; these inevitably touched on the sectarian discourse that underpinned this antiquarianism.[184] While Love's book was never completed, the broad conclusions at which he arrived were presented in two papers presented in New York and San Francisco in March and December 1965, respectively. Only the latter was published,[185] but the broader interpretive thrust of his project had already been outlined in New York.[186]

Love was intensely aware that the issues he was treating were not confined to Ireland. His obvious inclination toward "scientific" history was at odds with what he saw as the polemical intentions of most of those who had written about 1641: "Their interest has always been in the question 'should' it have happened, and they have usually come to their study with a resounding answer—[an answer] already arrived at."[187] Love identified the two confessional traditions that had dictated the interpretation of the rebellion—one Catholic, the other Protestant. He argued that Temple's notorious *Irish Rebellion* was the keystone of the "Protestant" tradition—a tradition which, especially in the nineteenth century, had linked the allegations of a massacre of Protestants to the eventual Cromwellian settlement. This linkage struck Love forcefully: "Since the settlement was the basis for the social, economic, and religious situation in Ireland right through the nineteenth century, the massacre was used over and over again as justification for the [Protestant] establishment."[188]

The opposing Catholic historiographical tradition sought to undermine the implications of this connection by attempting to demonstrate gross Protestant exaggeration of the massacres or even to deny their existence. The writings of Curry and Mathew Carey were inevitably identified as having been key texts in the formulation of this perspective. Love remarked that "the Catholic tradition remained . . . a kind of outsiders' interpretation and protest, while the Protestant tradition belonged to the establishment and was a sort of official line."[189] Thus, according to the Protestant line of reasoning, if 1641 was the proof of Irish Catholic degeneracy, then the Cromwellian settlement was a justifiable punishment. Love collected material on Cromwellian massacres, especially the events at Drogheda, presumably to provide a counterpoint to Protestant accounts of 1641. There was another story of another massacre that could potentially be told.

While the rise of "scientific" history in the nineteenth century held out the possibility of determining what had actually happened in 1641, the contrasting writings of Prendergast and Froude ("a muscular Protestant if there ever was one"[190]) showed that its inflammatory utility was too potent to be discarded so easily. A resolution of the debate also proved to be beyond the grasp of Lecky, despite his dismissal of the wilder allegations of a massacre. For despite his veneer of scientific methodology, Lecky had not looked at the deposition himself.[191] Lecky's arguments, influential as they proved to be, simply derived from the "Curry-Carey" tradition.[192] The subsequent writings of Mary Hickson ("a stern and prim little lady, probably in a velvet hat"[193]) were a reaction to this "reinforcement" of the Catholic tradition, but her conclusion was that the Protestant tradition was right after all, and that the depositions proved that in 1641 there had indeed been a massacre of Protestants in Ireland.

The issue remained unresolved. Hence his exhortation to examine the depositions, given that "the study of the massacre itself" was a task "never properly done."[194] Yet it seems obvious from his papers that Love was unlikely to have undertaken this task himself. He certainly had an interest in the contentious contemporary accounts of the rebellion, but only insofar as they contrasted with perceptions of it after the event. He was primarily concerned with the texts that shaped his subject, though over time he became increasingly preoccupied with the vexing utility of the original depositions and with their relationship to published polemics.[195] His primary objective was to examine the manner in which 1641 had been reconstructed and represented in the centuries since its occurrence. The realities that preoccupied nineteenth-century scholars did not capture Love's attention. But this omission belies his own conception of his project. As the authors of one well-known text on historical methodologies put it: "The cliché that history must be rewritten every generation should therefore run somewhat differently: the past cannot help being reconceived by every generation, but the earlier reports upon it are in the main as good and true as they ever were. He who would know the full history of any period will do well to read its successive treatments, just as the ordinary researcher who would know the truth of a single incident seeks out all of its witnesses. The revisionism of historians, rightly considered, does not substitute; it subtracts a little and adds more." This striking set of statements struck a responsive chord with Love, prompting him to ask, "Will my study bear this out?"[196]

It was understandable that he should ask such questions. Love was an American scholar trained in an American academic environment, and the ideal of "objectivity" had been firmly enshrined in the American historical discipline since its professionalization in the latter decades of the nineteenth century—long before its Irish counterpart. Yet Love was by no means an unabashed advocate of nonjudgmental, value-free history: "I would like to have it, I think, but perhaps it is giving up too much."[197]

There is precious little in his surviving papers with which to posit any linkages to either intellectual developments or historiographical trends. The scattered jottings and musings that he committed to paper provide no clues as to what had brought him to the point he reached, for the nature of his subject was in itself at odds with the dominant tenor of contemporary Irish historiography. Love was attempting to write a study of two opposing historical paradigms, of what people *thought* had happened as opposed to what had actually occurred.[198] Love was convinced of the relevance and vitality of what he was trying to do, and the manner in which he conceived of his work and intended to present it was harnessed to a definite purpose:

> The subject of the massacre is of tremendous interest and importance in the study of humanity, which I regard as the ultimate [purpose] of [all] historical work. Lecky could look for the truth "somewhere in the middle" because he rejected as unbelievable all suggestions of really monstrous human behavior. In the twentieth century, with contemporary actions of great horror so well documented by photographs, [to speak only of the most irrefutable] evidence, and with a profounder sense than Lecky possessed of the wolf that lurks in every man, we are more impressed by what we are told of extreme behaviour. And we want to know more about it.[199]

His chosen topic provided a means by which he might do so, and in a fashion explicitly colored by an awareness of twentieth-century horrors. At the very least he "might find out a lot about three centuries of conflict in that broken world of Irish life by studying the historiography of the massacre,"[200] for the simple reason that its afterlife "has more of a reality in men's minds than in actual fact, and even when it is seen as a malignant nightmare, it has a certain kind of reality—something to be observed as a part of other men's minds that tells something about them, that they hate Irish Catholics."[201]

Ultimately, it was the conscious and unconscious mentalities underlying the divergent histories of 1641 that were his subject. The rebellion, he remarked with much reason, "was for some three centuries the most celebrated, discussed, and controversial event in Irish history."[202] But interestingly, he was not impressed by traditional studies of historiography, which he dismissed as "not much more than dictionaries of historians and their works, in some rough chronological order. The *story*, the connected development of modern historical consciousness, has not been written; and we have very little sense of how men in other ages conceived the past."[203]

If this was the case, it permitted some leeway in presenting the past to a contemporary audience. Love even considered the possibility of making a film, possibly a documentary, about his subject "to see what extra and different resources could be brought into the enterprise of trying to take account of the past."[204] He was acutely aware of the inherent dramatic potential of his material; he contemplated using depictions of the actual massacres, the taking of depositions, and the preaching of commemorative sermons; he even mulled over dramatic reconstructions of the presentation of the remonstrance provided by Henry Jones to the English House of Commons in 1642, not to mention Froude's controversial American lecture tour in 1871. Love considered using a broad range of visual imagery, making links from woodcuts depicting the Irish rebellion to those portraying the parallel events of the Thirty Years' War; he also thought about using images of atrocities from the Second World War by way of "analogy": "I do have a deposition somewhere that talks about people laid in graves like herrings, and this could be coupled with a bulldozer scene for the bodies," presumably images from the Nazi concentration camps.[205] He mused that this project might be of interest to the Hibernophile movie director John Huston and could potentially serve as a companion piece to his book.[206] As for the projected book, it would begin by addressing the vexing historiographical issues that had first taken shape in the 1640s; "then," he said, "it will be possible to go into the treatment that I have been thinking of where I simply ignore whether it is true or not and deal with the contexts which determine upholding the myth and trying to break it down."[207]

Love's notes for his unfinished book display an inevitable concentration on moments of crisis: the events of the 1640s and 1650s, the settlement of the 1660s, the Popish Plot, the Glorious Revolution, the Jacobite rebellions of 1715 and 1745, the Whiteboy agitations of the late eighteenth century, Catholic emancipation in the 1820s, the rise of Irish nationalism in the mid-nineteenth century, the emergence of Home Rule, and finally, the Froude-Hickson-Lecky debate toward the end of the nineteenth century.[208] Fragments of the text survive in his papers in Trinity College, the most notable of which is a draft of the opening chapter; it began with a description of the state ceremony that had supposedly so exercised John Curry on 23 October 1746. The other surviving drafts concern themselves with the major historiographical controversies about the nature of the rebellion, namely, those revolving around the scholarly activities of Curry and O'Conor in the eighteenth century, and those of Froude and Lecky in the nineteenth.[209] But Love's sudden death ensured that the book was never completed, and thus his professional valediction came at the end of the single article that he had published on the subject that so exercised him:

> What was needed, I think, was not a sacred veil but a settled history that could be accepted by both sides as conveying approximately what actually happened, whatever might still be controverted in the area of interpretation. But the study of the historiography of 1641 shows that such was not to be,

though that study points to such an eventuality soon. Too late, of course; I
hope not too little to write a happy ending to the story of the appearances
of the Bloody Massacre.[210]

He never had the chance to attempt to do so. No doubt the scholarship that has
appeared on the subject since the 1960s has touched on at least some of the
ground that Walter Love sought to cover. But his singular effort to extract
meaning from the subject to which he had devoted himself before his untimely
demise ensured that his unfinished book would inadvertently but inevitably
become part of that same history.

In the meantime 1641 continued to cast its shadow.

Conclusion

On 31 January 1866 Thomas MacKnight arrived in Ireland at Kingstown, now Dun Laoghaire. Having made his name in London as a journalist and political writer, he was in Ireland to become the new editor of Belfast's *Northern Whig*. The next day, 1 February, he made his way to Westland Row to take the train to Belfast, and he reminisced about the journey thirty years later.[1] An English liberal who was both an admirer and a biographer of Edmund Burke, MacKnight was—at least at this juncture—sympathetic to Irish Catholics and deeply hostile to Irish "Toryism" and "Orangeism," viewing the Protestants of Ulster as little more than an "English garrison" and opposing both the "Protestant ascendancy" of the Church of Ireland and the "territorial ascendancy" of the Irish land system.[2] He was intent, as he prepared to take up his new position, on promoting what he described as "liberal reform" in Ireland. It was perhaps ironic, then, that on his journey to Belfast MacKnight should meet with a representative of many of the things he professed to oppose. As the train stopped briefly at Portadown in County Armagh, a "tall and solemn clergyman" engaged him in conversation:

"Ah! . . . there was bad work here. Have you ever read Foxe's *Book of Martyrs?*"

Foxe's great work had undergone an enthusiastic (if contentious) revival among English evangelicals in the Victorian era.[3] But MacKnight was unaffected; he replied that he had not read it, to which his new companion exclaimed, "Every Protestant ought to read it."

"How do you know that I am a Protestant?" said MacKnight.

"I did not say you were," replied the clergyman laughing, "all I said was that every Protestant ought to read Foxe's *Book of Martyrs*."

Presumably for a man of MacKnight's principles, this exhortation to read the great martyrology was incongruous. "Perhaps I may not agree with you," he replied. "It may be as well not to keep alive memories of evil deeds when they foster religious animosities." The unnamed clergyman deduced that MacKnight was a liberal and revealed in turn that he was both a conservative and an Orangeman.

"You are a gentleman of strong convictions," said MacKnight.

"Very: we have strong convictions in the north of Ireland."

Silence descended on the journey. But some minutes later, the clergyman struck up the conversation once again and began to discuss the "education controversy"—the issue of religious instruction in the Irish National School system. Indeed, this was essentially the reason for the clergyman's journey, as he was en route to address a meeting on this very subject in Belfast's Victoria Hall. He opposed any restrictions on religious instruction, being of the view that the National Schools were godless in the first place, but he was particularly concerned that behind the educational reforms being considered by the incumbent Liberal government lay the hand of the Catholic church. It was at this point that the train journey provided the clergyman with a more explicit reminder of why Catholicism should be opposed. As they passed Lurgan, he observed, "This town was all but destroyed in the rebellion of 1641. That was a frightful time. It showed what popery can do."

As a biographer of Edmund Burke, MacKnight responded by pointing out that "Burke always maintained that the rebellion of 1641 had been provoked by almost unbearable tyranny."

"Oh, did he? Well he knew nothing at all on the subject."

Having dismissed Burke, MacKnight's companion warmed to his theme as the train passed the bleaching fields of Lisburn. "This town too was destroyed in the rebellion of 1641. The Huguenots who were driven out of France when the Edict of Nantes was revoked did much for the trade of Lisburn. You can yet see the tombstones of these Huguenots who were obliged to leave their native country. This will show you what the Roman Catholics are."

MacKnight seemed unfazed in the face of such strident and presumably unfamiliar opinions. "It seems to me," he said, "that in Ireland you have good memories."

"Yes, sir, we have. We forget nothing."

"Would it not be better sometimes to forget?"

"Not at all under such circumstances," said the clergyman. "Macaulay says: 'A people which takes no pride in the achievements of remote ancestors will never achieve anything worthy to be remembered by remote descendants.' I have often quoted the sentence at our Twelfth of July meetings."

"But," replied MacKnight, "Macaulay was a liberal, and I think he added some qualifying words."

"Such qualifications are of little consequence, but here we are in Belfast."

And with that MacKnight's companion brought the conversation to an end. The train had indeed arrived in Belfast, and their time together was over. The clergyman disembarked and bid MacKnight goodbye.

Aside from his opinions, the reason for his journey, and the fact that he was from the "north of Ireland," MacKnight left no indication as to who this clergyman was, to what denomination he belonged, where he was from, or even where he got on the train. Writing thirty years after the encounter, the journalist may have allowed such details to fall by the wayside, or he may have ignored them for the sake of discretion. But MacKnight could possibly have recast the conversation for rhetorical purposes as a fitting introduction to a memoir in which he recounted his three decades of involvement in the public affairs of Ulster. In his journey toward Belfast he was introduced to a living embodiment of certain beliefs that had helped to shape Irish affairs since the middle of the seventeenth century, and that would continue to do so for the remainder of the nineteenth century and beyond. The quote from Macaulay that the clergyman reserved for traveling English liberals and the Twelfth of July came from the conclusion of his famous account of the siege and relief of Derry. Writing in the 1850s, Macaulay had indeed observed that "a people which takes no pride in the noble achievements of remote ancestors will never achieve anything worthy to be remembered with pride by remote descendants."[4] But as MacKnight correctly observed, Macaulay had immediately qualified it by commenting, "It is impossible for the moralist or the statesman to look with unmixed complacency on the solemnities with which Londonderry commemorates her deliverance." As he had tartly added, "Unhappily, the animosities of her brave champions have descended with their glory."[5]

Macaulay correctly observed that commemorating the siege helped to perpetuate sectarian strife. MacKnight may have had a point when he suggested that the past was best forgotten. But it was revealing both that the clergyman had dismissed this suggestion and that MacKnight later recalled it. The Siege of Derry, along with the slightly later Battle of the Boyne, became the events to remember par excellence in the pantheon and commemorative calendar of Protestant Ulster and Protestant Ireland.[6] Yet the entire point of commemorating the siege by the Catholic forces of James II was that it had failed. The Protestants within the walls of the "maiden city" had survived, but the city had become a haven for them in the first place precisely because they feared that they might be exterminated. The 1641 rebellion had provided the template for this fear; the recollection of the earlier event lurked behind the siege. Over a century after MacKnight's train journey, in 1989, the prominent Ulster unionist politician David Trimble told another audience in Belfast that "one of the enduring folk memories of the Ulster-British people is the fear of massacre—the fear that the people may cease to be, at least culturally."[7] This portentous comment may provide a clue as to why in 1991 the Orange Order in Portadown produced a video that explicitly compared 1641 to the Nazi Holocaust and asserted that what was presumed to have happened in 1641 was still crucial to understanding the "siege mentality of the Ulster Protestant."[8] This mentality surely is a significant element of an identity embraced by those who have perceived themselves (rightly or wrongly) as having being *under siege*. The point was made in a less measured fashion by Peter Robinson, deputy leader of the Democratic Unionist Party (and future First Minister of Northern Ireland) in 1988, when he wrote: "It was on Saturday, 23 October 1641, that the Catholic Irish had commenced an evil campaign of genocide . . . ; Over 100,000 were killed in a period of months. Hanging and burning were common, but stories surfaced of how children had been boiled to death, pregnant women split open, men buried alive, and hundreds drowned in rivers . . . ; Among the leading butchers were those who had long been regarded as 'friendly Irish,' an early term equivalent of today's 'moderate Catholics.'"[9] The willingness, at least in some quarters, to extract such disturbing notions from the past and apply them to the present was not dispelled by the "peace process" of the 1990s. One Protestant mural painted in Belfast at some point after the Good Friday Agreement of April 1998 contained an oblique depiction of what was termed the "persecution of the Protestant people by the Church of Rome [in] 1600." Within the mural was the declaration, "The ethnic cleansing still goes on today."[10] Though the date of 1600 was incorrect, both the message and the image of Protestant bodies scattered in the fields of Ulster echoed a particular version of 1641, updated to speak to a new dispensation.

   Perhaps this plasticity is the key to understanding the continued potency of such beliefs about 1641. Over three hundred years earlier, in November 1682, William Brooke of Portadown responded to a query from Dudley Loftus in Dublin about how many had actually been killed in Portadown in 1641. Brooke's answer, culled from his inquiries into an event still on the fringe of living memory, was that "7 score was the full number that lost their lives in that inhuman butchery, they too consisting for the most part of women and children, their husbands being sacrificed to a more early rage."[11] But this glimpse of reality made no impression; the version of 1641 that it contradicted spoke to the present with far greater force than Brooke's response ever would. Down through the generations little seems to have changed.

   From this consideration of the recent and much more distant past in the north of Ireland, we turn to the present. In 2001 the Irish historian Nicholas Canny

Loyalist mural, Hopewell Crescent, East Belfast, 1990s. (courtesy of Professor Bill Rolston)

published a colossal study of colonization in early modern Ireland, one that culminated with an account of 1641 that amply demonstrated the basis for Protestant fears that they were to be massacred by outlining the nature and extent of the violence directed at the settlers in 1641.[12] The depiction of the colonial experience contained in Canny's *Making Ireland British* was unprecedented in scope. When 1641 had attracted the attention of scholars in the latter decades of the twentieth century, the studies that resulted were, more often than not, relatively modest in scale. There had been numerous examinations of how the rebellion had been depicted in contemporary print culture,[13] along with studies of canonical authors such as Jones and Temple.[14] Other scholars tried to make sense of the cultural significance of the rebellion, sometimes extending their analysis beyond the seventeenth century as they did so.[15] Occasionally, studies of later periods touched on the significance of 1641.[16] And there had also been a number of studies of the historiography of the rebellion; these covered at least some of the ground that Walter Love had tried to make his own.[17] But they were studies of 1641 after the fact; what made Canny's contribution significant was that he had provided a massive account of the "insurrection" (as he termed it) itself, and that he had based it firmly on the depositions.

The notion of examining the depositions was usually observed in the breach rather than the observance. But the vexing question of finding out what had actually happened in 1641 (and von Ranke's dictum was borrowed by Canny and applied to this very question[18]) could only be answered by examining them. Canny was one of a tiny handful of scholars in the late twentieth century to examine the depositions in any great depth. Aidan Clarke of Trinity College devoted a considerable amount of time to a forensic examination of the collection in the 1980s. But while this inquiry would later inform Trinity's transcription and digitization project, of which Clarke was the principal editor, Canny's *Making Ireland British* was without precedent; no other historian had published a study that examined the rebellion in such detail, and Canny went far beyond anyone else in the manner in which he did so. As he argued, the depositions "constitute the only detailed information we have of what happened in Ireland during and immediately subsequent to October 1641."[19] Yet in Canny's view their significance in this regard remained neglected even by those scholars who had sought to examine the eruption of the rebellion with an appropriate level of scholarly sophistication, for "rather than study what actually happened in 1641, most academic historians have striven to explain why a major political disruption occurred in Ireland in 1641."[20] This contention was applicable to a number of studies arguing that the rebellion was precipitated by the crisis that had gripped the three Stuart kingdoms in the years immediately prior to 1641—an interpretative strategy that tended to emphasize short-term rather than long-run factors.[21]

Making Ireland British contained an unprecedented reconstruction of the course of events in 1641, based on an equally unprecedented forensic interrogation of the depositions. This systematic approach had two consequences. The first was that it enabled Canny to construct a remarkably sophisticated and richly detailed portrait of colonial society and the colonial economy in the years prior to 1641.[22] This in itself was a departure from the norm. Prior to the publication of Canny's work the most significant recent study of 1641 had been that of Michael Perceval-Maxwell, who used the depositions, along with a good deal of other source material, to construct a detailed narrative of the outbreak of the rebellion.[23] Canny, on the other hand, worked backward, using the depositions to shed light not merely on the course of events in 1641 but also on the realities of life in plantation Ireland. Thomas Fitzpatrick had first noted the potential value of the depositions for economic and social history in 1909, but Canny was the first scholar to mine them for that purpose in any substantive way (though his past approach in this matter had been subjected to some criticism).[24]

The second consequence of Canny's endeavors was that it allowed him to state with considerable authority that "while there may have been no 'massacre' in Ireland in 1641, there was certainly an outburst of Catholic fury which concentrated upon the expulsion of Protestants from within the Catholic community and the destruction of objects and places associated with Protestants and Protestantism. . . . This movement was unquestionably encouraged by priests and was marked by the involvement of women and children."[25] Canny's concentration on what had occurred on the ground in Ireland, as opposed to the machinations of high politics across three kingdoms, strongly suggested that the outbreak of the rebellion was prompted, at least in part, by simmering resentments that had accumulated over a much longer time among the dispossessed and fearful, eventually bursting forth with ferocious consequences. In this reading the 1641 rising was scarcely the product of recent circumstances.

This was a judgment that could be soundly based only on a thorough examination of the depositions. The very fact that a book such as Canny's could rightly be described as unprecedented in its use of the depositions is a sobering testament to the unreality of the debates about the nature of 1641 that had persisted over the centuries. And this sharp dichotomy brings us back to the point from which this study began, with the launch by Mary McAleese and Ian Paisley of digitized transcripts of the depositions that ensured for the first time that they could be fully accessible to scrutiny.

The transcription and digitization of the 1641 depositions was carried out between 2007 and 2010; the work was based primarily in Trinity College Dublin, with the involvement of both Irish and British funding bodies (the costs were in the region of €1 million), along with participation from the universities of Aberdeen and Cambridge.[26] According to Jane Ohlmeyer of Trinity College, who was one of the principal investigators on this remarkably sophisticated project, "what is so interesting about them [the depositions] is what they tell us about ordinary life in early seventeenth-century Ireland, albeit from the perspective largely of the Protestant community, the planter community." Also very revealing is "the indirect evidence that they give us into Gaelic Ireland or Catholic Ireland . . . and [into] the relationships that were enjoyed by the communities on the ground," even if the one-sided nature of the depositions requires (as Canny's critics had pointed out) that they must be handled with great caution.[27] But, says Ohlmeyer, "the end result . . . will give us a much fuller picture of the social, economic, religious, political, [and] military history of seventeenth-century Ireland."[28] This is a reasonable assumption in view of the example set by Canny. Indeed, the project could yet prove to have relevance far beyond Ireland. Perhaps, according to Ohlmeyer, the Irish experience of "ethnic cleansing, massacre, and atrocity," as reflected in the depositions, could be used "to speak to audiences in parts of the world today that are grappling with these issues."[29] This comment inexorably brings us back to the manner in which further study of the depositions might reshape the Catholic and Protestant interpretations of what happened in Ireland in 1641, with all the meanings that were attached to them. "This sort of project can promote understanding," observes Ohlmeyer, "and in that sense [it] is hugely important in terms of where we are [as] a political nation as we move forward in a very different world. . . . In terms of the project we are only approaching it in the spirit of wanting to promote dialogue and scholarly debate in a very constructive way. I would be very disappointed if this became sectarianised in any form or fashion. Because that is not what this project is about."[30]

The prospect that publishing the depositions in their entirety might salve an historic wound was the reason why McAleese and Paisley launched the project together. Indeed, even from the outset it had been greeted with occasionally breathless newspaper reports trumpeting the message that "one of the most hotly disputed controversies of Irish history may finally be settled" by "the ultimate cold-case investigation."[31] Perhaps it will, and if so, the debate about 1641 will have come full circle. But future study of what the depositions actually contain will require the most scrupulous care from researchers, and even then there will be limits to what is possible. The project was overseen on a day-to-day basis by Ohlmeyer's predecessor, Aidan Clarke, whose own examinations of the depositions have led to more tempered conclusions. One outcome of the publication of the depositions might be a set of calculations relating to the actual death toll from the rebellion. Given that the depositions are by their nature an incomplete and partial source, how might anyone derive trustworthy answers to the unresolved question of how many Protestants or Catholics were really killed in 1641? As Clarke observed, "we . . . need to keep in mind the confusion that the debate itself has created between what happened in the rebellion and the evidence of what happened."[32] The incompleteness of the evidence necessarily means that a full accounting of the death toll is unattainable. The depositions are indeed studded with incidents amounting to microhistories that are by their very nature "representative of nothing but themselves"; the bigger picture remains elusive.[33] Whether or not the new availability of the depositions will eventually shatter the long-cherished assumptions about what actually occurred in Ireland in 1641 is a question best left for another day. After all, as Clarke has pointed out, "the historiographical concentration on massacre had more to do with national and religious stereotyping than with history."[34] To paraphrase T. W. Moody, it remains to be seen whether "history" will triumph over "myth." Which will prove the stronger?

In the meantime there are enduring meanings to be elicited from the differing versions of the same events of 1641. Though Seamus Deane has rightly criticized Moody's "rudimentary dichotomy between myth and fact," it could also be argued that in the controversies over 1641 and its legacy the two went hand in hand.[35] The rising of 1641 defined the historical legitimacy of Ireland's two main religious communities; the divisions between them were "sectarian" (having to do with politics and culture) rather than theological, and the divergent versions of the rebellion that have been the subject of this book stayed remarkably constant throughout the turbulent course of Irish history. This fixity had a great deal to do with the nature of the communities that found those differing interpretations congenial. In the words of John Gillis, "The core meaning of any group identity, namely, a sense of sameness over time and space, is sustained by remembering."[36] Needless to say, what was being "remembered" did not have to bear any relation to reality. Facts were unlikely to get in the way of a tale when what was imagined could seem as traumatic to later generations as what had actually happened.[37] The 1641 revolt was of greater relevance to Irish Protestants since they had been the chief victims. It was an insurrection that had been directed at them. The Protestant interpretation remained valid through the centuries because it seemed to foreshadow the crises and predicaments that many Protestants of later eras felt that they continued to face in their own times.

The same could not be said for the opposing Catholic perspective, which was essentially a reaction to its Protestant counterpart. While the Protestant interpretation was detached from the broader pattern of Irish history, to be held up as a lurid beacon to the present, the opposite happened to its Catholic counterpart. As Irish nationalists defined their own past in terms of what Roy Foster has described as "a story of Ireland, with plot, narrative logic, and desired outcome," the Catholic version of 1641 was subsumed into a narrative of a nation on the march.[38] It was inevitable, then, that other events would take precedence over it. After 1922 the recollection of 1641 was of more significance to Protestants in the new statelet of Northern Ireland than to their coreligionists in the Irish Free State. But perhaps this is not a neutral issue. A southern Protestant (Brian Inglis) who wrote an admittedly brief account of Irish history told his readers that "when rebellion broke out in 1641, it took the form of an uprising of the Catholic gentry and peasants in Ulster, who were seizing the opportunity to take back the land which had been ejected by plantation and were little concerned with constitutional niceties."[39] Inglis mentioned no massacres—perhaps a discreet but deliberate omission, the better to avoid unwelcome controversy in a state that was not automatically congenial toward many of its Protestant inhabitants?[40] The 1641 rising cast no end of a shadow.

In the 1930s the Belfast poet John Hewitt wrote *The Bloody Brae*, a dramatic poem in which John Hill, an old soldier who had participated in the massacre at Islandmagee, remains wracked with guilt decades later and tries to tell his tale:

> Whenever the Irish meet with the Planters' breed
> there's always a sword between and black
> memories for both.[41]

Hill encounters the ghost of Bridget Magee, a young woman he killed at the Gobbin cliffs and whose forgiveness he implores, as,

> I murdered pity when I murdered you,
> and reason and mercy and hope for this vexed land.
> There was time that mercy should have appeared,
> if ever, between the clashing of our peoples,
> and from that mercy kindness seized a chance
> to weave together the broken halves of this land,
> to throw his shuttle across the separate threads,
> and make us a glittering web for God's delight,
> with joy in the placing of colours side by side.
> That sword-thrust made our opposition for ever,
> judged not me only but my kin and yours.[42]

Hill receives his forgiveness, but his victim enters a caveat:

> I have said that I pardon you. But the sword's edge
> Is marked with blood for ever. I am dead
> Who might have mothered crowding generations:
> For good or ill you altered the shape of things.
> You said there was a time for mercy once,
> but every moment is the time for mercy.

It is tempting to think of this story as a neat inversion of the ghosts at Portadown returning from the afterlife to demand vengeance; Bridget Magee returns instead with a warning for posterity. Hewitt came from a Protestant background but was a lifelong socialist; his ideological leanings might explain the reconciliatory undertone of *The Bloody Brae*, with its pregnant hope that the future might not remain in thrall to the past. But a very different vignette suggests the manner in which such hopes could be dashed. In the 1970s, as the Canadian historian Donald Akenson researched the history of Islandmagee in the nineteenth century, he was struck by the persistence of folklore pertaining to a massacre of Catholics within an overwhelmingly Presbyterian community. He mischievously concluded that within "the false history of a non-existent massacre . . . something else was at play, keeping the tale alive. The anti-Catholicism of an impacted Protestant community must have been contributory. And in a more general sense the instinctive exclusiveness of an isolated parish was involved: the cleansing of the community of alien elements left a pure community. A tiny, rural *herrenvolk* myth had been established."[43]

Such a slender thread could carry the heaviest of meanings.

The rebellion that erupted in Ireland in October 1641 is the single most notorious sequence of violence in what scholars now recognize as a remarkably violent era.[44] Stripped of the complexity of its background, the technical reality of an Irish Catholic rebellion against a British Protestant colony meant that the battle lines were drawn on religious grounds, especially as these lines emerged even more brightly with the benefit of hindsight. To claim that any one ethnic or religious group constituted the only victims of its violence is ludicrous, for there was no monopoly on violence in Ireland in 1641, or indeed at any other time. But the assumption that there was one played a part in shaping Ireland's history in the centuries after the event, as 1641 remained part of the recurring process by which Ireland's past was interrogated to give meaning and purpose to its present. What was considered the salvation of Ireland's Protestants at the Boyne in July 1690 was arguably salvation from the recurrence of an earlier catastrophe that was seen to afflict them, and them alone. But from a Catholic perspective, there was another tale to tell, of another catastrophe; it too would be told. And given the perennial reminders of historic divisions that become visible in Northern Ireland every summer, it should be borne in mind that behind 1690, and much else besides, lies the enduring shadow of 1641.

Notes

Introduction

1. The phrase was coined by the journalist Eoghan Harris in the course of the 1997 Irish presidential election; while he continued to affirm the statement as an expression of his view of McAleese at the time, he later admitted that her presidency had not conformed to his prediction and that she had "allayed my fears and aroused my admiration and even affection" (*Sunday Independent*, 19 June 2011).

2. *Irish Daily Mail*, 23 Oct. 2010; *Irish Times*, 23 Oct. 2010.

3. The terminology reflects differing interpretations. As William J. Smyth put it, "from most Irish points of view the event is an uprising; from the British point of view it is a rebellion." See William J. Smyth, *Map-Making, Landscapes, and Memory: A Geography of Colonial and Early Modern Ireland, c. 1530–1750* (Cork, 2006), 105. The use of the term "rebellion" in the title of the current work is based on its definition in the *Oxford American Dictionary* as "an act of violent or open resistance to an established government or order"—a definition that is sufficiently neutral to be appropriate to the events of 1641. For detailed modern accounts of 1641, on which my discussion draws freely, see Michael Perceval-Maxwell, *The Outbreak of the Irish Rebellion of 1641* (Montreal, 1994); Nicholas Canny, *Making Ireland British, 1580–1650* (Oxford, 2001), 461–550; Smyth, *Map-Making, Landscapes, and Memory*, 103–65.

4. Brian Mac Cuarta, "Religious Violence against Settlers in South Ulster, 1641–2," in *Age of Atrocity: Violent Death and Political Conflict in Early Modern Ireland*, ed. David Edwards, Padraig Lenihan, and Clodagh Tait (Dublin, 2007), 154–75.

5. *A Brief Narrative of the Several Popish Treasons and Cruelties against the Protestants in England, France, and Ireland* (London, [1678]), 1.

6. Ibid., 4–5.

7. Cited in David Fitzpatrick, "'I Will Acquire an Attitude Not Yours': Was Frederick Macniece a Home Ruler and Why Does This Matter?" *Field Day Review* 4 (2008): 160.

8. A. T. Q. Stewart, *The Narrow Ground: Aspects of Ulster, 1609–1969* (London, 1977), 48–49.

9. Walter Love, "Charles O'Conor of Belanagare and Thomas Leland's 'Philosophical' History of Ireland," *Irish Historical Studies* 13, no. 49 (Mar. 1962): 1.

10. See Toby Barnard, "The Uses of the 23rd of October 1641 and Irish Protestant Celebrations," *English Historical Review* 106 (Oct. 1991): 889–920; James Kelly, "'The Glorious and Immortal Memory': Commemoration and Protestant Identity in Ireland, 1660–1800," *Proceedings of the Royal Irish Academy* 94C/2 (1994): 25–52.

11. See [John Curry], *A Brief Account from the Most Authentic Protestant Writers of the Causes, Motives, and Mischiefs of the Irish Rebellion on the 23rd Day of October 1641, Deliver'd in a Dialogue between a Dissenter and a Member of the Church of Ireland as by Law Established* (London, 1747); idem, *Historical Memoirs of the Irish Rebellion in the Year 1641; Extracted from Parliamentary Journals, State-Acts, and the Most Eminent Protestant Historians . . . in a Letter to Walter Harris, Esq.* (London, 1758); idem, *Occasional Remarks on Certain Passages in Dr. Leland's History of Ireland Relative to the Irish Rebellion in 1641* (London, 1778); idem, *An Historical and Critical Review of the Civil Wars in Ireland from the Reign of Queen Elizabeth to the Settlement Under King William* (Dublin, 1775).

12. Walter Love, "The Irish Massacre of 1641: An Historiographical Study ('Paper to Be Delivered at the Conference on Irish Studies, 20 March 1965, New York City')," unpublished typescript dated 26 Feb. 1965, Trinity College Dublin (TCD) MSS 7,233–5, f. 108.

13. *Irish Independent*, 23 Oct. 2010.

14. Extensive details on the compilation and arrangement of the depositions, upon which I have drawn for this discussion, are to be found on the project website: http://1641.tcd.ie/ (accessed 17 Jan. 2010). The most comprehensive discussion of their technicalities is in the introduction to the forthcoming edition of the depositions being prepared under the general editorship of Aidan Clarke, to be published by the Irish Manuscripts Commission from 2013 onwards. I would like to thank Professor Clarke for providing me with an early draft of this work. At the time of writing, the standard description of the collection currently in print is Aidan Clarke, "The 1641 Depositions," in *Treasures of the Library: Trinity College Dublin*, ed. Peter Fox (Dublin, 1986), 111–22.

15. Interview with Jane Ohlmeyer, 17 Nov. 2010.

16. The fullest account of the complex relationship between the depositions and the representation of the rebellion in seventeenth-century print culture is Eamon Darcy, "Politics, Pogroms, and Print: The 1641 Depositions and Contemporary Print Culture" (Ph.D. dissertation, Trinity College Dublin, 2009).

17. TCD MSS 7,236–8, f. 244. The citation from the relevant edition is Guiseppe Tomasi di Lampedusa, *The Leopard* (London, 1960), 250.

18. For these and other biographical details I am indebted to Karl Bottigheimer. I would like to thank Professor Bottigheimer for sharing his recollections of Walter Love with me.

19. For Love and his unfinished project, see John Gibney, "Walter Love's 'Bloody

Massacre': An Unfinished Study in Irish Cultural History, 1641–1963," *Proceedings of the Royal Irish Academy* 110C (2010): 217–37.

20. Love's notes have been retained in TCD MSS 7,231–8.

21. The three dissertations that he had written as a graduate student were all of an historiographical nature: Walter D. Love, "The Philosophy of History of Alfred North Whitehead" (M.A. thesis, University of Chicago, 1950); idem, "Theories of History in England, 1550–1625" (M.A. thesis, University of California, 1952); idem, "Edmund Burke's Historical Thought" (Ph.D. dissertation, University of California, Berkeley, 1956). Love also published a monograph, presumably based on his doctoral thesis, titled *Edmund Burke's Idea of the Body Corporate: A Study in Imagery* (Notre Dame, 1965).

22. TCD MSS 7,236–8, f. 1,151–264.

23. Ibid., f. 1,258.

24. Ibid.

25. Ibid.

26. Ibid., f. 1,259.

27. Ibid., f. 266.

28. Valuable introductions to the subject that avoid such pitfalls are Ciaran Brady, "'Constructive and Instrumental': The Dilemma of Ireland's First 'New Historians,'" in *Interpreting Irish History: The Debate on Historical Revisionism, 1938–1994*, ed. Ciaran Brady (Dublin, 1994), 3–31, and Nicholas Canny, "Historians, Moral Judgement, and National Communities: The Irish Dilemma," *European Review* 14, no. 3 (2006): 401–10. The most comprehensive study of twentieth-century Irish historiography is Evi Gkotzaridis, *Trials of Irish History: Genesis and Evolution of a Reappraisal, 1938–2000* (London, 2006). Although this work contains much valuable material, it is extremely tendentious and should be treated with caution. For a polemical critique of "revisionism," see Kevin Whelan, "The Revisionist Debate in Ireland," *Boundary 2*, 31 (2004): 179–205. For a broader debate touching on the wider epistemological implications of "revisionism" (and much more besides), see Guy Beiner and Joep Leerssen, "Why Irish History Starved: A Virtual Historiography," *Field Day Review* 3 (2007): 67–81.

29. T. W. Moody, "Irish History and Irish Mythology," in Brady, *Interpreting Irish History*, 71–86.

30. William Carleton, *Traits and Stories of the Irish Peasantry* (2 vols., 1979 Garland facsimile edition), 1:199.

31. *Ordnance Survey Memoirs of Ireland: Vol. 22: Parishes of Co. Londonderry VI, 1831, 1833, 1835–6*, ed. Angélique Day and Patrick McWilliams (Belfast and Dublin, 1993), 15.

32. Carleton, *Traits and Stories*, 1:viii–ix.

33. Gustave de Beaumont, *Ireland: Social, Political, and Religious*, ed. W. C. Taylor (Cambridge, MA, 2006), 123.

34. Useful methodological overviews of these concepts are to be found in Alon Confino, "Collective Memory and Cultural History: Problems of Method," *American Historical Review* 102, no. 5 (1997): 1385–1403, and Wulf Kansteiner, "Finding Meaning in Memory: A Methodological Critique of Collective Memory Studies," *History and*

Theory 41 (2002): 179–97. For a recent synthesis of the voluminous literature on this subject, see Geoffrey Cubitt, *History and Memory* (Manchester, 2007).

35. Graham Dawson, *Making Peace with the Past? Memory, Trauma, and the Irish Troubles* (Manchester, 2007), 12.

36. Ibid., 13.

37. Paul Connerton, *How Societies Remember* (Cambridge, 1989), 13.

38. There is a strong case to be made that the allegedly value-free history expounded by such figures as Dudley Edwards and Moody was inherently conservative even by the standards of the 1930s. See Whelan, "Revisionist Debate in Ireland," 184–87. It should be said that in later phases of their careers Edwards and Moody were quite open to methodological innovation and became more willing to engage with contemporary events, as illustrated by their involvement in the Bureau of Military History set up by the Irish government to collect oral testimony from participants in the Irish "revolution" of 1913–21. See Gkotzaridis, *Trials of Irish History*, chap. 5.

39. David Gross, *The Past in Ruins: Tradition and the Critique of Modernity* (Amherst, 1992), 80.

40. Guy Beiner, *Remembering the Year of the French: Irish Folk History and Social Memory* (Madison, 2007).

41. Toby Barnard, "Reading in Eighteenth-Century Ireland: Public and Private Pleasures," in *The Experience of Reading: Irish Historical Perspectives*, ed. Bernadette Cunningham and Máire Kennedy (Dublin, 1999), 63.

42. Gerard Boate, *A Natural History of Ireland in Three Parts* (Dublin, 1755 [NLI IR 9141 B 10]), 5.

43. For example, see Toby Barnard, "Gathering Ideas: A Clerical Library in County Cork, 1774," in *Print Culture and Intellectual Life in Ireland, 1660–1941: Essays in Honour of Michael Adams*, ed. Martin Fanning and Raymond Gillespie (Dublin, 2006), 24–52.

44. Raymond Gillespie, "Temple's Fate: Reading *The Irish Rebellion* in Late Seventeenth-Century Ireland," in *British Interventions in Early Modern Ireland*, ed. Ciaran Brady and Jane Ohlmeyer (Cambridge, 2005), 324.

45. Jacques Le Goff, *History and Memory* (New York and Oxford, 1992), 58.

46. Pierre Nora, "Introduction: Between Memory and History," in *Realms of Memory: Contrasting the French Past* (3 vols., New York, 1996–98), 1:7.

47. James McConnel, "Remembering the 1605 Gunpowder Plot in Ireland," *Journal of British Studies* 50, no. 4 (Oct. 2011): 863–91; Ian McBride, *The Siege of Derry in Ulster Protestant Mythology* (Dublin, 1997); *The Sieges of Derry*, ed. William Kelly (Dublin, 2001); Kevin Whelan, *The Tree of Liberty: Radicalism, Catholicism, and the Construction of Irish Identity, 1760–1830* (Cork, 1996); Beiner, *Remembering the Year of the French*; Clair Wills, *Dublin 1916: The Siege of the GPO* (London, 2009); Anne Dolan, *Commemorating the Irish Civil War: History and Memory, 1923–2000* (Cambridge, 2003).

48. Kevin Cramer, *The Thirty Years War and German Memory in the Nineteenth Century* (Lincoln, 2007), 219.

49. Love, "The Irish Massacre of 1641: An Historiographical Study."

50. See Marianne Elliott, *When God Took Sides: Religion and Identity in Ireland* (Oxford, 2009), 65–68, 89, 139, 143, 218, 220.

51. TCD MSS 7,233–5, f. 125.

52. Hiram Morgan, "News from Ireland: Catalan, Portuguese, and Castilian Pamphlets on the Confederate War in Ireland," in *Ireland 1641: Contexts and Reactions*, ed. Jane Ohlmeyer and Micheál Ó Siochrú (Manchester, forthcoming). My thanks to Dr. Morgan for providing me with a copy of this article prior to its publication.

Chapter 1. "The Sad Story of Our Miseries"

1. John Gamble, *A View of Society and Manners in the North of Ireland in the Summer and Autumn of 1812* (London, 1813), 264–65. For Gamble, his travels in Ireland, and his accounts of them, see Breandán Mac Suibhne, "Afterworld: The Gothic Travels of John Gamble (1770–1831)," *Field Day Review* 4 (2008): 63–113.

2. Alfred Webb, *The Alleged Massacre of 1641* (London, 1887), 19.

3. Quoted in Conrad Russell, *The Fall of the British Monarchies, 1637–1642* (Oxford, 1991), 373.

4. Historical Manuscripts Commission (HMC), *Calendar of the Manuscripts of the Marquess of Ormonde* (8 vols., London, 1902–20) new ser., 2:7.

5. Ibid., 8.

6. Ibid., 12.

7. Ibid., 14.

8. Ibid., 18.

9. Ibid., 35.

10. Joad Raymond, *Pamphlets and Pamphleteering in Early Modern Britain* (Cambridge, 2004), 197–99; Keith J. Lindley, "The Impact of the 1641 Rebellion upon England and Wales, 1641–45," *Irish Historical Studies* 18, no. 70 (Sept. 1972): 144. According to Iain Donovan, "the 'typical' pamphlet is a letter from Ireland written by a gentleman from Dublin whose name is known but not well-known. It was printed in 1642 by an anonymous Londoner and sold by a publisher who is not renowned for a special interest in Irish affairs. And its half a dozen pages tell of widespread atrocities acted upon the Protestant settlers by the Catholic rebels, yet it provides concrete details of only a few isolated incidents." See Iain Donovan, "'Bloody News from Ireland': The Pamphlet Literature of the Irish Massacres of the 1640s" (M.Litt. thesis, Trinity College Dublin, 1995), 84. The technical details of the pamphlets are also outlined by Donovan, ibid., 57–84.

11. Lindley, "Impact of the 1641 Rebellion," 149. See also Joseph Cope, *England and the 1641 Irish Rebellion* (Woodbridge, 2009).

12. Thomas Crofton Croker, ed., *Narratives Illustrative of the Contests in Ireland in 1641 and 1690* (London, 1841), 16.

13. Important local studies of Armagh and Fermanagh are, respectively, Hilary Simms, "Violence in County Armagh," in *Ulster 1641: Aspects of the Rising*, ed. Brian Mac Cuarta (Belfast, 1997), 123–38; Charlene McCoy, "War and Revolution: County

Fermanagh and Its Borders, c. 1640–c. 1666" (Ph.D. dissertation, Trinity College, Dublin, 2007).

14. This is the subject of Darcy, "Politics, Pogroms, and Print."

15. *The Last Newes from Ireland* (London, 1641), [A3].

16. For a particularly lurid example of this kind of trope, see *The Antichristian Principle Fully Discovered* (London, 1679). The international context of such representations is explored in Cope, *England and the 1641 Irish Rebellion*, 76–101, and Darcy, "Politics, Pogroms, and Print," 167–222.

17. Ethan Howard Shagan, "Constructing Discord: Ideology, Propaganda, and English Responses to the Irish Rebellion of 1641," *Journal of British Studies* 36 (1997): 7, 9–17.

18. TCD MSS 7,236–8, ff. 400–409; Walter Love, "Civil War in Ireland: Appearances in Three Centuries of Historical Writing," *Emory University Quarterly* 22 (1966): 60–61.

19. *A Copy of a Letter Concerning the Traitorous Conspiracy of the Rebels in Ireland* (London, 1641), A5. See also *A True and Full Relation of the Horrible and Hellish Plot* (London, 1641).

20. For O'Connally's testimony, see TCD MS 809, ff. 11r-14v, http://1641.tcd.ie/deposition.php?depid<?php echo 809013r003?, accessed 11 Jan. 2011.

21. *Good and Bad News from Ireland* (London, 1642).

22. *The Rebels Turkish Tyranny* (London, 1641), A2r–A3.

23. *Worse and Worse Newes from Ireland* (London, 1641), 1–2.

24. *A Letter of the Earle of Corke to the State at Dublin* (London, 1642), 1–2.

25. "G.S.," *A Brief Declaration of the Barbarous and Inhumane Dealings of the Northerne Irish Rebels* (London, 1642), 2.

26. Ibid., 5. For the background to this set of events, see Raymond Gillespie, "The Murder of Arthur Champion and the 1641 Rising in Fermanagh," *Clogher Record* 14, no. 3 (1993): 52–66.

27. *Brief Declaration*, 10.

28. *A Continuation of the Irish Rebels Proceedings* (London, 1642), 2.

29. *The Happiest News from Ireland That Ever Came to England* (London, 1641).

30. *A Bloody Battell, or the Rebels Overthrow and Protestants Victorie* (London, 1641).

31. *Bloudy Newes from Ireland* (London, 1641), A3r.

32. *The Last News from Ireland*, 2.

33. *Still Worse News from Ireland* (London, 1641).

34. *The Irish Petition to the Parliament in England* (London, 1641).

35. For Wallington, see Cope, *England and the 1641 Irish Rebellion*, 76–88; Darcy, "Politics, Pogroms, and Print," 267–72; *The Notebooks of Nehemiah Wallington, 1618–1654*, ed. David Booy (Aldershot, 2007), 115–45.

36. Mairead O'Keefe, "The Politics of Irish Protestants, 1641–1660" (M.A. thesis, National University of Ireland, 1991), 1–17.

37. Joseph Cope, "Fashioning Victims: Dr. Henry Jones and the Plight of Irish Protestants, 1642," *Historical Research* 74 (2001): 370–91.

38. Darcy, "Politics, Pogroms, and Print," 72–75.

39. [Henry Jones], *A Remonstrance of Divers Remarkeable Passages Concerning the Church and Kingdom of Ireland* (London, 1642), 1.

40. Keith Thomas, *Religion and the Decline of Magic* (London, 1971), 490.

41. [Jones], *Remonstrance*, 4, 7.

42. Ibid., 8.

43. *Letters Written by His Excellency Arthur Capel, Earl of Essex, Lord Lieutenant of Ireland, in the Year 1675* (Dublin, 1770), 2.

44. British Library (BL), Stowe MS 82, f. 1 (©British Library Board).

45. John Dunton, *The Dublin Scuffle*, ed. Andrew Carpenter (Dublin, 2000), 180.

46. Sir John Temple, *The Irish Rebellion* (Dublin, 1713).

47. Temple, *The Irish Rebellion* (Dublin, 1716).

48. Temple, *The Irish Rebellion* (Dublin, 1724: Marsh's Library, G.4.3.39).

49. A recent exception is Gillespie, "Temple's Fate."

50. Temple, *Irish Rebellion* [1724], preface, A2v.

51. Ibid., A3v.

52. Ibid., A3r.

53. Temple's *Irish Rebellion* quoted from and drew upon eighty-three depositions, only some of which were printed *in extenso*. My thanks to Aidan Clarke for clarification on this point.

54. Barnard, "Uses of the 23rd of October 1641," 891.

55. Temple, *Irish Rebellion*, preface, A3v.

56. Ibid., A4v.

57. Darcy, "Politics, Pogroms, and Print," 1–4.

58. Donovan, "'Bloody News from Ireland,'" 28–29, 34–35, 88–94.

59. Temple, *Irish Rebellion*, 6.

60. Ibid., A4v.

61. Ibid., B1v.

62. Micheál Ó Siochrú, *Confederate Ireland, 1642–1649: A Constitutional and Political Analysis* (Dublin, 1999), 62–63.

63. Temple, *Irish Rebellion*, preface, B2r.

64. Ibid., 5.

65. Ibid., 6.

66. Ibid., 7.

67. John Adamson, "Strafford's Ghost: The British Context of Viscount Lisle's Lieutenancy of Ireland," in Ohlmeyer, *Ireland from Independence to Occupation*, 138–40.

68. Temple, *Irish Rebellion*, 90.

69. Gillespie, "Temple's Fate," 325–26.

70. Cromwell to William Lenthall, 17 Sept. 1649, in *The Writings and Speeches of Oliver Cromwell*, ed. W. C. Abbott (4 vols., Oxford, 1988), 2:127. Cromwell also provided a strategic justification for the actions of the New Model Army at Drogheda: "that it will tend to prevent the effusion of blood for the future, which are the satisfactory grounds to such actions, which otherwise cannot but work remorse and regret." John Morrill has suggested that the mention of "innocent blood" may also be a reference to those royalists

in Britain and Ireland who had been intent on prosecuting the second civil war. See John Morrill, "The Drogheda Massacre in Cromwellian Context," in Edwards et al., *Age of Atrocity*, 258–59.

71. Thomas Carlyle, *Oliver Cromwell's Letters and Speeches* (2 vols., London, 1846), 2:50.

72. Cromwell to General Council at Whitehall, 23 Mar. 1649, *Writings and Speeches of Oliver Cromwell*, 2:38.

73. Christopher Hill, "Seventeenth-Century English Radicals and Ireland," in *Radicals, Rebels, and Establishments*, ed. P. J. Corish (Belfast, 1985), 33–49.

74. Micheál Ó Siochrú, *God's Executioner: Oliver Cromwell and the Conquest of Ireland* (London, 2008), 63–64.

75. [T. Waring], *A Brief Narration of the Plotting, Beginning, & Carrying-on of That Execrable Rebellion and Butcherie in Ireland, with the Unheard of, Devilish Cruelties and Massacres by the Irish-Rebels Exercised upon the Protestants and English There* (London, 1650), 2–4.

76. Ibid., 42.

77. Ibid., 22.

78. Ó Siochrú, *God's Executioner*, 107–8.

79. Ibid., 116–17.

80. T. C. Barnard, "The Protestant Interest, 1641–1660," in Ohlmeyer, *Ireland from Independence to Occupation, 1641–1660*, 218–40.

81. *A Collection of the Several Papers Sent to His Highness the Lord-Protector Concerning the Bloody and Barbarous Massacres . . . Committed . . . in the Valleys of Piedmont* (London, 1655), 23, 27.

82. Cited in T. C. Barnard, "Crises of Identity among Irish Protestants, 1641–1685," *Past & Present* 127 (May 1990): 66.

83. "An Act of General Pardon and Oblivion," 24 Feb. 1651/2, in *Acts and Ordinances of the Interregnum, 1642–1660*, ed. C. H. Firth and R. S. Rait (3 vols., London, 1911), 2:574.

84. Ó Siochrú, *God's Executioner*, 206–7.

85. Robert Dunlop, *Ireland under the Commonwealth* (2 vols., Manchester, 1913), 1:179.

86. Ibid., 179–80.

87. *An Abstract of Some Few of Those Barbarous, Cruell Massacres and Murthers of the Protestants and English in Some Parts of Ireland, Committed since the 23 of October 1641* (London, 1652).

88. Dunlop, *Ireland under the Commonwealth*, 1:242.

89. "An Act for the Settling of Ireland," 12 Aug. 1652, in *Acts and Ordinances of the Interregnum*, 2:598–603.

90. R. P. Mahaffy, ed., *Calendar of the State Papers Relating to Ireland [in the Reign of Charles II] Preserved in the Public Record Office, 1660–(70), with Addenda, 1625–70* (4 vols. London, 1905–10), 1666–69:543–59.

91. Aidan Clarke, *Prelude to Restoration in Ireland: The End of the Commonwealth, 1659–1660* (Cambridge, 1999), 301, 305.

92. Ibid., 305–6.

93. Ibid., 317. See also Robert Armstrong, *Protestant War: The "British" of Ireland and the Wars of the Three Kingdoms* (Manchester, 2005), 230–34.

94. For example, see *The Irish Colours Displayed, in a Reply of an English Protestant to a Late Letter of an Irish Roman Catholique* (London, 1662), 4, 8, 12.

95. TCD MSS 587, ff. 205-11.

96. Ibid., f. 323.

97. "An Act for the Better Execution of His Majesties Gracious Declaration for the Settlement of His Kingdom of Ireland" (14 & 15 Charles II), in *The Statutes at Large Passed in the Parliaments Held in Ireland* (13 vols., Dublin, 1786), 2:239-45.

98. Sir William Temple, "An Essay on the Present State and Condition of Ireland," in *Select Letters to the Prince of Orange* (London [?], 1701), 197-216; William Petty, "The Political Anatomy of Ireland," in *The Economic Writings of Sir William Petty*, ed. C. H. Hull (2 vols., London, 1899), 2:167, 201-3.

99. Dublin Public Libraries, Gilbert MS 198, "Affairs of Ireland," f. 72.

100. Petty, "Political Anatomy," 154.

101. Ibid., 141.

102. Ibid., 164, 167.

103. Ibid., 201-3.

104. [H. Jones], *A Sermon of Antichrist Preached at Christ-Church, Dublin, Novemb. 12, 1676* (2nd ed., London, 1679), A2.

105. Ibid., 23.

106. Edmund Borlase, *The History of the Execrable Irish Rebellion Trac'd from Many Preceding Acts to the Grand Eruption [on] the 23 of October 1641* (London, 1680).

107. BL Sloane MS 1,008, f. 197. The appendices to Borlase's *History* are paginated separately from the main text; the reworked text of Jones's *Abstract* appears in the appendices at pages 109-25 (© British Library Board).

108. Dudley Loftus to Borlase, 25 Oct. 1679 (BL Sloane MS 1,008, f. 226 [© British Library Board]).

109. Royce Mcgillivray, "Edmund Borlase, Historian of the Irish Rebellion," *Studia Hibernica* 9 (1969): 89-91.

110. Raymond Gillespie, "The Irish Protestants and James II, 1688-90," *Irish Historical Studies* 38, no. 110 (Nov. 1992): 124-33; John Miller, "The Earl of Tyrconnell and James II's Irish Policy," *Historical Journal* 20 (1977): 803-23.

111. Patrick Melvin, ed., "Letters of Lord Longford and Others on Irish Affairs, 1687-1702," *Analecta Hibernica* 32 (1985): 53.

112. Cited in Stewart, *Narrow Ground*, 64-65.

113. Gillespie, "Irish Protestants and James II," 129.

114. *An Account of the Late Barbarous Proceedings of the Earl of Tyrconnel* (London, 1689); *A Brief and Modest Representation of the Present State and Condition of Ireland* (London, 1689); *A Letter from Monsieur Tyrconnel . . . to the Late Queen* (London, 1690), 4.

115. [Richard Tennison], *A Sermon Preached to the Protestants of Ireland in the City of London . . . by Richard, Lord Bishop of Killala* (London, 1691).

116. William King, *The State of the Protestants in Ireland under the Late King James' Government* (4th ed., London, 1692), 22.

117. For modern studies of the Penal Laws, see L. M. Cullen, "Catholics under the

Penal Laws," *Eighteenth-Century Ireland: Iris An Dá Chultúr* 1 (1986): 23–36; Thomas Bartlett, *The Fall and Rise of the Irish Nation: The Catholic Question, 1690–1830* (Dublin, 1992), 17–29; S. J. Connolly, *Religion, Law, and Power: The Making of Protestant Ireland, 1660–1760* (Oxford, 1992), 263–313; Charles Ivar Mcgrath, "Securing the Protestant Interest: The Origins and Purpose of the Penal Laws of 1695," *Irish Historical Studies* 30, no. 117 (May 1996): 25–46. See also the review of Bartlett's and Connolly's works by James Smyth: "The Making and Undoing of a Confessional State: Ireland, 1660–1829," *Journal of Ecclesiastical History* 44 (1993): 506–13.

118. *A Discourse Concerning the Rebellion in Ireland* (London, 1642), 14–19.

119. "Discourse Concerning the Securing the Government of the Kingdome of Ireland to the Interest of the English Nation" (BL Add. MS 28,724, f. 10v [© British Library Board]).

120. William King to Archbishop of Canterbury, 2 June 1719, cited in Thomas Bartlett, "The Origins and Progress of the Catholic Question in Ireland, 1690–1800," in *Endurance and Emergence: Catholics in Ireland in the Eighteenth Century*, ed. Thomas Bartlett and Kevin Whelan (Dublin, 1990), 3.

121. "An Episode in Irish History," *Journal of the Waterford & South-East of Ireland Archaeological Society* 6 (1900): 156; *Historical Register* 51 (July 1728): 194–95.

122. John Abernathy, *A Sermon Preached in Wood-Street, Dublin, on the 23rd of October, 1735* (Dublin, 1735), 40.

123. *An Act of State Made by the Lord Justices and Councell of Ireland for the Observation of the Three and Twentieth Day of October Yeerly* (Dublin, 1642), 6.

124. "An Act for the Keeping and Celebrating the Twenty-Third of October as an Anniversary Thanksgiving in This Kingdom" (14 & 15 Charles II), in *Statutes at Large*, 2:526–28.

125. John Hennig, "The Anglican Church in Ireland: Prayers against Irish 'Rebels,'" *Irish Ecclesiastical Record*, ser. 5, 64 (1944): 247–54.

126. Barnard, "Uses of the 23rd of October 1641," 892–93.

127. Barnard, "Crises of Identity," 54; BL Stowe MSS 82, f. 1 (© British Library Board).

128. Colin Haydon, *Anti-Catholicism in Eighteenth-Century England, c. 1714–1780: A Political and Social Study* (Manchester, 1993), 33.

129. Kelly, "Glorious and Immortal Memory"; idem, "The Emergence of Political Parading, 1660–1800," in *The Irish Parading Tradition: Following the Drum*, ed. T. G. Fraser (Basingstoke, 2000), 9–26; McConnell, "Gunpowder Plot."

130. *Freeman's Journal*, 24 Oct. 1775.

131. "Ulster's Office Diaries, 1698–1800" (NLI Genealogical Office [GO] MS 10, f. 19v), cited with the permission of the Board of the National Library of Ireland. My thanks to Robin Usher for bringing this source to my attention.

132. Cited in Kelly, "Glorious and Immortal Memory," 29.

133. Kelly, "Emergence of Political Parading," 17–18.

134. This discussion draws freely on Barnard, "Uses of 23 October 1641."

135. T. C. Barnard, "Athlone, 1685; Limerick, 1710: Religious Riots or Charivaris?" *Studia Hibernica* 27 (1993): 61–75.

136. Boyse, *Sermon Preached at Wood-Street*, 19–20.

137. John Abernathy, *Persecution Contrary to Christianity* (Dublin, 1735), 37.

138. NLI GO MS 10, [f. 9?] (cited with permission of the Board of the National Library of Ireland).

139. Jacqueline Hill, "National Festivals, the State, and 'Protestant Ascendancy' in Ireland," *Irish Historical Studies* 24, no. 93 (May 1984): 39; McConnell, "Gunpowder Plot," 875.

140. Daniel Defoe, *The Paralel, or the Persecution of Protestants the Shortest Way to Prevent the Growth of Popery in Ireland* (Dublin, 1705), 1.

141. Ibid.

142. *The Prose Works of John Milton* (2nd ed., 2 vols., Philadelphia, 1864), 1:495.

143. Linda Colley, *Britons: Forging the Nation, 1707–1837* (2nd ed., New Haven, 2005), 11–54; Colin Haydon, "'I Love My King and Country, but a Roman Catholic I Hate': Anti-Catholicism, Xenophobia, and National Identity in Eighteenth-Century England," in *Protestantism and National Identity: Britain and Ireland, c. 1650–c. 1850*, ed. Tony Claydon and Ian McBride (Cambridge, 1998), 33–52.

144. Patrick McNally, "'Irish and English Interests': National Conflict within the Church of Ireland Episcopate," *Irish Historical Studies* 29, no. 115 (May 1995): 302–3.

145. John Gibney, *Ireland and the Popish Plot* (Basingstoke, 2008), 99–114.

146. Bulstrode Whitelock, *Memorials of the English Affairs* (London, 1682), 46.

147. Ibid., 49.

148. [Edmund Hickeringill], *The History of Whiggism* (London, 1682), 21.

149. Edward, Earl of Clarendon, *The History of the Rebellion and Civil Wars in England Begun in the Year 1641*, ed. W. Dunn Macray (6 vols., Oxford, 1888).

150. Ibid., 1:397.

151. Ibid.

152. *A Vindication of the Royal Martyr King Charles I from the Irish Massacre in the Year 1641* (London, 3rd ed., 1704).

153. BL Stowe MS 82, f. 1 (© British Library Board). This is an annotated edition of the original printed text.

154. Ibid., ff. 52, 63, 68 (© British Library Board).

155. *London Journal*, 17 June 1721, 5.

156. Thomas Carte, *The Irish Massacre Set in a Clear Light* (London, 1715).

157. *The Grand Mystery Laid Open, Namely, the Dividing of the Protestants to Weaken the Hanover Succession, and by Weakening the Succession, to Extirpate the Protestant Religion* (London, 1714), 4–5.

158. *Vindication of the Royal Martyr*, 13; Carte, *Irish Massacre*, 41.

159. Carole Fabricant, "Swift as Irish Historian," in *Walking Naboth's Vineyard: New Studies on Swift*, ed. Chrisopher Fox and Brenda Tooley (Notre Dame, 1995), 63–66; Christopher Fox, "Swift and the Passions of Posterity," in *Reading Swift: Papers from the*

Sixth Munster Symposium on Jonathan Swift, ed. Kristin Juhas, Hermann J. Real, and Sandra Simon (Munich, forthcoming). My thanks to Professor Fox for providing me with a copy of this article prior to its publication.

160. David Hume, *The History of Great Britain from the Accession of James I to the Revolution in 1688* (8 vols., London, 1770).

161. Ibid., 6:474.

162. Ibid.

163. Ibid., 482.

164. Ibid., 484.

165. Graham Gargett, "Voltaire and Irish History," *Eighteenth-Century Ireland* 5 (1990): 122–26. An attempt to mitigate his stance by the editors of a later edition of his *Account of the Stuart Family* was vigorously contested by "a Protestant Hanoverian" who sought to implicate Charles I and the pope in 1641 yet again. See *The Political Register and Impartial Review of New Books* 7, no. 43 (1770): 206–9.

166. Catharine Macaulay, *The History of England from the Accession of James I to That of the Brunswick Line* (8 vols., London, 1763–83).

167. Ibid., 5:56.

168. Ibid., 61–62.

169. Ibid., 71.

170. Ibid., 58n.

171. This was the technique used in *Popish Cruelty Display'd by Facts* (London, 1745).

172. *A Warning to English Protestants on [the] Occasion of the Present More Than Ordinary Growth of Popery* (London, 1780). The account of 1641 in this work, which was ultimately drawn from that of Temple, with additional material from Hume and others, is at pages 1–14.

173. Kathleen Wilson, *The Sense of the People: Politics, Culture, and Imperialism in England, 1715–1785* (Cambridge, 1995), 366–68.

174. *The Protestant Packet, or British Monitor* 10 (8 Dec. 1780): 228–40; 11 (22 Dec. 1780): 253–62; 12 (5 Jan. 1781): 281–86.

175. Ibid., 10:228.

176. Ibid., 229.

177. Ibid., 233.

178. Ibid., 239.

179. Ibid., 11:259–62.

180. Ibid., 12:185n.

181. *Proceedings of the Irish House of Lords, 1771–1795*, ed. James Kelly (3 vols., Dublin, 2008), 2:386.

182. Ibid., 388.

183. Thomas P. Power, "Publishing and Sectarian Tension in South Munster in the 1760s," *Eighteenth-Century Ireland* 18 (2004): 88.

184. James Kelly, "The Whiteboys in 1762: A Contemporary Account," *Journal of the Cork Historical and Archaeological Society* 94, no. 253 (1989): 22, 24; Thomas Bartlett, "An Account of the Whiteboys from the 1790s," *Tipperary Historical Journal* (1991): 144–45.

185. Power, "Publishing and Sectarian Tension," 90–91.

186. John Temple, *The Irish Rebellion* (London, 1812), v.

187. Ibid., vi.

188. Ibid., vii.

189. Ibid., viii.

190. Ibid., 234.

191. The figures are those of Tom Dunne, who has been among the most forceful recent advocates of the interpretation of 1798 in sectarian terms. See Dunne, *Rebellions: Memoir, Memory, and 1798* (Dublin, 2004), 247–64. See also James S. Donnelly, Jr., "Sectarianism in 1798 and in Catholic Nationalist Memory," in *Rebellion and Remembrance in Modern Ireland*, ed. Laurence M. Geary (Dublin, 2001), 15–37.

192. Cited in Kyla Madden, *Forkhill Protestants and Forkhill Catholics, 1787–1858* (Liverpool, 2006), 23. See also David W. Miller, *Peep O'Day Boys and Defenders: Selected Documents on the Disturbances in County Armagh, 1784–1796* (Belfast, 1990), 75–108. Other versions of the surname of the main victims were in use, including Barkley and Barkeley. My thanks to Jim Donnelly for clarification on this point.

193. Madden, *Forkhill Protestants and Forkhill Catholics*, 23–27.

194. Ibid., 156–59.

195. Temple, *Irish Rebellion*, viii. The extracts from Musgrave are at pages 181–236.

196. For the *Memoirs*, see Jim Smyth, "Anti-Catholicism, Conservatism, and Conspiracy: Sir Richard Musgrave's *Memoirs of the Different Rebellions in Ireland*," *Eighteenth-Century Life* 22 (1998): 62–73; James Kelly, *Sir Richard Musgrave, 1746–1818: Ultra-Protestant Ideologue* (Dublin, 2009), 90–150.

197. Cited in Kelly, *Musgrave*, 40.

198. Ibid., 34.

199. Ibid., 91–92, 104–5.

200. For Musgrave's influence in the nineteenth century, see Stuart Andrews, *Irish Rebellion: Protestant Polemic, 1798–1900* (Basingstoke, 2007).

201. *"A Volley of Execrations": The Letters and Papers of John Fitzgibbon, Earl of Clare, 1772–1802*, ed. D. A. Fleming and A. P. W. Malcomson (Dublin, 2005), 83.

202. Kelly, *Proceedings of the Irish House of Lords*, 2:360.

203. Ibid., 3:13.

204. Fleming and Malcomson, *"A Volley of Execrations,"* 244–45.

205. For suggestive comments on the manner in which 1641 could be evoked in 1798, see James Kelly, "'We Were All to Have Been Massacred': Irish Protestants and the Experience of Rebellion," in *1798: A Bicentenary Perspective*, ed. Thomas Bartlett, David Dickson, Daire Keogh, and Kevin Whelan (Dublin, 2003), 312–30; Beiner, *Remembering the Year of the French*, 318.

206. "Veridicus" [Sir Richard Musgrave], *A Concise Account of the Material Events and Atrocities Which Occurred in the Present Rebellion, with the Causes Which Produced Them, and an Answer to Veritas's Vindication of the Roman Catholic Clergy of the Town of Wexford* (2nd ed. [?], Dublin, 1799; NLI JP 2252), 12. Musgrave gave a total of 221 killed at Scullabogue (ibid., 12n.).

207. See Joep Leerssen, "1798: The Recurrence of Violence and Two Conceptualizations of History," *Irish Review* 22 (Summer 1998): 37–45.

208. Kelly, *Proceedings of the Irish House of Lords*, 3:413.

209. George Taylor, *An Historical Account of the Rise, Progress, and Suppression of the Rebellion in the County of Wexford in the Year 1798* (Dublin, 1800), 24.

210. Ibid., 44.

211. Ibid., 51–52.

212. Ibid., 181.

213. For example, see *A Memento for Protestants Containing the English, Piedmontese, Irish, and French Massacres* (London, 1813), 44–62. The account of 1641 contained in this work is identical to the text of *An Accompt of the Bloody Massacre in Ireland* (1678) and is followed by extracts from Musgrave in order to flesh out a section entitled "Popish Massacres in Ireland, 1523 to 1798." For an account of 1641 that draws a specific comparison with the massacre at Scullabogue in 1798, see John De Falkirk, *Annals of Irish Popery* (Dublin, 1814), 257–63.

214. *Williamite Scrap Book; or, Chronicle of the Times, No. 1* (2 vols., Dublin, 1823), 15.

215. Ibid., 16.

216. Irene Whelan, *The Bible War in Ireland: The "Second Reformation" and the Polarization of Protestant-Catholic Relations, 1800–1840* (Dublin, 2005), 142.

217. Stephen R. Gibbons, ed., *Captain Rock, Night Errant: The Threatening Letters of Pre-Famine Ireland, 1801–1845* (Dublin, 2004), 119–20.

218. Ibid., 120.

219. James S. Donnelly, Jr., "Pastorini and Captain Rock: Millenarianism and Sectarianism in the Rockite Movement of 1821–4," in *Irish Peasants: Violence and Political Unrest, 1780–1914*, ed. Samuel Clark and James S. Donnelly, Jr. (Madison, 1983), 102–39.

220. Earl of Rosse to Lord Redesdale, 19 Apr. 1822, cited in Whelan, *Bible War in Ireland*, 147.

221. *The Prophecies of Pastorini Analyzed and Refuted, and the Powerful Tendency of Inflammatory Predictions to Excite Insurrection Satisfactorily Demonstrated from Incontrovertible Historical Records, with a Cursory View of the Dangerous State of Ireland from an Exclusively Popish Conspiracy* (Dublin, 1823), 18.

222. Ibid., 33.

223. Allan Blackstock, *Loyalism in Ireland, 1789–1829* (Woodbridge, 2007), 248.

224. *Prophecies of Pastorini*, 38.

225. Ibid., 41.

226. *Dublin Evening Post*, 13 Nov. 1824, cited in Donnelly, "Pastorini and Captain Rock," 127.

227. Gibbons, *Captain Rock, Night Errant*, 248.

228. S. J. Connolly, "The 'Blessed Turf': Cholera and Popular Panic in Ireland, June 1832," *Irish Historical Studies* 23, no. 91 (May 1983): 224.

229. Ibid., 225–26.

230. Sir James Graham (home secretary) to Wellington, 18 Oct. 1843, cited in Gibbons, *Captain Rock, Night Errant*, 35–36.

231. James Meikle, *Killinchy, or the Days of Livingston: A Tale of the Ulster Presbyterians* (Belfast, 1839).

232. Ibid., 83.

233. Ibid., 97.

234. Ibid., 106.

235. Ibid., 111–12.

236. Ibid., 112.

237. Ibid., 133.

238. Ibid., 138.

239. This is the attribution in the *Wellesley Index to Victorian Periodicals* (accessed 22 Jan. 2008).

240. "A Legend of Ulster in 1641," *Dublin University Magazine* 15, no. 86 (Feb. 1840): 295.

241. Ibid., 15, no. 92 (Aug. 1840): 207–8.

242. Ibid., 215.

243. Ibid., 217.

244. Ibid.

245. Ibid.

246. Ibid., 15, no. 94 (Oct. 1840): 427–28.

247. Ibid., 430.

248. Ibid., 431.

249. Ibid., 15, no. 95 (Nov. 1840): 568.

250. Ibid., 569.

251. Ibid., 571.

252. R. F. Foster, *Words Alone: Yeats and His Inheritances* (Oxford, 2011), 35–36, 52–53.

253. Richard Mant, *History of the Church of Ireland from the Reformation to the Revolution* (2nd ed., 2 vols., London, 1841), 2:55.

254. Gamble, *View of Society and Manners*, 265.

255. Ibid., 267–68.

Chapter 2. "The Naked Truth of This Tragical History"

1. Charles O'Conor, "Account of the Author," in Curry, *Historical and Critical Review of the Civil Wars in Ireland*.

2. TCD MSS 7,236–8, ff. 1,152–59.

3. Kenneth Nicholls, "The Other Massacre: English Killings of Irish, 1641–2," in Edwards et al., *Age of Atrocity*, 176–91.

4. *No Pamphlet, but a Detestation against All Such Pamphlets as Are Printed Concerning the Irish Rebellion* (London, 1642), A2.

5. *A Bibliography of Royal Proclamations of the Tudor and Stuart Sovereigns, 1485–1714*, ed. Richard Steel (2 vols., Oxford, 1910), 2:40.

6. Ibid.

7. "Morgan, "News from Ireland."

8. Huntington Library, San Marino, Hastings MS 15,000; *A Declaration Made by the Rebels in Ireland* (London, 1644), 3–4.

9. Aidan Clarke, ed., "A Discourse between Two Councillors of State, the One of England, and the Other of Ireland (1642)," *Analecta Hibernica* 26 (1970): 171.

10. Clarke, "Discourse between Two Councillors of State," 171–72. For the composition of the *Remonstrance*, see Cope, "Fashioning Victims."

11. Clarke, "Discourse between Two Councillors of State," 172.

12. Temple, *Irish Rebellion*, A4r.

13. *A Contemporary History of Affairs in Ireland from 1641 to 1652*, ed. John T. Gilbert (5 vols., Dublin, 1879–80), 1:11.

14. Ó Siochrú, *God's Executioner*, 19.

15. Gilbert, *Contemporary History*, 1:11–12.

16. Ibid., 1:12.

17. Ibid.

18. Ibid., 1:14.

19. Ibid., 1:360.

20. Ibid.

21. Nicholls, "Other Massacre."

22. Gilbert, *Contemporary History*, 1:13. For Coote, see Kevin Forkan, "Inventing a Protestant Icon: The Strange Death of Sir Charles Coote, 1642," in Edwards et al., *Age of Atrocity*, 204–18.

23. "An Account of Murders Committed by Scots upon the Irish, 1641" (BL Add. MS 4,819, f. 318 [© British Library Board]). My thanks to Kevin Forkan for bringing this source to my attention.

24. Ibid., f. 319.

25. "R.S.," *A Collection of Some of the Murthers and Massacres Committed on the Irish in Ireland since the 23d of October 1641* (London, 1662).

26. Ibid., 6.

27. Ibid., B1.

28. Toby Barnard, "1641: A Bibliographical Essay," in Mac Cuarta, *Ulster 1641*, 178.

29. Anne Creighton, "The Remonstrance of December 1661 and Catholic Politics in Restoration Ireland," *Irish Historical Studies* 34, no. 133 (May 2004): 16–41.

30. *A Brief Narrative [of] How Things Were Carried at the Beginning of the Troubles in the Year 1641 in Ireland* (Dublin [?], 1660).

31. Karl Bottigheimer, "The Restoration Land Settlement in Ireland: A Structural View," *Irish Historical Studies* 18, no. 69 (Mar. 1972): 19–20.

32. *The Speech of Sir Audley Mervyn, Knight . . . , Containing the Sum of Affairs in Ireland, but More Especially the Interest of Adventurers and Soldiers* (Dublin, 1663), 11.

33. Richard Bellings, *History of the Irish Confederation and the War in Ireland, 1641–1643*, ed. John T. Gilbert (7 vols., Dublin, 1882–91), 1:2–3.

34. Ibid., 15.

35. Ibid., 9.

36. Raymond Gillespie, "The Social Thought of Richard Bellings," in *Kingdoms in Crisis: Ireland in the 1640s*, ed. Micheál Ó Siochrú (Dublin, 2001), 213–14.

37. John Lynch, *Cambrensis Eversus*, ed. Matthew Kelly (2 vols., Dublin, 1848), 1:35, 59.

38. Nicholas French, "The Bleeding Iphigenia," in *The Historical Works of the Right Rev. Nicholas French, D.D.*, ed. S. H. Bindon (2 vols., Dublin, 1846), 1:19.

39. Historical Manuscripts Commission (HMC), *Calendar of the manuscripts of the marquess of Ormonde*, old ser. (2 vols., London, 1895–99), 2:279.

40. Historical Manuscripts Commission (HMC), *Report on the manuscripts of F. W. Leyborne-Popham, esq.* (London, 1899), 242–43.

41. *The Earl of Castlehaven's Review, or His Memoirs of His Engagement and Carriage in the Irish Wars* (London, 1684), 10–14, 22–23. This work was the subject of a scathing commentary by Borlase: "Reflections on Lord Castlehaven's Memoirs, 1682," BL Add. MS 1,105 (© British Library Board).

42. French, "Bleeding Iphigenia," 1:28.

43. French, "A Narrative of the Earl of Clarendon's Settlement and Sale of Ireland," in Bindon, *Historical Works of the Right Rev. Nicholas French*, 1:108.

44. Clarke, "1641 Depositions," 111.

45. *The History of the Warr of Ireland from 1641 to 1653*, ed. Edward Hogan (Dublin, 1873), 7.

46. Ibid., 7–8.

47. Ibid., 8–9.

48. Ibid., 6, 9–10.

49. Barnard, "Uses of 23rd October 1641," 914–17.

50. Melvin, "Letters of Lord Longford and Others," 40.

51. Barnard, "Uses of 23rd October 1641," 894. For the later account of Davis, see James Quinn, "Thomas Davis and the Patriot Parliament of 1689," in Kelly et al., *People, Politics, and Power*, 190–202.

52. The edition used here is Hugh Reily, *Genuine History of Ireland, Containing a Summary Account of All the Battles, Sieges, Rebellions, and Massacres, with the Most Remarkable Transactions Both in Church and State since the Reformation, in Which the Valour and Loyalty of the Irish Are Proved, and the Calumnies on Them and Their Country Refuted* (Dublin, 1830s [?]: NLI IR 94106 R5). Reily's original text is reproduced in this edition at pages 1–62. It also contains the texts of the 1661 remonstrance and Oliver Plunkett's speech from the gallows, and was updated with addendums bringing it up to the 1830s, including a potted biography of Daniel O'Connell.

53. Ibid., 5.

54. Ibid., 18–20.

55. Ibid., 23.

56. Ibid.

57. Ibid., 25.

58. Ibid.

59. Ibid., 26.

60. Ibid., 34.

61. For an insightful discussion of the Synge-Nary dispute and its broader implications, see James Livesey, *Civil Society and Empire: Ireland and Scotland in the Eighteenth-Century Atlantic World* (New Haven, 2009), 95–108.

62. Eoin Mac Cárthaigh, ed., "Dia Libh, A Uaisle Éireann (1641)," *Ériu* 52 (2002): 89–121; Michael Hartnett, *Haicéad* (Oldcastle, Co. Meath, 1993), 55–59.

63. *Duanaire Dháibhidh Uí Bhruadair: The Poems of David Ó Bruadair*, ed. John C. MacErlean (3 vols., London, 1910–13), 3:12–23, 164–79; Michael Hartnett, *Ó Rathaille* (Oldcastle, Co. Meath, 1998), 43–48.

64. Niall Ó Ciosáin, *Print and Popular Culture in Ireland, 1750–1850* (Basingstoke, 1997), 102–6.

65. [John Curry], *Brief Account*.

66. TCD MSS 7,236–8, ff. 1,166–7. The passage in question is from Daniel Corkery, *The Hidden Ireland* (Dublin, 1941), 54.

67. C. D. A. Leighton, *Catholicism in a Protestant Kingdom: A Study of the Irish Ancien Regime* (Basingstoke, 1994), 89–127.

68. Love, "Hibernian Antiquarian Society," 424. Antiquarian activity in late eighteenth-century Ireland is comprehensively examined in Clare O'Halloran, *Golden Ages and Barbarous Nations: Antiquarian Debate and Cultural Politics in Ireland, c. 1750–1800* (Cork, 2004).

69. Clare O'Halloran, "Historical Writings, 1690–1890," in *The Cambridge History of Irish Literature*, ed. Margaret Kelleher and Philip O'Leary (2 vols., Cambridge, 2006), 1:599.

70. Walter D. Love, "Edmund Burke and an Irish Historiographical Controversy," *History and Theory* 2 (1962): 181–82.

71. "Tracts Relating to the Popery Laws, 1765," *The Writings and Speeches of Edmund Burke, Volume IX, [Part] I: The Revolutionary War, 1794–1797; [Part] II: Ireland*, ed. R. B. McDowell (Oxford, 1991), 478–79.

72. Curry, *Brief Account*, 3.

73. Ibid., 4.

74. Ibid., 15.

75. Ibid., 17–19.

76. Ibid., 20–21.

77. Ibid., 22n.

78. Ibid., 29.

79. Ibid., 47.

80. Ibid., 62–63n., 49–53. The tract itself is reproduced at pages 90–120.

81. Ibid., 61.

82. Walter Harris, *Fiction Unmasked: or an Answer to a Dialogue Lately Published by a Popish Physician and Pretended to Have Passed between a Dissenter and a Member of the Church of Ireland, Wherein the Causes, Motives, and Mischiefs of the Irish Rebellion and Massacres in 1641 Are Laid Thick upon the Protestants* (Dublin, 1752), iii. For a fuller account of both Harris and the

composition of this work, see Eoin Magennis, "A 'Beleagured Protestant'? Walter Harris and the Writing of *Fiction Unmasked* in Mid-Eighteenth-Century Ireland," *Eighteenth-Century Ireland* 13 (1998): 86–111.

83. Harris, *Fiction Unmasked*, vii.

84. Ibid., viii.

85. Ibid., 1.

86. Ibid., 14.

87. Ibid., 16.

88. Ibid., 37.

89. Ibid., 162.

90. Ibid., 163.

91. Ibid., 211.

92. Curry, *Historical Memoirs*.

93. Ibid., xi.

94. Ibid., xii–xv, xxiv.

95. Ibid., 33.

96. Ibid., xxiv. For the details of Curry's dealings with Hume, see David Berman, "David Hume on the 1641 Rebellion in Ireland," *Studies: An Irish Quarterly Review* 65 (Summer 1976): 103–8.

97. Curry, *Historical Memoirs*, 34.

98. Ibid., 145–54, 172–74.

99. Ibid., 40–68.

100. Ibid., 105–29.

101. Ibid., 78–80.

102. O'Halloran, *Golden Ages and Barbarous Nations*, 145.

103. Curry, *Historical Memoirs*, 78–80.

104. Ibid., 95–96.

105. Ibid., 193–94.

106. Ibid., 197.

107. *Monthly Review* 37 (Aug. 1767): 139.

108. O'Halloran, *Golden Ages and Barbarous Nations*, 145.

109. Charles Lucas, *The Political Constitutions of Great-Britain and Ireland Asserted and Vindicated* (London, 1751), 555.

110. Ibid., 556.

111. Ferdinando Warner, *The History of Ireland to the Year 1171* (n.p., 1763).

112. The edition used here is Ferdinando Warner, *The History of the Rebellion and Civil-War in Ireland* (2 vols., Dublin, 1768).

113. Ibid., 1:xi.

114. Ibid.

115. Ibid., xi–xii. Clanricarde's memoirs had been published in 1757.

116. Ibid., xii–xiii.

117. Ibid., xv.

118. Ibid., xviii.

119. Ibid., 14.

120. Ibid., 23.

121. Ibid., 72–73.

122. Ibid., 113–14.

123. Ibid., xiv–xvii.

124. Ibid., 2:6–11.

125. Ibid., 7.

126. Ibid., 7–8. The manuscript in question is presumably BL Harliean MS 5,999. My thanks to Aidan Clarke for clarifying this point.

127. Warner, *History of the Rebellion and Civil-War*, 2:8.

128. Ibid., 8–9.

129. Ibid., 9.

130. Aidan Clarke, "The 1641 Massacres," in *Ireland 1641: Contexts and Reactions*, ed. Jane Ohlmeyer and Micheál Ó Siochrú (Manchester, forthcoming). My thanks to Professor Clarke for providing me with a copy of this article prior to its publication.

131. Warner, *History of the Rebellion and Civil-War*, 2:10.

132. *Desiderata Curiosa Hibernica, or a Select Collection of State Papers* (2 vols., Dublin, 1772), 2:78–118.

133. Joseph Liechty, "Testing the Depth of Catholic/Protestant Conflict: The Case of Thomas Leland's 'History of Ireland,' 1773," *Archivium Hibernicum* 42 (1987): 17; Barnard, "Uses of 23 October 1641," 909.

134. Thomas Leland, *The History of Ireland from the Invasion of Henry II* (3 vols., London, 1779 ed.), 3:89–91.

135. Ibid., 128.

136. Ibid.

137. [John Curry], *Occasional Remarks*.

138. Curry, *Historical and Critical Review of the Civil Wars*.

139. Ibid., 149–53, 165–74.

140. Ibid., 175–81.

141. *Monthly Review* 55 (Dec. 1776): 445.

142. Ibid.

143. *Public Register, or Freeman's Journal*, 3–5 Feb. 1778.

144. Ibid.

145. "Account of the Murder of Lord Maguire," *Irish Magazine and Monthly Asylum for Neglected Biography* 1 (Mar. 1808): 137.

146. Martin J. Burke, "The Poetics and Politics of Nationalist Historiography: Mathew Carey and the *Vindiciae Hibernicae*," in *Forging in the Smithy: National Identity and Representation in Anglo-Irish Literary History*, ed. Joep Leerssen, A. H. Van Der Weel, and Bart Westerweel (Amsterdam, 1995), 183–94.

147. Mathew Carey, *Vindiciae Hibernicae, or Ireland Vindicated: An Attempt to Develop and Expose a Few of the Multifarious Errors and Falsehoods Respecting Ireland in the Histories of May, Temple, Whitelock, Borlase, Rushworth, Clarendon, Cox, Carte, Leland, Warner, Macaulay, Hume,*

and Others, Particularly in the Legendary Tales of the Conspiracy and Pretended Massacre of 1641 (Philadelphia, 1819). Unless otherwise specified, all quotations in the text are from this edition.

148. William Godwin, *Mandeville: A Tale of the Seventeenth Century in England* (3 vols., Edinburgh, 1817).

149. Ibid., 1:15.

150. Ibid., 27–28.

151. Ibid., 11.

152. Ibid., 29.

153. Ibid., 37.

154. "To those superior spirits who scorn the yoke of fraud, imposture, bigotry, and delusion; who at the sacred shrine of truth will offer up their prejudices, how inveterate soever, when her bright torch illuminates their minds; who, possessing the inestimable blessings of thrice-holy and revered liberty acquired by an arduous struggle against a mere incipient despotism, will sympathize with those who contended ardently, although unsuccessfully, against as grievous an oppression as ever pressed to the earth a noble and generous nation, which embarked in the same glorious cause as Leonidas, Epaminondas, Brutus, the Prince of Orange, William Tell, [La]Fayette, Hancock, Adams, Franklin, and Washington, this work is dedicated" (Carey, *Vindiciae*, iv). Furthermore, Carey proclaimed: "It is likewise dedicated to the immortal memory of the Desmond's, the O'Niall's, the O'Donnell's, the O'Moore's, the Prestons, the Mountgarrets, the Castle-havens, the Fitzgeralds, the Sheareses, the Tones, the Emmetts, and the myriads of illustrious Irishmen who sacrificed life or fortune in the unsuccessful effort to emancipate a country endowed by heaven with as many and as choice blessings as any part of the terraqueous globe, but for ages a hopeless and helpless victim to a form of government transcendently pernicious" (ibid., v).

155. Ibid., ix.

156. Ibid., xii–xiii.

157. Burke, "Poetics and Politics of Nationalist Historiography," 193–94.

158. Carey, *Vindiciae*, xiv–xv.

159. Ibid., xvii.

160. Ibid., xviii.

161. Ibid., 90–91.

162. Ibid., 373.

163. Ibid., 505–10.

164. *Legend of the Irish Conspiracy of 1641* (Philadelphia, 1833).

165. Carey, *Vindiciae* (1837 ed.), 2.

166. Ibid., 3–4.

167. Gearóid Ó Tuathaigh, "Gaelic Ireland, Popular Politics, and Daniel O'Connell," *Journal of the Galway Archaeological and Historical Society* 34 (1974–75): 21–34.

168. Daniel O'Connell, *A Memoir on Ireland Native and Saxon* (London, 1843), ix.

169. Ibid., 253.

170. Ibid., 251–323.

171. Ibid., 323.

172. Ibid., 324–25.

173. Ibid., 328. O'Connell was in error; Warner was never a fellow of TCD. Lecky repeated the mistake some decades later.

174. Ibid., 331.

175. Ibid., 336.

176. See Tom Dunne, "Subaltern Voices? Poetry in Irish, Popular Insurgency, and the 1798 Rebellion," *Eighteenth-Century Life* 22, no. 3 (1998): 31–44, and especially Breandán Ó Buachalla, "From Jacobite to Jacobin," in Bartlett et al., *1798*, 75–96.

177. Miller, *Peep O'Day Boys and Defenders*, 44. The observer in question, one "J. Byrne," identified himself as a "dyer and publican" from Armagh; he was possibly the John Byrne who in 1790 was elected as the representative of Armagh to the Catholic Committee (ibid., 5–6).

178. Ibid., 45.

179. Donal McCartney, "The Writing of History in Ireland, 1800–30," *Irish Historical Studies* 10, no. 40 (Sept. 1957): 357–59.

180. *A Sketch of Irish History Compiled by Way of Question and Answer for the Use of Schools* (Dublin [?], 1815: NLI JP 2243), 13.

181. Ibid., 21.

182. Thomas Crofton Croker, *Researches in the South of Ireland* (Dublin, 1824), 328–29.

183. Vincent Morley, "Views of the Past in Irish Vernacular Literature, 1650–1850," in *Unity and Diversity in European Culture*, ed. Tim Blanning and Hagen Schulze (Oxford, 2006), 174.

184. Thomas Moore, *Memoirs of Captain Rock*, ed. Emer Nolan (Dublin, 2008).

185. Ibid., 1.

186. Ibid., 37n.

187. Julia M. Wright, "'The Same Dull Round Over Again': Colonial History in Moore's *Memoirs of Captain Rock*," *European Romantic Review* 14 (2003): 239–49.

188. Moore, *Memoirs of Captain Rock*, 48–49.

189. Ibid., 53.

190. Ibid., 49.

191. Ibid., 54.

192. Ibid., 54n.

193. Ibid., 84–85.

194. Ibid., 179.

195. Gillian M. Doherty, *The Irish Ordnance Survey: History, Culture, and Memory* (Dublin, 2004), 11.

196. Ibid., 44–54.

197. Ibid., 158.

198. Ibid., 27.

199. *Ordnance Survey Memoirs, Vol. 10: Parishes of County Antrim III, 1833, 1835, 1839–40*, ed. Angélique Day and Patrick McWilliams (Belfast and Dublin, 1991), 42.

200. For earlier descriptions, see "An Account of Island Magee Taken in 1809," *Belfast Monthly Magazine* 3, no. 13 (31 Aug. 1809): 104–6; Gamble, *View of Society and Manners*, 78, 83.

201. *Ordnance Survey Memoirs . . . , County Antrim III*, 64.

202. Ibid., 65.

203. Ibid.

204. Ibid., 66.

205. Donald H. Akenson, *Between Two Revolutions: Islandmagee, Co. Antrim, 1798–1920* (Port Credit, Ontario, 1979), 21.

206. For the elision of 1798 from Presbyterian memory, see Ian McBride, "Memory and Forgetting: Ulster Presbyterians and 1798," in Bartlett et al., *1798*, 478–96.

207. *Ordnance Survey Memoirs . . . County Antrim III*, 104.

208. *Ordnance Survey Memoirs, Vol. 15: Parishes of Co. Londonderry IV, 1824, 1833–5*, ed. Angélique Day and Patrick McWilliams (Belfast and Dublin, 1992), 34.

209. See Mary Helen Thuente, "The Folklore of Irish Nationalism," in *Perspectives on Irish Nationalism*, ed. Thomas E. Hachey and Lawrence J. McCaffrey (Lexington, 1989), 42–60.

210. Christopher Morash, *A History of the Media in Ireland* (Cambridge, 2010), 83.

211. Charles Gavan Duffy, *The Ballad Poetry of Ireland* (4th ed., Dublin, 1845). This was a circumscribed (if enormously popular) collection predominantly consisting of "Anglo-Irish ballads, the production of educated men, with English tongues but Irish hearts" (xv). It did not include "old bardic songs" (xi) or "the common ballads of the people" (xiii), which were collected elsewhere by such figures as Thomas Crofton Croker.

212. Ibid., 91.

213. Edward Hayes, *The Ballads of Ireland* (2 vols., Dublin, Edinburgh, and London, 1855), 1:178. The introductory note stated: "The present ballad is founded on the rising of Ulster in 1641, at the commencement of the ten years' war. We have always denied the alleged massacre of that era and the atrocious calumnies on Sir Phelim O'Neill; but that the natives, in ejecting the English from their towns and castles, committed various excesses, is undeniable—as is equally the bitter provocation—in the plunder of their properties by James I and the long persecution that ensued. The object of the ballad is not to excuse these excesses, which we condemn and deplore, but to give a vivid picture of the feelings of an outraged people in the first madness of successful resistance" (ibid., 177). The ballad was being reproduced as late as 1927. See Stephen J. Brown, *Poetry of Irish History* (Dublin and Cork, 1927), 166.

214. James French, *Clongibbon, or the White Knight of the Forest* (Dublin, 1845), 5.

215. Ibid., 72.

216. C. P. Meehan, *The Confederation of Kilkenny* (Dublin, 1846), ix.

217. Ibid., 16–19.

218. This suggestion has been made by David Lloyd in his *Anomalous States: Irish Writing and the Post-Colonial Moment* (Dublin, 1993), 89–100.

219. The distinction between these concepts of nationalism is a key theme of many of the essays collected in Hugh Kearney, *Ireland: Contested Ideas of Nationalism and History* (Cork, 2007).

220. "Mrs. J. Sadlier" [Mary Anne Madden], *The Confederate Chieftains: A Tale of the Irish Rebellion of 1641* (New York, 1864), 3. For biographical details, see Rolf Loeber and Magda Loeber, *A Guide to Irish Fiction, 1650–1900* (Dublin, 2006), 1155–56.

221. [Madden], *Confederate Chieftains*, 32.

222. Ibid., 35.

223. Ibid., 40.

224. Ibid., 41.

225. Ibid., 41n.

226. Ibid., 90.

227. Ibid., 100.

228. Ibid.

229. Ibid., 102, 107–9.

230. Ibid., 118, 121.

231. Ibid., 121.

232. Ibid., 191.

233. Ibid.

234. Tom Garvin, *Nationalist Revolutionaries in Ireland, 1858–1928* (Oxford, 1987), 111.

235. Joep Leerssen, *Remembrance and Imagination: Patterns in the Historical and Literary Representation of Ireland in the Nineteenth Century* (Cork, 1996), 156.

236. James S. Donnelly, Jr., "The Construction of the Memory of the Famine in Ireland and the Irish Diaspora, 1850–1900," *Éire-Ireland* 31, no. 1–2 (1996): 26–61.

Chapter 3. "Historical Facts" and "Stupendous Falsehoods"

1. J. P. Prendergast, "Autobiography" (unpublished typescript), Prendergast Papers, King's Inns, Dublin, chap. 9, 3. Prendergast provided more details about the context in his published work. In 1846, while on the Leinster circuit, he had been commissioned to make "pedigree researches" in County Tipperary on behalf of an unspecified individual whose family had left Ireland just after the Battle of the Boyne in 1690. The family was originally of Old English extraction and in the 1650s had managed to retain the family seat on the banks of the River Suir, south of Clonmel. But the estate was subsequently forfeited. The stories arising from the family's unsuccessful struggle to retain its estate reportedly spurred Prendergast's interest; on his return to Dublin he began to consult the sources, such as they were, and noticed that a significant gap existed between 1640 and 1652. See J. P. Prendergast, *The Cromwellian Settlement of Ireland* (London, 1865), xii–xviii.

2. Prendergast, "Autobiography," chap. 9, 5.

3. Ibid.

4. Ibid., 8.

5. Ibid., Prendergast, *Cromwellian Settlement*, iv.

6. Ibid., v–vi.

7. Ibid., ix.

8. Ibid., 1.

9. Ibid., 2.

10. Ibid., 3–4.

11. Ibid., 4.

12. Ibid., 5–7.

13. Ibid., 7.

14. John Cunningham, "The Transplanters' Certificates and the Historiography of Cromwellian Ireland," *Irish Historical Studies* 37, no. 147 (May 2011): 384.

15. "Cromwell's Conquest and Settlement of Ireland," *Dublin Review* 6, no. 11 (Jan. 1866): 125. See also the review of Prendergast by H.S. Fagan in *Fortnightly Review* 5, no. 30 (Aug. 1866): 758–63.

16. "The Cromwellian Settlement of Ireland," *Fraser's Magazine for Town and Country* 75, no. 445 (Jan. 1867): 33.

17. Prendergast, "Autobiography," chap. 9, 10.

18. Donal McCartney, "James Anthony Froude and Ireland: A Historiographical Controversy of the Nineteenth Century," *Irish University Review* 1 (Spring 1971): 240–42. See also Ciaran Brady, "Offering Offence: James Anthony Froude (1818–1894), Moral Obligation, and the Uses of Irish History," in *Taking Sides? Colonial and Confessional Mentalities in Early Modern Ireland*, ed. Vincent P. Carey and Ute Lotz-Heumann (Dublin, 2003), 266–90; Ciaran Brady, "Destinies Intertwined: The Metaphysical Unionism of James Anthony Froude," in *Social Thought on Ireland in the Nineteenth Century*, ed. Seamus Ó Síocháin (Dublin, 2009), 108–34.

19. McCartney, "Froude and Ireland," 241.

20. Brady, "Offering Offence," 270.

21. McCartney, "Froude and Ireland," 245.

22. *Philadelphia Inquirer*, 16 Jan. 1873.

23. For details, see McCartney, "Froude in Ireland," 243, n. 16.

24. *Freeman's Journal*, 11 Nov. 1872.

25. Ibid., 19 Nov. 1872.

26. Prendergast, "Autobiography," chap. 9, 14.

27. *The Nation*, 14 Dec. 1872.

28. *Freeman's Journal*, 19 Nov. 1872.

29. James Anthony Froude, *The English in Ireland in the Eighteenth Century* (3 vols., London, 1872–74), 1:2.

30. Ibid., 10.

31. Ibid., 11.

32. Ibid., 12.

33. Ibid., 13.

34. Ibid., 15.

35. Ibid., 15–16.

36. Ibid., 18.
37. Ibid., 21.
38. Ibid., 22–23.
39. Ibid., 31.
40. Ibid., 51.
41. Ibid.
42. Ibid., 62–64.
43. Ibid., 65.
44. McCartney, "Froude and Ireland," 241; Tom Dunne, "La Trahison des Clercs: British Intellectuals and the First Home Rule Crisis," *Irish Historical Studies* 23, no. 90 (Nov. 1982): 134–73.
45. Brady, "Offering Offence," 270.
46. Froude, *English in Ireland*, 1:83.
47. Ibid.
48. Ibid., 94–96.
49. Ibid., 116.
50. Ibid., 100–101.
51. Ibid., 110.
52. Ibid., 103–5.
53. Ibid., 106.
54. Ibid., 102.
55. Ibid., 107.
56. Ibid.
57. Ibid., 108–9.
58. Ibid., 111, n. 1.
59. Ibid., 112.
60. Ibid., 113.
61. Ibid., 114.
62. Ibid., 121.
63. Ibid., 125.
64. Ibid., 126.
65. Ibid., 137.
66. Ibid., 138.
67. Ibid., 140.
68. "Mr. Froude on the English in Ireland," *Dublin Review* 20, no. 40 (Apr. 1873): 428.
69. Ibid., 448.
70. "Froude's *English in Ireland*," *Quarterly Review* 134, no. 267 (Jan. 1873): 178.
71. T. N. Burke, *Ireland's Case Stated in Reply to Mr. Froude* (New York, 1873), 109–18; John Mitchel, *The Crusade of the Period, and Last Conquest of Ireland (Perhaps)* (New York, 1873), 38; *New York Times*, 21 Dec. 1872.
72. Donal McCartney, *W. E. H. Lecky: Historian and Politician, 1838–1903* (Dublin, 1993), 87. Lecky's dispute with Froude over 1641 is discussed at pages 71–77.

73. W. E. H. Lecky, "Mr. Froude's English in Ireland," *Macmillan's Magazine* 27 (Nov. 1872–Apr. 1873): 246–64.

74. Ibid., 247.

75. Ibid., 253.

76. Ibid., 264.

77. McCartney, "Froude and Ireland," 77–79; Dunne, "La Trahison des Clercs," 143–44.

78. W. E. H. Lecky, *A History of Ireland in the Eighteenth Century* (5 vols., London, 1892), 1:v.

79. Ibid., 36.

80. Ibid., 36–40.

81. Ibid., 41.

82. Ibid., 71.

83. Ibid., 43.

84. Ibid., 45.

85. Ibid., 46.

86. Ibid., 47.

87. Ibid., 47–52.

88. Ibid., 55.

89. Ibid., 59–60.

90. Ibid., 60.

91. Ibid., 69–70.

92. Ibid., 61.

93. Ibid., 73.

94. Ibid., 69.

95. Ibid., 74–76.

96. Ibid., 89.

97. Love, "Irish Massacre of 1641," f. 103.

98. Ibid., f. 104; McCartney, *Lecky*, 74.

99. *Alfred Webb: The Autobiography of a Quaker Nationalist*, ed. Mary-Louise Legg (Cork, 1999), 37.

100. Ibid., 35.

101. James Loughlin, "The Irish Protestant Home Rule Association and Nationalist Politics, 1886–93," *Irish Historical Studies* 24, no. 95 (May 1985): 341–60.

102. Alfred Webb, *The Opinions of Some Protestants Regarding Their Irish Catholic Fellow-Countrymen, Collected by Alfred Webb, . . . with Resolutions of the Irish Protestant Home Rule Association* (2nd ed., Dublin, 1886), 2.

103. Alice Milligan, "When I Was a Little Girl," cited in Owen McGee, *The IRB: The Irish Republican Brotherhood from the Land League to Sinn Féin* (Dublin, 2005), 37.

104. Nicholas Canny, *The Politics of History: Writing Early Modern History in Parnellian Ireland* (Cambridge, 2005), 12–13.

105. "Catholic Rule in Ireland, 1641–48," *Edinburgh Review* 151 (Jan.–Apr. 1880): 473.

106. Legg, *Alfred Webb*, 32.

107. Webb, *Alleged Massacre of 1641*, 1.

108. Ibid., 4 n.

109. Ibid., 7, 10.

110. Ibid., 10–11.

111. Ibid., 19–20.

112. Ibid., 30.

113. For examples, see Gamble, *View of Society and Manners*, 301–2; Henry Hallam, *The Constitutional History of England from the Accession of Henry VII to the Death of George II* (2 vols., London, 1827), 2:751–52.

114. "The Shamrock, or Recollections of Ireland by Slow Jamie," *National Era*, 2 June 1859.

115. O'Halloran, "Historical Writings, 1690–1890," 621–22.

116. J. T. Gilbert, "The Manuscripts of Trinity College Dublin," *Historical Manuscripts Commission, Eighth Report* (London, 1881), 572–76. See also Toby Barnard, "Sir John Gilbert and Irish Historiography," in *Sir John Gilbert, 1829–1898: Historian, Archivist, and Librarian*, ed. Mary Clark, Yvonne Desmond, and Nollaig P. Hardiman (Dublin, 1999), 92–110.

117. Canny, *Politics of History*, 12–20.

118. For example, J. O'Laverty, *An Historical Account of the Diocese of Down and Connor, Ancient and Modern* (5 vols., Dublin, 1878–95), 3:128–33; James Frost, *The History and Topography of the County of Clare* (Dublin, 1893), 355–70.

119. Mary Hickson, *Ireland in the Seventeenth Century, or the Irish Massacres of 1641–2* (2 vols., London, 1884).

120. Ibid., 1:v.

121. "T.C.D," "The Irish Rebellion of 1641," *British Quarterly Review* 80 (July–Oct. 1884): 353.

122. Ibid.

123. Ibid., 364.

124. "P.F.M.[oran?]," "The Irish Massacre of 1641," *Irish Ecclesiastical Record*, 2nd ser., 9 (Apr. 1873): 297.

125. Robert Dunlop, "The Depositions Relating to the Irish Massacres of 1641," *English Historical Review* 1, no. 4 (Oct. 1886): 740.

126. Ibid., 741.

127. *The Academy*, new ser., 642 (23 Aug. 1884): 121–22. Lecky's critique of the depositions, with particular reference to Hickson, was incorporated into later editions of his history.

128. *The Academy*, new ser., 644 (6 Sept. 1884): 153–54. Her conclusions about the technicalities of the depositions are outlined in Hickson, *Ireland in the Seventeenth Century*, 1:128–33.

129. *The Academy*, new ser., 644 (6 Sept. 1884): 153.

130. Mary Hickson, "The Depositions Relating to the Irish Massacres of 1641," *English Historical Review* 2, no. 5 (Jan. 1887): 135.

131. Robert Dunlop, "The Depositions Relating to the Irish Massacres of 1641," *English Historical Review* 2, no. 6 (Apr. 1887): 339.

132. Hickson, *Ireland in the Seventeenth Century*, 1:162–63.

133. J. P. Prendergast to W. E. H. Lecky, 12 [?] 1887 (month illegible), TCD MSS 1,827–36, f. 492.

134. Thomas Fitzpatrick, *The Bloody Bridge and Other Papers Relating to the Insurrection of 1641* (Dublin, 1903), xi–x. Fitzpatrick's view of the rebellion is usefully summarized in the *Irish Independent*, 20 Oct. 1906. His papers, which include an extensive unpublished manuscript about the attack on Islandmagee, are retained in the University College Dublin archives.

135. Thomas Fitzpatrick, "The T.C.D. Depositions (1641)," *Irish Rosary* 12, no. 9 (Sept. 1908): 662.

136. "The 'Massacre' of 1641," *New Ireland Review* 19 (Mar.–Aug. 1903): 379.

137. Ibid., 381.

138. TCD MSS 7,233–5, f. 162.

139. Love, "Irish Massacre of 1641," f. 110.

140. For example, James Frost's assessment of the depositions, published in 1893, was that "no doubt can be entertained that in several particulars they are charged with exaggeration, and perhaps with deliberate falsehoods; they are nevertheless deserving of attention as the testimony of contemporary witnesses." See Frost, *History and Topography of the County of Clare*, 355.

141. Dunlop, *Ireland under the Commonwealth*, 1:vii.

142. T. S. C. Dagg to McNeill, 7 Dec. 1934, cited in *Reconstructing Ireland's Past: A History of the Irish Manuscripts Commission*, ed. Michael Kennedy and Deirdre McMahon (Dublin, 2009), 72.

143. Ibid., 73.

144. Love, "Irish Massacre of 1641," f. 108.

145. Rev. Augustine J. Thébaud, S.J., *The Irish Race in the Past and the Present* (New York, 1883), 265.

146. Rev. George R. Wedgwood, "Ireland: Old and New," *Wesleyan-Methodist Magazine* (Dec. 1891): 931.

147. J. P. Mahaffy, *An Epoch in Irish History: Trinity College, Dublin: Its Foundation and Early Fortunes, 1591–1660* (London, 1903), 275. His preface to another work on the Glorious Revolution gave the distinct impression that his opinion of his contemporaries was somewhat low: "The present population of Ireland is not a people that reads anything beyond the daily gossip of the newspapers or the poor stuff of the current novel. If such people are to be induced to buy and read historical books, they must be violent and exciting books, such as tirades upon the misconduct of England, panegyrics of Ireland, and the like." See "Introduction," R. H. Murray, *Revolutionary Ireland and Its Settlement* (London, 1911), xv.

148. R. Barry O'Brien, "The Rebellion of 1641," *Irish Ecclesiastical Record*, 4th ser., 17 (May 1905): 424.

149. Justin McCarthy, *Ireland and Her Story* (New York, 1903), iii.

150. Ibid., 73.

151. Richard Bagwell, *Ireland under the Stuarts* (3 vols., Dublin, 1909–16), 3:334–35.

152. For good examples of this trend from opposing perspectives, see T. A. Emmet, *Ireland under English Rule, or a Plea for the Plaintiff* (2nd ed., 2 vols., New York and London, 1909), and Rev. James Barkley Woodburn, *The Ulster Scot: His History and Religion* (London, 1914).

153. "C.W.C.," "The Wrongs of Ulster," *Blackwood's Magazine* 193 (Jan. 1913): 30–48.

154. *Parliamentary Debates (Official Report)*, 5th ser., *House of Commons*, vol. 46, col. 2153 (15 Jan. 1913).

155. J. B. Williams, "The Depositions about the Rebellion of 1641," *Irish Ecclesiastical Record*, 5th ser., 15 (Jan. 1920): 15–23.

156. Peter Hart, "The Protestant Experience of Revolution in Southern Ireland," in *Unionism in Modern Ireland: New Perspectives on Politics and Culture*, ed. Richard English and Graham Walker (Basingstoke, 1996), 81–98.

157. Paul McMahon, *British Spies and Irish Rebels: British Intelligence and Ireland, 1916–1945* (Woodbridge, 2008), 75–76. For the meeting at Multyfarnham, see Perceval-Maxwell, *Outbreak of the Irish Rebellion*, 238, n. 95; Froude, *English in Ireland*, 1:94–96; Lecky, *Ireland in the Eighteenth Century*, 1:95.

158. Cited in McMahon, *British Spies and Irish Rebels*, 88.

159. Hugh O'Grady, *Strafford and Ireland: The History of His Vice-Royalty with an Account of His Trial* (2 vols., Dublin, 1923), 1:234.

160. TCD MSS 7,233–5, ff. 489–91.

161. Lord Ernest Hamilton, *The Irish Rebellion of 1641* (London, 1920), vi.

162. Niamh Brennan, "A Political Minefield: Southern Loyalists, the Irish Grants Committee, and the British Government, 1922–31," *Irish Historical Studies* 30, no. 119 (May 1997): 406–19.

163. For a discussion of the development of a specifically "southern" nationalism in the Free State and Republic after 1922, see John M. Regan, "Southern Irish Nationalism as a Historical Problem," *Historical Journal* 50, no. 1 (2007): 197–223.

164. For studies of this phenomenon, see Brian Walker, "1641, 1689, 1690 and All That: The Unionist Sense of History" in his *Dancing to History's Tune: History, Myth, and Politics in Ireland* (Belfast, 1996), 1–14; Alvin Jackson, "Unionist History," in Brady, *Interpreting Irish History*, 253–68; Mary Burgess, "Mapping the Narrow Ground: Geography, History, and Partition," *Field Day Review* 1 (2005): 121–32.

165. Lord Ernest Hamilton, *The Soul of Ulster* (London, 1917), 39–40.

166. Ibid., 48–51.

167. Ibid., 52.

168. Ibid., 75.

169. Ibid., 109.

170. Ibid., 114.

171. Ibid., 164–76.

172. Ibid., 110–11.

173. Lord Ernest Hamilton, *The Irish Rebellion of 1641* (London, 1920).

174. *Catholic Bulletin* 10 (Dec. 1920): 791.

175. See the stories collected in Lord Ernest Hamilton, *Tales of the Troubles* (London, 1925), some of which fictionalized incidents recounted in the original depositions.

176. *The Parliamentary Debates, Official Report*, 1st ser., *Northern Ireland . . . , House of Commons*, vol. 2 (1922), col. 613–14.

177. Ibid., vol. 6 (1926), col. 1883–84.

178. Maude Glasgow, *The Scotch-Irish in North America and in the American Colonies* (New York, 1936), 57–64.

179. Beckett, *The Making of Modern Ireland, 1603–1923* (London, 1966), 83.

180. TCD MSS 7,233–5, f. 224.

181. Ibid.

182. See Jacqueline Hill, "Popery and Protestantism, Civil and Religious Liberty: The Disputed Lessons of Irish History, 1690–1812," *Past and Present* 118 (1988): 96–129; and especially O'Halloran, *Golden Ages and Barbarous Nations*.

183. Love, "Edmund Burke and an Irish Historiographical Controversy," 180–98.

184. Love, "Edmund Burke, Charles Vallancey, and the Sebright Manuscripts," *Hermathena* 95 (July 1961): 21–35; idem, "The Hibernian Antiquarian Society: A Forgotten Predecessor to the Royal Irish Academy," *Studies: An Irish Quarterly Review* 51 (Autumn 1962): 419–31.

185. These papers were given as part a panel that Love shared with Karl Bottigheimer at the annual conference of the American Historical Association. While Bottigheimer dealt with the reality of events in Munster in the 1640s, Love addressed perceptions of the rebellion as revealed in the work of Jones and Temple. See Karl Bottigheimer, "Civil War in Ireland: The Reality in Munster," *Emory University Quarterly* 22 (1966): 46–56; Love, "Civil War in Ireland," 57–72.

186. Love, "Irish Massacre of 1641," ff. 97–117.

187. Ibid., f. 98.

188. Ibid., f. 99.

189. Ibid., f. 100.

190. Ibid., f. 103.

191. Ibid.

192. Ibid., f. 104.

193. Ibid., f. 105.

194. Ibid., f. 110.

195. TCD MSS 7,233–5, f. 218.

196. Ibid., f. 234. The extract is from Jacques Barzun and H. F. Graff, *The Modern Researcher* (New York, 1957), 165.

197. TCD MS 7,233–5, f. 125.

198. Ibid., f. 226r.

199. Ibid., f. 119v-r.

200. Ibid., f. 125.

201. Ibid., f. 156.

202. Ibid., f. 215.

203. Ibid., f. 221.

204. TCD MS 7,236–8, f. 243.

205. Ibid., f. 242.

206. Ibid., f. 243.

207. Ibid., ff. 266–67.

208. Ibid., f. 267.

209. TCD MS 7231–4, ff. 60–86; MSS 7,233–5, ff. 191–213.

210. Love, "Civil War in Ireland," 72.

Conclusion

1. Unless otherwise specified, all details and quotations here are taken from Thomas MacKnight, *Ulster as It Is, or Twenty-Eight Years' Experience as an Irish Editor* (2 vols., London, 1896), 1:1–10.

2. By the time that he came to write his memoirs in the 1890s, MacKnight's views had changed radically; he had become an enthusiastic unionist with a deep contempt for nationalist Ireland. His concluding remarks were revealing. On the subject of Home Rule he maintained that unionists were of the view that "having abolished one ascendancy, . . . parliament can have no moral, no constitutional right to virtually substitute another, which would really be an ascendancy of ignorance, poverty, and disaffection" (ibid., 2:381). Arguing that "the Bulgarian Christians were far the superior of their Turkish oppressors," he observed that "the superiority of the unionists in Ireland to the southern peasants is at least quite as indisputable" (ibid., 386). In a rather dubious testament to their loyalty MacKnight also suggested that unionists would be happier with an "impartial" German army governing them rather than an "Irish Home Rule parliament," and that "in their resolution to resist such a fate they will be supported by all the queen's subjects devoted to the British empire throughout the world" (ibid., 392–93, 401).

3. Vivienne Westbrook, "Mid-Victorian Foxe," in John Foxe, *Acts and Monuments . . . : The Variorum Edition* (Sheffield, 2004). Available at http://www.hrionline.ac.uk/foxe/ (accessed 1 Oct. 2008).

4. T. B. Macaulay, *The History of England*, ed. C. H. Firth (6 vols., London, 1913–15), 3:1526.

5. Ibid.

6. Anthony Buckley, "Uses of History amongst Ulster Protestants" in *The Poet's Place: Ulster Literature and Society*, ed. Gerald Dawe and John Wilson Foster (Belfast, 1991), 262. See also McBride, *Siege of Derry*; Kelly, *Sieges of Derry*.

7. Cited in *Cultural Traditions in Northern Ireland*, ed. Maura Crozier (Belfast, 1989), 50.

8. "Mini-Twelfth and Re-enactment, 15 June 1991," New Way Video, Portadown. My thanks to Elizabethanne Boran for providing me with a copy of this film. The significance of such totemic events to the self-perception of distinct communities is the subject

of Jeffrey C. Alexander, "Towards a Theory of Cultural Trauma," in *Cultural Trauma and Collective Identity*, ed. Jeffrey C. Alexander et al. (Berkeley, 2001), 1–30.

9. Peter Robinson, *Their Cry Was No Surrender* (Belfast, 1988).

10. Bill Rolston, *Drawing Support 3: Murals and Transition in the North of Ireland* (Belfast, 2003), 52.

11. William Brooke to Dudley Loftus, 26 Nov. 1682, quoted in *Journal of the Royal Historical and Archaeological Association of Ireland* 4, no. 2 (1877): 176.

12. Canny, *Making Ireland British*, 461–550.

13. McGillivray, "Edmund Borlase, Historian of the Irish Rebellion"; Donovan, "'Bloody News from Ireland'"; Tom O'Gorman, "'Occurrences from Ireland': Contemporary Pamphlet Reactions to the Confederate War, 1641–1649" (M.Litt. thesis, National University of Ireland, 1999); David A. O'Hara, *English Newsbooks and Irish Rebellion, 1641–1649* (Dublin, 2006); Shagan, "Constructing Discord"; Kathleen M. Noonan, "'The Cruell Pressure of an Enraged, Barbarous People': Irish and English Identity in Seventeenth-Century Policy and Propaganda," *Historical Journal* 41 (1998), 151–77.

14. Cope, "Fashioning Victims"; Gillespie, "Temple's Fate."

15. Aidan Clarke, "The 1641 Rebellion and Anti-Popery in Ireland," in Mac Cuarta, *Ulster 1641*, 139–57; Barnard, "Uses of 23 October 1641"; Walker, "1641, 1689, 1690, and All That."

16. Kelly, "'Glorious and Immortal Memory'"; idem, "'We Were All to Have Been Massacred.'"

17. Hill, "Popery and Protestantism, Civil and Religious Liberty"; idem, "1641 and the Quest for Catholic Emancipation, 1691–1829," in Mac Cuarta, *Ulster 1641*, 159–71; Barnard, "1641: A Bibliographical Essay," in Mac Cuarta, *Ulster 1641*, 173–86; idem, "'Parlour Entertainment in an Evening?' Histories of the 1640s," in *Kingdoms in Crisis: Ireland in the 1640s*, ed. Micheál Ó Siochrú (Dublin, 2001), 20–43; O'Halloran, *Golden Ages and Barbarous Nations*, 141–57.

18. Nicholas Canny, "What Really Happened in Ireland in 1641?," in Ohlmeyer, *Ireland from Independence to Occupation*, 24–42.

19. Canny, *Making Ireland British*, 468.

20. Ibid., 464.

21. Aidan Clarke, "The Genesis of the Ulster Rising of 1641," in *Plantation to Partition: Essays in Ulster History in Honour of J.L. McCracken*, ed. Peter Roebuck (Belfast, 1981), 29–45; Raymond Gillespie, "The End of an Era: Ulster and the Outbreak of the 1641 Rising," in *Natives and Newcomers: Essays on the Making of Irish Colonial Society*, ed. Ciaran Brady and Raymond Gillespie (Dublin, 1986), 191–213.

22. Canny, *Making Ireland British*, esp. 336–401. This aspect of his study was foreshadowed in Nicholas Canny, "The 1641 Depositions as a Source for the Writing of Social History: County Cork as a Case Study," in *Cork: History and Society*, ed. Patrick O'Flanagan and Cornelius G. Buttimer (Dublin, 1993), 249–308.

23. Perceval-Maxwell, *Outbreak of the Irish Rebellion*.

24. Raymond Gillespie, "Migration and Opportunity: A Comment," *Irish Economic and Social History* 13 (1986): 90–95; Nicholas Canny, "A Reply," *Irish Economic and Social*

History 13 (1986): 96–100; Michael Perceval-Maxwell, "Migration and Opportunity: A Further Comment," *Irish Economic and Social History* 14 (1987): 59–61.

25. Canny, *Making Ireland British*, 547.

26. The project is accessible at http://1641.tcd.ie (accessed 30 Jan. 2011).

27. Interview with Jane Ohlmeyer, 17 Nov. 2010.

28. Ibid.

29. Ibid.

30. Ibid.

31. *Irish Independent (Metro Edition)*, 18 Oct. 2007; *Daily Mirror* (Northern Ireland), 18 Oct. 2007.

32. Clarke, "1641 Massacres."

33. For examples of this approach, see Gillespie, "Murder of Arthur Champion"; Michael Perceval-Maxwell, "The Ulster Rising of 1641 and the Depositions," *Irish Historical Studies* 21, no. 82 (1978): 144–67.

34. Clarke, "1641 Massacres."

35. Seamus Deane, "'To See Again the Stars': The *Dictionary of Irish Biography: From the Earliest Times to the Year 2002*," *Field Day Review* 6 (2010): 181. Elizabeth Tonkin, "History and the Myth of Realism" in *The Myths We Live By*, ed. Raphael Samuel and Paul Thompson (London, 1990), 25–35.

36. John R. Gillis, "Memory and Identity: The History of a Relationship," in *Commemorations: The Politics of National Identity*, ed. John R. Gillis (Princeton, 1994), 3.

37. Alexander, "Towards a Theory of Cultural Trauma," 8–10.

38. R. F. Foster, *The Irish Story: Telling Tales and Making It Up in Ireland* (London, 2002), 3, 7.

39. Brian Inglis, *The Story of Ireland* (2nd ed., London, 1965), 55.

40. For an introduction to the experiences of southern Protestants both before and after independence and partition, see Ian d'Alton, "'A Vestigial Population'? Perspectives on Southern Irish Protestants in the Twentieth Century," *Éire-Ireland* 44, no. 3–4 (Fall/Winter 2009): 9–42.

41. John Hewitt, "The Bloody Brae," in *The Collected Poems of John Hewitt*, ed. Frank Ormsby (Belfast, 1991), 408.

42. Ibid., 411.

43. Akenson, *Between Two Revolutions*, 139–40.

44. David Edward, Clodagh Tait, and Padraig Lenihan, "Early Modern Ireland: A History of Violence," in their *Age of Atrocity*, 9–33.

Bibliography

Manuscripts

British Library (BL), London
 "Reflections on Lord Castlehaven's Memoirs, 1682" (Add. MS 1,105)
 Pococke Papers (Add. MS 4,819)
 "Discourse Concerning the Securing [of] the Government of the Kingdome of Ireland to the Interest of the English Nation" (Add. MS 28,724)
 Edmund Borlase Papers (Sloane MS 1,008)
 Borlases's "History of the Execrable Irish Rebellion" (Stowe MS 82)
Dublin City Archives
 "Affairs of Ireland" (Gilbert MS 198)
Huntington Library, San Marino
 Hastings Papers
King's Inns, Dublin
 Prendergast Papers
National Library of Ireland (NLI), Dublin
 Ulster Officers' Diaries, 1698–1800 (GO MS 10)
Trinity College Dublin (TCD)
 Lecky Papers (MSS 1,827–36)
 Walter Love Papers (MSS 7,231–38)
 "Proceedings . . . Relating to the Settlement of Ireland" (MS 587)

Official Publications and Editions of Texts

Abbott, W. C., ed. *The Writings and Speeches of Oliver Cromwell.* 4 vols. Cambridge, MA: Harvard University Press, 1937–47; Oxford: Oxford University Press, 1988.
Bartlett, Thomas, ed. "An Account of the Whiteboys from the 1790s." *Tipperary Historical Journal* (1991): 140–47.

Bellings, Richard. *History of the Irish Confederation and the War in Ireland, 1641–1643*, ed. John T. Gilbert. 7 vols. Dublin, 1882–91.

Booy, David, ed. *The Notebooks of Nehemiah Wallington, 1618–1654*. Aldershot: Ashgate, 2007.

Brown, Stephen J., ed. *Poetry of Irish History*. Dublin and Cork: Talbot Press, 1927.

Burke, Edmund. *The Writings and Speeches of Edmund Burke, Volume IX: I: The Revolutionary War, 1794–1797; II: Ireland*, ed. R. B. McDowell. Oxford: Oxford University Press, 1991.

Carlyle, Thomas, ed. *Oliver Cromwell's Letters and Speeches*. 2 vols. London, 1846.

Clarke, Aidan, ed. "A Discourse between Two Councillors of State, the One of England, and the Other of Ireland (1642)." *Analecta Hibernica* 26 (1970): 159–75.

Crofton Croker, Thomas, ed. *Narratives Illustrative of the Contests in Ireland in 1641 and 1690*. London, 1841.

Day, Angélique, and Patrick McWilliams, eds. *Ordnance Survey Memoirs of Ireland, Vol. 10: Parishes of County Antrim III, 1833, 1835, 1839–40*. Belfast and Dublin: Institute of Irish Studies, Queen's University in association with the Royal Irish Academy, 1991.

———. *Ordnance Survey Memoirs of Ireland, Vol. 15: Parishes of County Londonderry IV, 1824, 1833–5*. Belfast and Dublin: Institute of Irish Studies, Queen's University in association with the Royal Irish Academy, 1992.

———. *Ordnance Survey Memoirs of Ireland, Vol. 22: Parishes of County Londonderry VI, 1831, 1833, 1835–6*. Belfast and Dublin: Institute of Irish Studies, Queen's University in association with the Royal Irish Academy, 1993.

Desiderata Curiosa Hibernica, or a Select Collection of State Papers. 2 vols. Dublin, 1772.

Dunlop, Robert, ed. *Ireland under the Commonwealth*. 2 vols. Manchester: Manchester University Press, 1913.

Dunton, John. *The Dublin Scuffle*, ed. Andrew Carpenter. Dublin: Four Courts Press, 2000.

Firth, C. H., and R. S. Rait, eds. *Acts and Ordinances of the Interregnum, 1642–1660*. 3 vols. London: H.M. Stationery Office, 1911.

Fleming, D. A., and A. P. W. Malcolmson, eds. *"A Volley of Execrations": The Letters and Papers of John Fitzgibbon, Earl of Clare, 1772–1802*. Dublin: Irish Manuscripts Commission, 2005.

French, Nicholas. *The Historical Works of the Right Rev. Nicholas French, D.D.*, ed. S. H. Bindon. 2 vols. Dublin, 1846.

Gavan Duffy, Charles. *The Ballad Poetry of Ireland*. Dublin, 1845.

Gibbons, Stephen R., ed. *Captain Rock, Night Errant: The Threatening Letters of Pre-Famine Ireland, 1801–1845*. Dublin: Four Courts Press, 2004.

Gilbert, John T., ed. *A Contemporary History of Affairs in Ireland from 1641 to 1652*. 5 vols. Dublin, 1879–80.

Hartnett, Michael. *Haicéad*. Oldcastle, Co. Meath: Gallery Press, 1993.

———. *O Rathaille*. Oldcastle, Co. Meath: Gallery Press, 1998.

Hayes, Edward. *The Ballads of Ireland*. 2 vols. Dublin, Edinburgh, and London, 1855.

Hewitt, John. *The Collected Poems of John Hewitt*, ed. Frank Ormsby. Belfast: Blackstaff Press, 1991.

Historical Manuscripts Commission. *Eighth Report*. London, 1881.

——. *Calendar of the Manuscripts of the Marquess of Ormonde*. Old series, 2 vols., London, 1895–99; New series, 8 vols., London: Historical Manuscripts Commission, 1902–20.

——. *Report on the Manuscripts of F.W. Leyborne-Popham, Esq*. London, 1899.

Hickson, Mary. *Ireland in the Seventeenth Century; or, the Irish Massacres of 1641–2*. 2 vols. London, 1884.

Hogan, Edward, ed. *The History of the Warr of Ireland from 1641 to 1653*. Dublin, 1873.

Kelly, James, ed. "The Whiteboys in 1762: A Contemporary Account." *Journal of the Cork Historical and Archaeological Society* 94, no. 253 (1989): 19–26.

——, ed. *Proceedings of the Irish House of Lords, 1771–1795*. 3 vols. Dublin: Irish Manuscripts Commission, 2008.

Legg, Mary-Louise, ed. *Alfred Webb: The Autobiography of a Quaker Nationalist*. Cork: Cork University Press, 1999.

Letters Written by His Excellency Arthur Capel, Earl of Essex, Lord Lieutenant of Ireland, in the Year 1675. Dublin, 1770.

Lynch, John. *Cambrensis Eversus*, ed. Matthew Kelly. 2 vols. Dublin, 1848.

Mac Cárthaigh, Eoin, ed. "Dia libh, a Uaisle Éireann (1641)." *Ériu* 52 (2002): 89–121.

MacErlean, John C., ed. *Duanaire Dháibhidh Uí Bhruadair: The Poems of David Ó Bruadair*. 3 vols. London: Irish Texts Society, 1910–13.

Mahaffy, R. P., ed. *Calendar of the State Papers Relating to Ireland [in the Reign of Charles II] Preserved in the Public Record Office, 1660–(70), with Addenda, 1625–70*. 4 vols. London: H.M. Stationery Office, 1905–10.

Melvin, Patrick, ed. "Letters of Lord Longford and Others on Irish Affairs, 1687–1702." *Analecta Hibernica* 32 (1985): 35–124.

Miller, David W., ed. *Peep O'Day Boys and Defenders: Selected Documents on the County Armagh Disturbances, 1784–96*. Belfast: PRONI, 1990.

Milton, John. *The Prose Works of John Milton*. 2 vols. Philadelphia, 1864.

Moore, Thomas. *Memoirs of Captain Rock*, ed. Emer Nolan. Dublin: Field Day, 2008.

The Parliamentary Debates (Official Report). 5th ser., *House of Commons*, vol. 46.

The Parliamentary Debates, Official Report. 1st ser., *Northern Ireland . . . , House of Commons*, vol. 2. Belfast: H.M. Stationery Office, 1922.

Petty, William. *The Economic Writings of Sir William Petty*, ed. C. H. Hull. 2 vols. London, 1899.

The Statutes at Large Passed in the Parliaments Held in Ireland. 13 vols. Dublin, 1786.

Steele, Richard, ed. *A Bibliography of Royal Proclamations of the Tudor and Stuart Sovereigns, 1485–1714*. 2 vols. Oxford: Clarendon Press, 1910.

Newspapers and Periodicals

The Academy (London)
Belfast Monthly Magazine
Blackwood's Magazine (Edinburgh)

British Quarterly Review (London)
Daily Mirror (Northern Ireland)
Dublin Review
Dublin University Magazine
Edinburgh Review
Fortnightly Review (London)
Fraser's Magazine for Town and Country (London)
Freeman's Journal (Dublin)
The Historical Register (London)
Irish Daily Mail
Irish Independent
Irish Independent (Metro Edition)
Irish Magazine and Monthly Asylum for Neglected Biography
Irish Times
London Journal
Macmillan's Magazine (London)
The Monthly Review (London)
The Nation (Dublin)
The National Era (Washington, D.C.)
New Ireland Review
New York Times
Philadelphia Inquirer
The Political Register and Impartial Review of New Books (London)
The Protestant Packet, or British Monitor (Newcastle)
Quarterly Review (London)
Sunday Independent
The Wesleyan-Methodist Magazine (London)

Articles, Books, and Pamphlets

Abernathy, John. *Persecution Contrary to Christianity*. Dublin, 1735.
———. *A Sermon Preached in Wood-Street, Dublin, on the 23rd of October 1735*. Dublin, 1735.
Adamson, John. "Strafford's Ghost: The British Context of Viscount Lisle's Lieutenancy of Ireland." In *Ireland from Independence to Occupation, 1641–1660*, ed. Jane Ohlmeyer, 128–59. Cambridge: Cambridge University Press, 1995.
Akenson, Donald H. *Between Two Revolutions: Islandmagee, Co. Antrim, 1798–1920*. Port Credit, Ontario: P.D. Meany, 1979.
Alexander, Jeffrey C. "Towards a Theory of Cultural Trauma." In *Cultural Trauma and Collective Identity*, ed. Jeffrey C. Alexander et al., 1–30. Berkeley: University of California Press, 2001.
Andrews, Stuart. *Irish Rebellion: Protestant Polemic, 1798–1900*. Basingstoke: Palgrave Macmillan, 2007.
Anon. *An Accompt of the Bloody Massacre in Ireland*. London, 1678.
Anon. *An Account of the Late Barbarous Proceedings of the Earl of Tyrconnel*. Dublin, 1689.

Anon. *An Act of State Made by the Lord Justices and Councell of Ireland for the Observation of the Three and Twentieth Day of October Yeerly.* Dublin, 1642.

Anon. *The Antichristian Principle Fully Discovered.* London, 1679.

Anon. *A Bloody Battell, or the Rebels Overthrow and Protestants Victorie.* London, 1641.

Anon. *Bloudy Newes from Ireland.* London, 1641.

Anon. *A Brief Declaration of the Barbarous and Inhumane Dealings of the Northerne Irish Rebels.* London, 1642.

Anon. *A Brief and Modest Representation of the Present State and Condition of Ireland.* London, 1689.

Anon. *A Brief Narrative [of] How Things Were Carried at the Beginning of the Troubles in the Year 1641 in Ireland.* Dublin [?], 1660.

Anon. *A Brief Narrative of the Several Popish Treasons and Cruelties against the Protestants in England, France, and Ireland.* London, [1678].

Anon. *A Collection of the Several Papers Sent to His Highness the Lord-Protector Concerning the Bloody and Barbarous Massacres . . . Committed . . . in the Valleys of Piedmont.* London, 1655.

Anon. *A Continuation of the Irish Rebels' Proceedings.* London, 1642.

Anon. *A Copy of a Letter Concerning the Traitorous Conspiracy of the Rebels in Ireland.* London, 1641.

Anon. *A Declaration Made by the Rebels in Ireland.* London, 1644.

Anon. *A Discourse Concerning the Rebellion in Ireland.* London, 1642.

Anon. "An Episode in Irish History." *Journal of the Waterford and South-East of Ireland Archaeological Society* 6 (1900): 155–58.

Anon. *Good and Bad News from Ireland.* London, 1642.

Anon. *The Grand Mystery Laid Open, Namely, the Dividing of the Protestants to Weaken the Hanover Succession, and by Weakening the Succession, to Extirpate the Protestant Religion.* London, 1714.

Anon. *The Happiest News from Ireland That Ever Came to England.* London, 1641.

Anon. *Ireland's Lamentation for the Late Destructive Cessation.* London, 1644.

Anon. *The Irish Petition to the Parliament in England.* London, 1641.

Anon. *The Last Newes from Ireland.* London, 1641.

Anon. *Legend of the Irish Conspiracy of 1641.* Philadelphia, 1833.

Anon. *A Letter from Monsieur Tyrconnel . . . to the Late Queen.* London, 1690.

Anon. *A Letter of the Earle of Corke to the State at Dublin.* London, 1642.

Anon. "Letter of William Brooke to Dudley Loftus, 26 November 1682." *Journal of the Royal Historical and Archaeological Association of Ireland* 4, part 2 (1877): 176.

Anon. *A Memento for Protestants Containing the English, Piedmontese, Irish, and French Massacres.* London, 1813.

Anon. *No Pamphlet, but a Detestation against All Such Pamphlets as Are Printed Concerning the Irish Rebellion.* London, 1642.

Anon. *Popish Cruelty Display'd by Facts.* London, 1745.

Anon. *The Prophecies of Pastorini Analyzed and Refuted, and the Powerful Tendency of Inflammatory Predictions to Excite Insurrection Satisfactorily Demonstrated from Incontrovertible Historical Records, with a Cursory View of the Dangerous State of Ireland from an Exclusively Popish Conspiracy.* Dublin, 1823.

Anon. *The Rebels' Turkish Tyranny*. London, 1641.

Anon. *A Sketch of Irish History Compiled by Way of Question and Answer for the Use of Schools*. Dublin [?], 1815 (NLI JP 2243).

Anon. *Still Worse News from Ireland*. London, 1641.

Anon. *A True and Full Relation of the Horrible and Hellish Plot*. London, 1641.

Anon. *A Vindication of the Royal Martyr King Charles I from the Irish Massacre in the Year 1641*. 3rd ed., London, 1704.

Anon. *A Warning to English Protestants on Occasion of the Present More Than Ordinary Growth of Popery*. London, 1780.

Anon. *Williamite Scrap Book*, 1. Dublin, 1823.

Anon. *Worse and Worse Newes from Ireland*. London, 1641.

Armstrong, Robert. *Protestant War: The "British" of Ireland and the Wars of the Three Kingdoms*. Manchester: Manchester University Press, 2005.

Bagwell, Richard. *Ireland under the Stuarts*. 3 vols. Dublin, 1909–16.

Barnard, T. C. [Toby]. "Athlone, 1685; Limerick, 1710: Religious Riots or Charivaris?" *Studia Hibernica* 27 (1993): 61–75.

———. "Crises of Identity among Irish Protestants, 1641–1685." *Past and Present* 127 (May 1990): 39–83.

———. *Cromwellian Ireland: English Government and Reform in Ireland, 1649–1660*. Oxford: Clarendon Press, 1975.

———. "The Protestant Interest, 1641–1660." In *Ireland from Independence to Occupation, 1641–1660*, ed. Jane Ohlmeyer, 218–40. Cambridge: Cambridge University Press, 1995.

———. "The Uses of the 23rd of October 1641 and Irish Protestant Celebrations." *English Historical Review* 106 (Oct. 1991): 889–920.

Barnard, Toby. "1641: A Bibliographical Essay." In *Ulster 1641: Aspects of the Rising*, ed. Brian Mac Cuarta, 173–86. Belfast: Institute of Irish Studies, 1997.

———. "Gathering Ideas: A Clerical Library in County Cork, 1774." In *Print Culture and Intellectual Life in Ireland, 1660–1941: Essays in Honour of Michael Adams*, ed. Martin Fanning and Raymond Gillespie, 24–52. Dublin: Woodfield Press, 2006.

———. "'Parlour Entertainment in an Evening?' Histories of the 1640s." In *Kingdoms in Crisis: Ireland in the 1640s*, ed. Micheál Ó Siochrú, 20–43. Dublin: Four Courts Press, 2001.

———. "Reading in Eighteenth-Century Ireland: Public and Private Pleasures." In *The Experience of Reading: Irish Historical Perspectives*, ed. Bernadette Cunningham and Máire Kennedy, 60–77. Dublin: Rare Books Group of the Library Association of Ireland, 1999.

———. "Sir John Gilbert and Irish Historiography." In *Sir John Gilbert, 1829–1898: Historian, Archivist, and Librarian*, ed. Mary Clark, Yvonne Desmond, and Nollaig P. Hardiman, 92–110. Dublin: Four Courts Press, 1999.

Bartlett, Thomas. *The Fall and Rise of the Irish Nation: The Catholic Question, 1690–1830*. Dublin: Gill and Macmillan, 1992.

———. "The Origins and Progress of the Catholic Question in Ireland, 1690–1800." In

Endurance and Emergence: Catholics in Ireland in the Eighteenth Century, ed. Thomas P. Power and Kevin Whelan, 179–201. Dublin: Irish Academic Press, 1990.

Barzun, Jacques, and H. F. Graff. *The Modern Researcher*. New York: Harcourt Brace and World 1957.

Beckett, J. C. *The Making of Modern Ireland, 1603–1923*. London: Faber, 1966.

Beiner, Guy. "Between Trauma and Triumphalism: The Easter Rising, the Somme, and the Crux of Deep Memory in Modern Ireland." *Journal of British Studies* 46 (April 2007): 366–89.

———. *Remembering the Year of the French: Irish Folk History and Social Memory*. Madison: University of Wisconsin Press, 2007.

Beiner, Guy, and Joep Leerssen. "Why Irish History Starved: A Virtual Historiography." *Field Day Review* 3 (2007): 67–81.

Berman, David. "David Hume on the 1641 Rebellion in Ireland." *Studies: An Irish Quarterly Review* 65 (1976): 103–8.

Blackstock, Allan. *Loyalism in Ireland, 1789–1829*. Woodbridge: Boydell Press, 2007.

Boate, Gerard. *A Natural History of Ireland in Three Parts*. Dublin, 1755 (NLI IR 9141 B 10).

Borlase, Edmund. *The History of the Execrable Irish Rebellion Trac'd from Many Preceding Acts to the Grand Eruption [on] the 23 of October 1641*. London, 1680.

Bottigheimer, Karl. "Civil War in Ireland: The Reality in Munster." *Emory University Quarterly* 22 (1966): 46–56.

———. "The Restoration Land Settlement in Ireland: A Structural View." *Irish Historical Studies* 18, no. 69 (March 1972): 1–21.

[Boyle, Roger, Earl of Orrery]. *The Irish Colours Displayed in a Reply of an English Protestant to a Late Letter of an Irish Roman Catholique*. London, 1662.

Boyse, J. *A Sermon Preached at Wood-Street on the 23rd October 1716*. Dublin, 1716.

Brady, Ciaran. "'Constructive and Instrumental': The Dilemma of Ireland's First 'New Historians.'" In *Interpreting Irish History: The Debate on Historical Revisionism, 1938–1994*, ed. Ciaran Brady, 3–31. Dublin: Irish Academic Press, 1994.

———. "Destinies Intertwined: The Metaphysical Unionism of James Anthony Froude." In *Social Thought on Ireland in the Nineteenth Century*, ed. Seamus Ó Síocháin, 108–34. Dublin: University College Dublin Press, 2009.

———. "Offering Offence: James Anthony Froude (1818–1894), Moral Obligation, and the Uses of Irish History." In *Taking Sides? Colonial and Confessional Mentalities in Early Modern Ireland*, ed. Vincent P. Carey and Ute Lotz-Heumann, 266–90. Dublin: Four Courts Press, 2003.

Brennan, Niamh. "A Political Minefield: Southern Loyalists, the Irish Grants Committee, and the British Government, 1922–31." *Irish Historical Studies* 30, no. 119 (May 1997): 406–19.

Buckley, Anthony. "Uses of History amongst Ulster Protestants." In *The Poet's Place: Ulster Literature and Society*, ed. Gerald Dawe and John Wilson Foster. Belfast: Institute of Irish Studies, 1991.

Burgess, Mary. "Mapping the Narrow Ground: Geography, History, and Partition." *Field Day Review* 1 (2005): 121–32.

Burke, Martin J. "The Poetics and Politics of Nationalist Historiography: Mathew
    Carey and the *Vindiciae Hibernicae.*" In *Forging in the Smithy: National Identity and Repre-
    sentation in Anglo-Irish Literary History*, ed. Joep Leerssen, A. H. Van Der Weel, and
    Bart Westerweel, 183–94. Amsterdam: Rodopi, 1995.
Burke, T. N. *Ireland's Case Stated in Reply to Mr. Froude*. New York, 1873.
Canny, Nicholas. "The 1641 Depositions as a Source for the Writing of Social History:
    County Cork as a Case Study." In *Cork: History and Society*, ed. Patrick O'Flanagan
    and Cornelius G. Buttimer, 249–308. Dublin: Geography Publications, 1993.
———. "Historians, Moral Judgement, and National Communities: The Irish Dilemma."
    European Review 14, no. 3 (2006): 401–10.
———. *Making Ireland British, 1580–1650*. Oxford: Oxford University Press, 2001.
———. *The Politics of History: Writing Early Modern History in Parnellian Ireland*. Cambridge:
    Magdalene College, 2005.
———. "A Reply." *Irish Economic and Social History* 13 (1986): 96–100.
———. "What Really Happened in Ireland in 1641?" In *Ireland from Independence to
    Occupation, 1641–1660*, ed. Jane Ohlmeyer, 24–42. Cambridge: Cambridge University
    Press, 1995.
Carey, Mathew, *Vindiciae Hibernicae, or Ireland Vindicated: An Attempt to Develop and Expose a
    Few of the Multifarious Errors and Falsehoods Respecting Ireland in the Histories of May, Temple,
    Whitelock, Borlase, Rushworth, Clarendon, Cox, Carte, Leland, Warner, Macaulay, Hume, and
    Others, Particularly in the Legendary Tales of the Conspiracy and Pretended Massacre of 1641*.
    Philadelphia, 1819.
Carleton, William. *Traits and Stories of the Irish Peasantry*. 2 vols. New York and London:
    Garland Publications, 1979.
Carte, Thomas. *The Irish Massacre Set in a Clear Light*. London, 1715.
Castlehaven, Richard, Earl of. *The Earl of Castlehaven's Review, or His Memoirs of His Engage-
    ment and Carriage in the Irish Wars*. London, 1684.
Clarendon, Edward, Earl of. *The History of the Rebellion and Civil Wars in England Begun in
    the Year 1641*. 6 vols. Oxford, 1888.
Clarke, Aidan. "The 1641 Depositions." In *Treasures of the Library: Trinity College Dublin*,
    ed. Peter Fox, 111–22. Dublin: Trinity College Dublin, 1986.
———. "The 1641 Massacres." In *Ireland 1641: Contexts and Reactions*, ed. Jane Ohlmeyer
    and Micheál Ó Siochrú. Manchester: Manchester University Press, forthcoming.
———. "The 1641 Rebellion and Anti-Popery in Ireland." In *Ulster 1641*, ed. Mac
    Cuarta, 139–157. Belfast: Institute of Irish Studies, 1997.
———. "The Genesis of the Ulster Rising of 1641." In *Plantation to Partition: Essays in Ulster
    History in Honour of J. L. McCracken*, ed. Peter Roebuck, 29–45. Belfast: Blackstaff
    Press, 1981.
———. *Prelude to Restoration in Ireland: The End of the Commonwealth, 1659–1660*. Cambridge:
    Cambridge University Press, 1999.
Colley, Linda. *Britons: Forging the Nation, 1707–1837*. 2nd ed. New Haven, CT: Yale Univer-
    sity Press, 2005.
Confino, Alon. "Collective Memory and Cultural History: Problems of Method."
    American Historical Review 102, no. 5 (Dec. 1997): 1385–1403.

Connerton, Paul. *How Societies Remember.* Cambridge: Cambridge University Press, 1989.

Connolly, S. J. "The 'Blessed Turf': Cholera and Popular Panic in Ireland, June 1832." *Irish Historical Studies* 23, no. 91 (May 1983): 214–32.

———. *Religion, Law, and Power: The Making of Protestant Ireland, 1660–1760.* Oxford: Oxford University Press, 1992.

Cope, Joseph. *England and the 1641 Irish Rebellion.* Woodbridge: Boydell Press, 2009.

———. "Fashioning Victims: Dr. Henry Jones and the Plight of Irish Protestants, 1642." *Historical Research* 74 (2001): 370–91.

Corkery, Daniel. *The Hidden Ireland.* Dublin: M.H. Gill, 1941.

Cramer, Kevin. *The Thirty Years' War and German Memory in the Nineteenth Century.* Lincoln: University of Nebraska Press, 2007.

Creighton, Anne. "The Remonstrance of December 1661 and Catholic Politics in Restoration Ireland." *Irish Historical Studies* 34, no. 133 (May 2004): 16–41.

Croker, Thomas Crofton. *Researches in the South of Ireland.* Dublin, 1824.

Crozier, Maura, ed. *Cultural Traditions in Northern Ireland.* Belfast: Institute of Irish Studies, 1989.

Cubitt, Geoffrey. *History and Memory.* Manchester: Manchester University Press, 2007.

Cullen, L. M. "Catholics under the Penal Laws." *Eighteenth-Century Ireland: Iris An Dá Chultúr* 1 (1986): 23–36.

Cunningham, John. "The Transplanters' Certificates and the Historiography of Cromwellian Ireland." *Irish Historical Studies* 37, no. 147 (May 2011): 376–95.

[Curry, John]. *A Brief Account from the Most Authentic Protestant Writers of the Causes, Motives, and Mischiefs of the Irish Rebellion on the 23rd Day of October 1641, Deliver'd in a Dialogue between a Dissenter and a Member of the Church of Ireland as by Law Established.* London, 1747.

———. *An Historical and Critical Review of the Civil Wars in Ireland from the Reign of Queen Elizabeth to the Settlement under King William.* Dublin, 1775; reprinted 1810.

———. *Historical Memoirs of the Irish Rebellion in the Year 1641 Extracted from Parliamentary Journals, State-Acts, and the Most Eminent Protestant Historians . . . , in a Letter to Walter Harris, Esq.* London, 1758.

———. *Occasional Remarks on Certain Passages in Dr. Leland's History of Ireland Relative to the Irish Rebellion in 1641.* London, 1778.

d'Alton, Ian. "'A Vestigial Population'? Perspectives on Southern Irish Protestants in the Twentieth Century." *Éire-Ireland* 44, no. 3–4 (Fall/Winter 2009): 9–42.

Darcy, Eamon. "Politics, Pogroms, and Print: The 1641 Depositions and Contemporary Print Culture." Ph.D. Dissertation, Trinity College Dublin, 2009.

Dawson, Graham. *Making Peace with the Past? Memory, Trauma, and the Irish Troubles.* Manchester: Manchester University Press, 2007.

Deane, Seamus. "'To See Again the Stars'": *The Dictionary of Irish Biography: From the Earliest Times to the Year 2002.*" *Field Day Review* 6 (2010): 179–205.

De Beaumont, Gustave. *Ireland: Social, Political, and Religious,* ed. W. C. Taylor. Cambridge, MA: Harvard University Press, 2006.

De Falkirk, John. *Annals of Irish Popery.* Dublin, 1814.

Defoe, Daniel. *The Parallel, or the Persecution of Protestants the Shortest Way to Prevent the Growth of Popery in Ireland.* Dublin, 1705.

di Lampedusa, Guiseppe Tomasi. *The Leopard*. London: Collins and Harvill Press, 1960.

Doherty, Gillian M. *The Irish Ordnance Survey: History, Culture, and Memory*. Dublin: Four Courts Press, 2004.

Dolan, Anne. *Commemorating the Irish Civil War: History and Memory, 1923–2000*. Cambridge: Cambridge University Press, 2003.

Donnelly, James S., Jr. "The Construction of the Memory of the Famine in Ireland and the Irish Diaspora, 1850–1900." *Éire-Ireland* 31, no. 1–2 (1996): 26–61.

———. "Pastorini and Captain Rock: Millenarianism and Sectarianism in the Rockite Movement of 1821–4." In *Irish Peasants: Violence and Political Unrest, 1780–1914*, ed. Samuel Clark and James S. Donnelly, Jr., 102–39. Madison: University of Wisconsin Press, 1983.

———. "Sectarianism in 1798 and in Catholic Nationalist Memory." In *Rebellion and Remembrance in Modern Ireland*, ed. Laurence M. Geary, 15–37. Dublin: Four Courts Press, 2001.

Donovan, Iain. "'Bloody News from Ireland': The Pamphlet Literature of the Irish Massacres of the 1640s." M.Litt. Thesis, Trinity College Dublin, 1995.

Dunlop, Robert. "The Depositions Relating to the Irish Massacres of 1641." *English Historical Review* 1, no. 4 (Oct. 1886): 740–44.

———. "The Depositions Relating to the Irish Massacres of 1641." *English Historical Review* 2, no. 6 (April 1887): 338–40.

Dunne, Tom. "La Trahison des Clercs: British Intellectuals and the First Home Rule Crisis." *Irish Historical Studies* 23, no. 90 (Nov. 1982): 134–73.

———. *Rebellions: Memoir, Memory, and 1798*. Dublin: Lilliput Press, 2004.

———. "Subaltern Voices? Poetry in Irish, Popular Insurgency, and the 1798 Rebellion." *Eighteenth-Century Life* 22, no. 3 (1998): 31–44.

Edwards, David, Clodagh Tait, and Padraig Lenihan. "Early Modern Ireland: A History of Violence." In *Age of Atrocity: Violence and Political Conflict in Early Modern Ireland*, ed. Edwards, Tait, and Lenihan, 9–33. Dublin: Four Courts Press, 2007.

Elliot, Marianne. *When God Took Sides: Religion and Identity in Ireland*. Oxford: Oxford University Press, 2009.

Emmet, T. A. *Ireland under English Rule, or a Plea for the Plaintiff*. 2nd ed. 2 vols. New York and London: G.P. Putnam's Sons, 1909.

Fabricant, Carole. "Swift as Irish Historian." In *Walking Naboth's Vineyard: New Studies on Swift*, ed. Christopher Fox and Brenda Tooley, 40–72. Notre Dame, IN: University of Notre Dame Press, 1995.

Fitzpatrick, David. "'I Will Acquire an Attitude Not Yours': Was Frederick MacNiece a Home Ruler and Why Does This Matter?" *Field Day Review* 4 (2008): 146–62.

Fitzpatrick, Thomas. *The Bloody Bridge and Other Papers Relating to the Insurrection of 1641*. Dublin: Sealey, Bryers and Walker, 1903.

———. "The T.C.D. Depositions (1641)." *Irish Rosary* 12, no. 9 (Sept. 1908): 657–66.

Forkan, Kevin. "Inventing a Protestant Icon: The Strange Death of Sir Charles Coote, 1642." In *Age of Atrocity*, ed. Edwards, Tait, and Lenihan, 204–18. Dublin: Four Courts Press, 2007.

Foster, R. F. *The Irish Story: Telling Tales and Making It Up in Ireland.* London: Allen Lane, 2002.

————. *Words Alone: Yeats and His Inheritances.* Oxford: Oxford University Press, 2011.

Fox, Christopher. "Swift and the Passions of Posterity." In *Reading Swift: Papers from the Sixth Munster Symposium on Jonathan Swift,* ed. Kristin Juhas, Hermann J. Real, and Sandra Simon. Munich: Wilhelm Fink Verlag, forthcoming.

French, James. *Clongibbon, or the White Knight of the Forest.* Dublin, 1845.

Frost, James. *The History and Topography of the County of Clare.* Dublin, 1893.

Froude, James Anthony. *The English in Ireland in the Eighteenth Century.* 3 vols. London, 1872–74.

Gamble, John. *A View of Society and Manners in the North of Ireland in the Summer and Autumn of 1812.* London, 1813.

Gargett, Graham. "Voltaire and Irish History." *Eighteenth-Century Ireland* 5 (1990): 117–41.

Garvin, Tom. *Nationalist Revolutionaries in Ireland, 1858–1928.* Oxford: Clarendon Press, 1987.

Gibney, John. "1641 and Protestant Identity in Restoration and Jacobite Ireland." In *Irish Protestant Identities,* ed. Mervyn Busteed, Frank Neal, and Jonathan Tonge, 13–27. Manchester: Manchester University Press, 2008.

————. "'Facts Newly *Stated*': John Curry, the 1641 Rebellion, and Catholic Revisionism in Eighteenth-Century Ireland, 1747–80." *Éire-Ireland* 44, no. 3–4 (Fall/Winter 2009): 248–77.

————. *Ireland and the Popish Plot.* Basingstoke: Palgrave Macmillan, 2009.

————. "Protestant Interests? The 1641 Rebellion and State Formation in Early Modern Ireland." *Historical Research* 84 (Feb. 2011): 67–86.

————. "Walter Love's 'Bloody Massacre': An Unfinished Study in Irish Cultural History, 1641–1963." *Proceedings of the Royal Irish Academy* 110C (2010): 217–37.

Gillespie, Raymond. "The End of an Era: Ulster and the Outbreak of the 1641 Rising." In *Natives and Newcomers: Essays on the Making of Irish Colonial Society,* ed. Ciaran Brady and Raymond Gillespie, 191–213. Dublin: Irish Academic Press, 1986.

————. "The Irish Protestants and James II, 1688–90." *Irish Historical Studies* 38, no. 110 (Nov. 1992): 124–33.

————. "Migration and Opportunity: A Comment." *Irish Economic and Social History* 13 (1986): 90–95.

————. "The Murder of Arthur Champion and the 1641 Rising in Fermanagh." *Clogher Record* 14, no. 3 (1993): 52–66.

————. "The Social Thought of Richard Bellings." In *Kingdoms in Crisis,* ed. Ó Siochrú, 212–28. Dublin: Four Courts Press, 2001.

————. "Temple's Fate: Reading *The Irish Rebellion* in Late Seventeenth-Century Ireland." In *British Interventions in Early Modern Ireland,* ed. Ciaran Brady and Jane Ohlmeyer, 315–33. Cambridge: Cambridge University Press, 2005.

Gillis, John R. "Memory and Identity: The History of a Relationship." In *Commemorations: The Politics of National Identity,* ed. John R. Gillis, 3–24. Princeton, NJ: Princeton University Press, 1994.

Gkotzaridis, Evi. *Trials of Irish History: Genesis and Evolution of a Reappraisal, 1938–2000.* London: Routledge, 2006.

Glasgow, Maude. *The Scotch-Irish in North America and in the American Colonies.* New York: G.P. Putnam's Sons, 1936.

Godwin, William. *Mandeville: A Tale of the Seventeenth Century in England.* 3 vols. Edinburgh, 1817.

Gross, David. *The Past in Ruins: Tradition and the Critique of Modernity.* Amherst: University of Massachusetts Press, 1992.

Halbwachs, Maurice. *The Collective Memory.* Trans. Francis J. Ditter and Vida Yazdi Ditter. New York: Harper Colophon Books, 1980.

Hallam, Henry. *The Constitutional History of England from the Accession of Henry VII to the Death of George II.* 2 vols. London, 1827.

Hamilton, Lord Ernest. *The Irish Rebellion of 1641.* London: John Murray, 1920.

———. *The Soul of Ulster.* London: Hurst and Blackett, 1917.

———. *Tales of the Troubles.* London: Unwin, 1925.

Harris, Walter, *Fiction Unmasked, or an Answer to a Dialogue Lately Published by a Popish Physician and Pretended to Have Passed between a Dissenter and a Member of the Church of Ireland, Wherein the Causes, Motives, and Mischiefs of the Irish Rebellion and Massacres in 1641 Are Laid Thick upon the Protestants.* Dublin, 1752.

Hart, Peter. "The Protestant Experience of Revolution in Southern Ireland." In *Unionism in Modern Ireland: New Perspectives on Politics and Culture,* ed. Richard English and Graham Walker, 81–98. Basingstoke: Macmillan, 1996.

Haydon, Colin. *Anti-Catholicism in Eighteenth-Century England, c. 1714–1780: A Political and Social Study.* Manchester: Manchester University Press, 1993.

———. "'I Love My King and Country, but a Roman Catholic I Hate': Anti-Catholicism, Xenophobia, and National Identity in Eighteenth-Century England." In *Protestantism and National Identity: Britain and Ireland, c. 1650–c. 1850,* ed. Tony Claydon and Ian McBride, 33–52. Cambridge: Cambridge University Press, 1998.

Hennig, John. "The Anglican Church in Ireland: Prayers against Irish 'Rebels.'" *Irish Ecclesiastical Record,* 5th ser., 64 (1944): 247–54.

[Hickeringill, Edmund]. *The History of Whiggism.* London, 1682.

Hickson, Mary. "The Depositions Relating to the Irish Massacres of 1641." *English Historical Review* 2, no. 5 (Jan. 1887): 133–37.

Hill, Christopher. "Seventeenth-Century English Radicals and Ireland." In *Radicals, Rebels, and Establishments,* ed. P. J. Corish, 33–49. Belfast: Appletree Press, 1985.

Hill, Jacqueline. "1641 and the Quest for Catholic Emancipation, 1691–1829." In *Ulster 1641,* ed. Mac Cuarta, 159–71. Belfast: Institute of Irish Studies, 1997.

———. "National Festivals, the State, and 'Protestant Ascendancy' in Ireland." *Irish Historical Studies* 24, no. 93 (May 1984): 30–51.

———. "Popery and Protestantism, Civil and Religious Liberty: The Disputed Lessons of Irish History, 1690–1812." *Past and Present* 118 (1988): 96–129.

Hume, David. *The History of Great Britain from the Accession of James I to the Revolution in 1688.* 8 vols. London, 1770.

Inglis, Brian. *The Story of Ireland.* 2nd ed. London: Faber, 1966.

Jackson, Alvin. "Unionist History." In *Interpreting Irish History*, ed. Brady, 253–68. Dublin: Irish Academic Press, 1994.

[Jones, Henry]. *An Abstract of Some Few of Those Barbarous, Cruell Massacres and Murthers of the Protestants and English in Some Parts of Ireland, Committed since the 23 of October 1641.* London, 1652.

———. *A Remonstrance of Divers Remarkeable Passages Concerning the Church and Kingdom of Ireland.* London, 1642.

———. *A Sermon of Antichrist Preached at Christ-Church, Dublin, Novemb. 12, 1676.* 2nd ed. London, 1679.

Kansteiner, Wulf. "Finding Meaning in Memory: A Methodological Critique of Collective Memory Studies." *History and Theory* 41 (2002): 179–97.

Kearney, Hugh. *Ireland: Contested Ideas of Nationalism and History.* Cork: Cork University Press, 2007.

Kelly, James. "The Emergence of Political Parading, 1660–1800." In *The Irish Parading Tradition: Following the Drum*, ed. T. G. Fraser, 9–26. Basingstoke: Macmillan, 2000.

———. "'The Glorious and Immortal Memory': Commemoration and Protestant Identity in Ireland, 1660–1800." *Proceedings of the Royal Irish Academy* 94C/2 (1994): 25–52.

———. *Sir Richard Musgrave, 1746–1818: Ultra-Protestant Ideologue.* Dublin: Four Courts Press, 2009.

———. "'We Were All to Have Been Massacred': Irish Protestants and the Experience of Rebellion." In *1798: A Bicentenary Perspective*, ed. Thomas Bartlett, David Dickson, Daire Keogh, and Kevin Whelan, 312–30. Dublin: Four Courts Press, 2003.

Kelly, William, ed. *The Sieges of Derry.* Dublin: Four Courts Press, 2001.

Kennedy, Michael, and Deirdre McMahon. *Reconstructing Ireland's Past: A History of the Irish Manuscripts Commission.* Dublin: Irish Manuscripts Commission, 2009.

King, William. *The State of the Protestants in Ireland under the Late King James's Government.* 4th ed. London, 1692.

Lecky, W. E. H. *A History of Ireland in the Eighteenth Century.* 5 vols. London, 1892.

———. "Mr. Froude's English in Ireland." *Macmillan's Magazine* 27 (Nov. 1872–Apr. 1873): 246–64.

Leerssen, Joep. "1798: The Recurrence of Violence and Two Conceptualizations of History." *Irish Review* 22 (Summer 1998): 37–45.

———. *Remembrance and Imagination: Patterns in the Historical and Literary Representation of Ireland in the Nineteenth-Century.* Cork: Cork University Press, 1996.

Le Goff, Jacques. *History and Memory.* New York and Oxford: Columbia University Press, 1992.

Leighton, C. D. A. *Catholicism in a Protestant Kingdom: A Study of the Irish Ancien Regime.* Basingstoke: Macmillan, 1994.

Leland, Thomas. *The History of Ireland from the Invasion of Henry II.* 3 vols. London, 1779.

Liechty, Joseph. "Testing the Depth of Catholic/Protestant Conflict: The Case of Thomas Leland's 'History of Ireland,' 1773." *Archivium Hibernicum* 42 (1987): 13–28.

Lindley, Keith J. "The Impact of the 1641 Rebellion upon England and Wales, 1641–45." *Irish Historical Studies* 18, no. 70 (Sept. 1972): 143–76.

Livesey, James. *Civil Society and Empire: Ireland and Scotland in the Eighteenth-Century Atlantic World.* New Haven, CT: Yale University Press, 2009.

Lloyd, David. *Anomalous States: Irish Writing and the Post-Colonial Moment.* Dublin: Lilliput Press, 1993.

Loeber, Rolf, and Magda Loeber. *A Guide to Irish Fiction, 1650–1900.* Dublin: Four Courts Press, 2006.

Loughlin, James. "The Irish Protestant Home Rule Association and Nationalist Politics, 1886–93." *Irish Historical Studies* 24, no. 95 (May 1985): 341–60.

Love, Walter D. "Charles O'Conor of Belanagare and Thomas Leland's 'Philosophical' History of Ireland." *Irish Historical Studies* 13, no. 49 (March 1962): 1–25.

———. "Civil War in Ireland: Appearances in Three Centuries of Historical Writing." *Emory University Quarterly* 22 (1966): 57–72.

———. "Edmund Burke, Charles Vallancey, and the Sebright Manuscripts." *Hermathena* 95 (July 1961): 21–35.

———. "Edmund Burke and an Irish Historiographical Controversy." *History and Theory* 2 (1962): 180–98.

———. "The Hibernian Antiquarian Society: A Forgotten Predecessor to the Royal Irish Academy." *Studies: An Irish Quarterly Review* 51 (Autumn 1962): 419–31.

Lucas, Charles. *The Political Constitutions of Great-Britain and Ireland Asserted and Vindicated.* London, 1751.

Macaulay, Catharine. *The History of England from the Accession of James I to That of the Brunswick Line.* 8 vols. London, 1763–83.

Macaulay, T. B. *The History of England,* ed. C. H. Firth. 6 vols. London: Macmillan, 1913–15.

Madden, Kyla. *Forkhill Protestants and Forkhill Catholics, 1787–1858.* Liverpool: Liverpool University Press, 2006.

McBride, Ian. "Memory and Forgetting: Ulster Presbyterians and 1798." In *1798: A Bicentenary Perspective,* ed. Thomas Bartlett, David Dickson, Daire Keogh, and Kevin Whelan, 478–96. Dublin: Four Courts Press, 2003.

———. *The Siege of Derry in Ulster Protestant Mythology.* Dublin: Four Courts Press, 1997.

McCarthy, Justin. *Ireland and Her Story.* New York: Funk and Wagnalis, 1903.

McCartney, Donal. "James Anthony Froude and Ireland: A Historiographical Controversy of the Nineteenth Century." *Irish University Review* 1 (Spring 1971): 238–57.

———. *W. E. H. Lecky: Historian and Politician, 1838–1903.* Dublin: Lilliput Press, 1993.

———. "The Writing of History in Ireland, 1800–30." *Irish Historical Studies* 10, no. 40 (Sept. 1957): 347–62.

McConnel, James. "Remembering the 1605 Gunpowder Plot in Ireland." *Journal of British Studies* 50, no. 4 (Oct. 2011): 863–91.

McCoy, Charlene. "War and Revolution: County Fermanagh and Its Borders, c. 1640–c. 1666." Ph.D. Dissertation, Trinity College Dublin, 2007.

Mac Cuarta, Brian. "Religious Violence against Settlers in South Ulster, 1641–2." In *Age of Atrocity,* ed. Edwards, Tait, and Lenihan, 154–75. Dublin: Four Courts Press, 2007.

————, ed. *Ulster 1641: Aspects of the Rising*. 2nd ed. Belfast: Institute of Irish Studies, 1997.

McGee, Owen. *The IRB: The Irish Republican Brotherhood from the Land League to Sinn Féin*. Dublin: Four Courts Press, 2005.

McGillivray, Royce. "Edmund Borlase, Historian of the Irish Rebellion." *Studia Hibernica* 9 (1969): 89–91.

McGrath, Charles Ivar. "Securing the Protestant Interest: The Origins and Purpose of the Penal Laws of 1695." *Irish Historical Studies* 30, no. 117 (May 1996): 25–46.

Macknight, Thomas. *Ulster as It Is, or Twenty-Eight Years' Experience as an Irish Editor*. 2 vols. London, 1896.

McMahon, Paul. *British Spies and Irish Rebels: British Intelligence and Ireland, 1916–1945*. Woodbridge: Boydell and Brewer, 2008.

McNally, Patrick. "'Irish and English Interests': National Conflict within the Church of Ireland Episcopate." *Irish Historical Studies* 29, no. 115 (May 1995): 295–314.

Mac Suibhne, Breandán. "Afterworld: The Gothic Travels of John Gamble (1770–1831)." *Field Day Review* 4 (2008): 63–113.

Magennis, Eoin. "A 'Beleaguered Protestant'? Walter Harris and the Writing of *Fiction Unmasked* in Mid-Eighteenth-Century Ireland." *Eighteenth-Century Ireland* 13 (1998): 86–111.

Mahaffy, J. P. *An Epoch in Irish History: Trinity College, Dublin: Its Foundation and Early Fortunes, 1591–1660*. London: T. Fisher Unwin, 1903.

Mant, Richard. *History of the Church of Ireland from the Reformation to the Revolution*. 2nd ed. 2 vols. London, 1841.

Meehan, C. P. *The Confederation of Kilkenny*. Dublin, 1846.

Meikle, James. *Killinchy, or the Days of Livingston: A Tale of the Ulster Presbyterians*. Belfast, 1839.

Mervyn, Audley. *The Speech of Sir Audley Mervyn, Knight, . . . Containing the Sum of Affairs in Ireland*. Dublin, 1663.

Miller, John. "The Earl of Tyrconnell and James II's Irish Policy." *Historical Journal* 20 (1977): 803–23.

Mitchel, John. *The Crusade of the Period, and Last Conquest of Ireland (Perhaps)*. New York, 1873.

Moody, T. W. "Irish History and Irish Mythology." In *Interpreting Irish History*, ed. Brady, 71–86. Dublin: Irish Academic Press, 1994.

Morash, Christopher. *A History of the Media in Ireland*. Cambridge: Cambridge University Press, 2010.

Morgan, Hiram. "News from Ireland: Catalan, Portuguese, and Castilian Pamphlets on the Confederate War in Ireland." In *Ireland 1641: Contexts and Reactions*, ed. Jane Ohlmeyer and Micheál Ó Siochrú. Manchester: Manchester University Press, forthcoming.

Morley, Vincent. "Views of the Past in Irish Vernacular Literature, 1650–1850." In *Unity and Diversity in European Culture c. 1800*, ed. Tim Blanning and Hagen Schulze, 174–98. Oxford: Oxford University Press, 2006.

Morrill, John. "The Drogheda Massacre in Cromwellian Context." In *Age of Atrocity*, ed. Edwards, Tait, and Lenihan, 242–65. Dublin: Four Courts Press, 2007.

Murray, R. H. *Revolutionary Ireland and Its Settlement*. London: Macmillan, 1911.

[Musgrave, Sir Richard]. *"Veridicus'" a Concise Account of the Material Events and Atrocities Which Occurred in the Present Rebellion, with the Causes Which Produced Them, and an Answer to Veritas's Vindication of the Roman Catholic Clergy of the Town of Wexford."* 2nd ed. Dublin, 1799 (NLI JP 2252).

Nicholls, Kenneth. "The Other Massacre: English Killings of Irish, 1641–2." In *Age of Atrocity*, ed. Edwards, Tait, and Lenihan, 176–91. Dublin: Four Courts Press, 2007.

Noonan, Kathleen M. "'The Cruell Pressure of an Enraged, Barbarous People': Irish and English Identity in Seventeenth-Century Policy and Propaganda." *Historical Journal* 41 (1998): 151–77.

Nora, Pierre, ed. *Realms of Memory: Constructing the French Past*, trans. Arthur J. Goldhammer. 3 vols. New York: Columbia University Press, 1996–98.

O'Brien, R. Barry. "The Rebellion of 1641." *Irish Ecclesiastical Record*, 4th ser., 17 (May 1905): 409–24.

Ó Buachalla, Breandán. "From Jacobite to Jacobin." In *1798: A Bicentenary Perspective*, ed. Thomas Bartlett, David Dickson, Daire Keogh, and Kevin Whelan, 75–96. Dublin: Four Courts Press, 2003.

Ó Ciosáin, Niall. *Print and Popular Culture in Ireland, 1750–1850*. London: Macmillan, 1997.

O'Connell, Daniel. *A Memoir on Ireland Native and Saxon*. London, 1843.

O'Gorman, Tom. "'Occurrences from Ireland': Contemporary Pamphlet Reactions to the Confederate War, 1641–1649." M.Litt. Thesis, National University of Ireland, 1999.

O'Grady, Hugh. *Strafford and Ireland: The History of His Vice-Royalty with an Account of His Trial*. 2 vols. Dublin: Hodges, Figgis, 1923.

O'Halloran, Clare. *Golden Ages and Barbarous Nations: Antiquarian Debate and Cultural Politics in Ireland, c. 1750–1800*. Cork: Cork University Press, 2004.

———. "Historical Writings, 1690–1890." In *The Cambridge History of Irish Literature*, ed. Margaret Kelleher and Philip O'Leary. 2 vols. Cambridge: Cambridge University Press, 2006.

O'Hara, David A. *English Newsbooks and Irish Rebellion, 1641–1649*. Dublin: Four Courts Press, 2006.

O'Keefe, Mairead. "The Politics of Irish Protestants, 1641–1660." M.A. Thesis, National University of Ireland, 1991.

O'Laverty, J. *An Historical Account of the Diocese of Down and Connor, Ancient and Modern*. 5 vols. Dublin, 1878–95.

Ó Siochrú, Micheál. *Confederate Ireland, 1642–1649: A Constitutional and Political Analysis*. Dublin: Four Courts Press, 1999.

———. *God's Executioner: Oliver Cromwell and the Conquest of Ireland*. London: Faber, 2008.

Ó Tuathaigh, Gearóid. "Gaelic Ireland, Popular Politics, and Daniel O'Connell." *Journal of the Galway Archaeological and Historical Society* 34 (1974–75): 21–34.

Perceval-Maxwell, Michael. "Migration and Opportunity: A Further Comment." *Irish Economic and Social History* 14 (1987): 59–61.

———. *The Outbreak of the Irish Rebellion of 1641*. Montreal: McGill-Queen's University Press, 1994.

———. "The Ulster Rising of 1641 and the Depositions." *Irish Historical Studies* 21, no. 82 (1978): 144–67.

"P.F.M.[oran?]." "The Irish Massacre of 1641." *Irish Ecclesiastical Record*, 2nd ser., 9 (April 1873): 299–319.

Power, Thomas P. "Publishing and Sectarian Tension in South Munster in the 1760s." *Eighteenth-Century Ireland* 18 (2004): 75–110.

Prendergast, J. P. *The Cromwellian Settlement of Ireland*. London, 1865.

Quinn, James. "Thomas Davis and the Patriot Parliament of 1689." In *People, Politics, and Power: Essays in Irish History, 1660–1850, in Honour of James I. McGuire*, ed. James Kelly, John McCafferty, and Charles Ivar McGrath, 190–202. Dublin: University College Dublin Press, 2009.

"R.S." *A Collection of Some of the Murthers and Massacres Committed on the Irish in Ireland since the 23d of October 1641*. London, 1662.

Raymond, Joad. *Pamphlets and Pamphleteering in Early Modern Britain*. Cambridge: Cambridge University Press, 2004.

Regan, John M. "Southern Irish Nationalism as a Historical Problem." *Historical Journal* 50, no. 1 (2007): 197–223.

Reily, Hugh. *Genuine History of Ireland Containing a Summary Account of All the Battles, Sieges, Rebellions, and Massacres, with the Most Remarkable Transactions Both in Church and State since the Reformation, in Which the Valour and Loyalty of the Irish Are Proved, and the Calumnies on Them and Their Country Refuted*. Dublin, 1830s [?] (NLI IR 94106 R5).

Robinson, Peter. *Their Cry Was "No Surrender": An Account of the Siege of Londonderry, 1688–1689*. Belfast: Crown Publications, 1988.

Rolston, Bill. *Drawing Support, 3: Murals and Transition in the North of Ireland*. Belfast: Beyond the Pale, 2003.

Russell, Conrad. *The Fall of the British Monarchies, 1637–1642*. Oxford: Clarendon Press, 1991.

"Sadlier, Mrs. J." [Mary Anne Madden]. *The Confederate Chieftains: A Tale of the Irish Rebellion of 1641*. New York, 1864.

Shagan, Ethan Howard. "Constructing Discord: Ideology, Propaganda, and English Responses to the Irish Rebellion of 1641." *Journal of British Studies* 36 (1997): 4–34.

Simms, Hilary. "Violence in County Armagh." In *Ulster 1641*, ed. Mac Cuarta, 123–38. Belfast: Institute of Irish Studies, 1997.

Smyth, James. "Anti-Catholicism, Conservatism, and Conspiracy: Sir Richard Musgrave's *Memoirs of the Different Rebellions in Ireland*." *Eighteenth-Century Life* 22 (1998): 62–73.

———. "The Making and Undoing of a Confessional State: Ireland 1660–1829." *Journal of Ecclesiastical History* 44 (1993): 506–13.

Smyth, William J. *Map-Making, Landscapes, and Memory: A Geography of Colonial and Early Modern Ireland, c. 1530–1750*. Cork: Cork University Press, 2006.

Stewart, A. T. Q. *The Narrow Ground: Aspects of Ulster, 1609–1969*. London: Faber, 1977.

Taylor, George. *An Historical Account of the Rise, Progress, and Suppression of the Rebellion in the County of Wexford in the Year 1798*. Dublin, 1800.

Temple, Sir John. *The Irish Rebellion.* London, 1646, 1745, 1766, and 1812; Dublin, 1713, 1716, and 1724.

Temple, Sir William. "An Essay on the Present State and Condition of Ireland." In Temple, *Select Letters to the Prince of Orange*, 197–216. London, 1701.

[Tennison, Richard]. *A Sermon Preached to the Protestants of Ireland in the City of London . . . by Richard, Lord Bishop of Killala.* London, 1691.

Thébaud, Rev. Augustine J., S.J. *The Irish Race in the Past and the Present.* New York, 1883.

Thomas, Keith. *Religion and the Decline of Magic.* London: Weidenfeld and Nicolson, 1971.

Thuente, Mary Helen. "The Folklore of Irish Nationalism." In *Perspectives on Irish Nationalism*, ed. Thomas E. Hachey and Lawrence J. McCaffrey, 42–60. Lexington: University Press of Kentucky, 1989.

Tonkin, Elizabeth. "History and the Myth of Realism." In *The Myths We Live By*, ed. Raphael Samuel and Paul Thompson, 25–35. London: Routledge, 1990.

Walker, Brian. "1641, 1689, 1690, and All That: The Unionist Sense of History." In Walker, *Dancing to History's Tune: History, Myth, and Politics in Ireland*, 1–14. Belfast: Institute of Irish Studies, 1996.

[Waring, Thomas]. *A Brief Narration of the Plotting, Beginning, and Carrying-on of That Execrable Rebellion and Butcherie in Ireland, with the Unheard of, Devilish Cruelties and Massacres by the Irish-Rebels Exercised upon the Protestants and English There.* London, 1650.

Warner, Ferdinando. *The History of Ireland to the Year 1171.* London [?], 1763.

———. *The History of the Rebellion and Civil-War in Ireland.* 2 vols. Dublin, 1768.

Webb, Alfred. *The Alleged Massacre of 1641.* London, 1887.

———. *The Opinions of Some Protestants Regarding Their Irish Catholic Fellow-Countrymen, Collected by Alfred Webb . . . , with Resolutions of the Irish Protestant Home Rule Association.* 2nd ed. Dublin, 1886.

Whelan, Irene. *The Bible War in Ireland: The "Second Reformation" and the Polarization of Protestant-Catholic Relations, 1800–1840.* Dublin: Lilliput Press, 2005.

Whelan, Kevin. "The Revisionist Debate in Ireland." *Boundary 2*, 31 (2004): 179–205.

———. *The Tree of Liberty: Radicalism, Catholicism, and the Construction of Irish Identity, 1760–1830.* Cork: Cork University Press, 1996.

Whitelock, Bulstrode. *Memorials of the English Affairs.* London, 1682.

Williams, J. B. "The Depositions about the Rebellion of 1641." *Irish Ecclesiastical Record*, 5th ser., 15 (Jan. 1920): 15–23.

Wills, Claire. *Dublin 1916: The Siege of the GPO.* London: Profile, 2009.

Wilson, Kathleen. *The Sense of the People: Politics, Culture, and Imperialism in England, 1715–1785.* Cambridge: Cambridge University Press, 1995.

Woodburn, Rev. James Barkley. *The Ulster Scot: His History and Religion.* London: H.R. Allenson, 1914.

Wright, Julia M. "'The Same Dull Round Over Again': Colonial History in Moore's *Memoirs of Captain Rock*." *European Romantic Review* 14 (2003): 239–49.

Index

History of Ireland and
the Irish Diaspora